Dr. Chandra Bhanu Gupta is an eminent scholar of Sanskrit and Linguistics. He is specialist in the History of Drama and Theatre and Ancient Indian History and Culture. He taught Sanskrit at Hindu College and University of Delhi. He has attended several international conferences and contributed important research papers. He has also guided several research students.

The Indian Theatre

Fig. 1: Nataraja, Tanjore
(Courtesy: Archaeological Survey of India, New Delhi)

The Indian Theatre

Chandra Bhan Gupta
Professor Emeritus in Sanskrit
University of Delhi

with a foreword by
Dr Ludo Rocher

Munshiram Manoharlal
Publishers Pvt Ltd

ISBN 81–215–0483–4
Second revised edition 1991
FIRST PUBLISHED 1954

Published by Munshiram Manoharlal Publishers Pvt. Ltd., Post Box 5715, 54 Rani Jhansi Road, New Delhi-1100 055 and printed at Gayatri Offset Press, Noida-201 301

To

Professor Ramachandra Narayan Dandekar
"Padma Bhushan," "Vacaspati"
Emeritus Professor of Sanskrit, University of Poona
Honorary Secretary, Bhandarkar Oriental Research Institute, Poona
General Secretary, All India Oriental Conference
President, International Association of Sanskrit Studies
President, International Union for Oriental and Asian Studies
President, World Sanskrit Conference

Contents

Foreword x

Preface xi

List of Illustrations xiii

Abbreviations xiv

CHAPTER ONE

THE ORIGIN OF THE INDIAN DRAMA 1
The Indian Tradition 1
Genesis of Indian Drama 2
Theories 5

CHAPTER TWO

SANSKRIT PLAYS 9
Significance 9
Object 9
Occasions for Enactment 15
Places for Performance 18

CHAPTER THREE

CONSTRUCTION OF THE THEATRE 23
Types and Measurements 23
Raṅgapīṭha and Decoration 27
Raṅgaśīrṣa, Green Room and Mattavāraṇīs 36
Pillars and Seating Arrangements 38
Doors and Roof 40

CHAPTER FOUR

SCENIC REPRESENTATION 43
The Curtain 43
Origin of the Curtain 48
Employment of Painting 50
Time of Presentation 53

CHAPTER FIVE

PARAPHERNALIA **56**
Significance of Āhāryābhinaya 56
Pusta 57
Alaṅkāra 60
Aṅgaracanā 64
Sañjīva 67

CHAPTER SIX

ACCESSORY ARTS **69**
Music and Orchestra 69
Histrionics 76
Dancing 79
Dialogue 81

CHAPTER SEVEN

THE TROUPE **87**
Roles of Characters *(Bhūmikā)* 87
Nāṭyācāryas 88
Actors and Actresses 90
Spectators and Judges 93
Social Position of Actors and Actresses 96

CHAPTER EIGHT

CONVENTIONS **99**
Pūrvaraṅga 99
Religious Ceremonies 103
Dialects 105
Injunctions and Prohibitions 107

CHAPTER NINE

NATURE AND TYPES OF THE DRAMA **112**
Nṛtta, Nṛtya and Nāṭya 112
Major Types of Drama (Rūpakas) 114
Minor Types (Uparūpakas) 118
Art of Writing a Sanskrit Play 121

CHAPTER TEN

PRESENTATION OF PLAYS **127**
Actual Performance 127
Portrayal of Sentiments (*Rasa*) 131
Success 133

CHAPTER ELEVEN

NATIONAL THEATRE **138**
Idea of National Theatre 138

CHAPTER TWELVE

EPILOGUE **145**

Bibliography 151

Index 161

Foreword

I am happy to write a brief foreword to the revised edition of Professor Chandra Bhan Gupta's book *The Indian Theatre* which was first published in 1954.

This is not a historical and descriptive presentation of Indian dramatic literature. It is a thorough and detailed analysis of the theory and practice of Indian Theatre, mainly classical. As such I can see a wide variety of readers using the book to their advantage. On the one hand, students of comparative dramaturgy will find in it, in English, ample details on anything that made Indian theatre and theatrical performances specially Indian; the theatre itself, its form, measurements and accessories; the actors and the rules and conventions they are supposed to follow; the types of plays and their respective characteristics; and so forth. On the other hand, students of Sanskrit and readers of plays in the Sanskrit original will benefit not only from the body of the book but, even more so, from the copious footnotes. For any concept, the material element or technical term connected with Sanskrit theatre, they will not only find a clear description, but also references to guide them to the relevant passages in the theoretical treatises on dramaturgy for more ample and technical information.

The book also serves a more practical purpose; to demonstrate that there has been—and still can be—a typically Indian form of theatre. Thus, in the first chapter the author, briefly but rightly, reacts against those theories that attempted to explain the origin of Indian drama as a result of extraneous influences. In the last chapter he not only surveys the forms of theatre in the several vernaculars; he also pleads for the establishment of a contemporary Indian national theatre, drawing on and adapting the various forms of theatre India has known in the past, and free from foreign elements which have made their appearance on the Indian stage in recent times.

The first edition of Professor Gupta's *The Indian Theatre* has been out of print for some time. I am sure that this revised edition will fill a vacuum, and be well received by all those interested in classical—and modern—Indian drama.

LUDO ROCHER
W. Norman Brown Professor
of South Asian Studies

Philadelphia
February 15, 1987

Preface

Sanskrit drama in general has received a great deal of attention at the hands of European Scholars since the *Abhijñānaśākuntala* was translated into English by William Jones in 1789. The origin of the Sanskrit drama has been the subject of elaborate investigation by professors Von Schroedar, Pischel, Hertel, W. Ridgeway, Lévi, Lüder, Konow, Jacobi and Keith, and the significance and value of the Indian theory of dramatic art have been brought out by them. I have also come across certain articles, pamphlets and books in connection with some aspects of the Indian theatre, which I have mentioned in the Bibliography. Mulk Raj Anand's book *The Indian Theatre* deals only with the different theatres in modern times in India in a stylish but sketchy way. It has nothing to do with the ancient Indian theatre, and so it cannot establish any connected study of the development of the theatre in India, R.K. Yajnik's book on *The Indian Theatre* deals mainly with the influence of British drama on the Indian stage of today with special reference to Western India. D.R. Mankad's *Ancient Indian Theatre* was published in August 1950, and only interpreted the second chapter of *Nāṭyaśāstra*. The English translation of the *Nāṭyaśāstra*, vol. I (chapters I–XXVII) and vol. II (chapters XXVIII–XXXVI) were published in 1951 and 1961, respectively. There are certain aspects of Indian theatre, which have not yet received much attention, for example, the actual scenic arrangement, stage paraphernalia etc. The present study deals with the Indian theory of dramatic art as employed in the actual performance or presentation of a play. The title of this work was, therefore, given as "Presentation of Sanskrit plays", and was published under the title *The Indian Theatre* in 1954. It was highly appreciated by learned scholars and drama critics and was utilized by researchers throughout the world.

This work mainly depends on the *Nāṭyaśāstra*, the *Abhinavabhāratī*, other works on dramaturgy and the experience gained by the author by visiting caves of Ellora, Ajanta, Elephanta and Sanchi stupa etc., and joining Uday Shanker India Culture Centre, Almora to study histrionics and dancing in detail. It deals with the 'Ancient Theatre' and has twelve chapters.

The general plan of the work is arranged in the following manner. Names of all books as well as Sanskrit words have been italicized. Quotations of translated passages have been given in inverted commas. In the case of dramas, names of books containing translations have not been referred to in the footnotes as those translations are very popular.

Diagrams of different types of theatres mentioned in the *Nāṭyaśāstra* and seating arrangement in a palace theatre as mentioned in the *Saṅgītaratnākara* were prepared according to the plan given by the author.

Diagram of seating arrangement of musicians in an orchestra *(Kutapa)* on the Raṅgaśīrṣa as well as seating arrangement of spectators in the Auditorium as mentioned in the *Nāṭyaśāstra,* are drawn by Shri Jagmohan Singh Bisht, Artist, according to the plan supplied by the author.

The photographs of Bronze image of Naṭarāja, Tanjore and images of Nāṭamandira in Konarak and Darbarhall in Belur temple, dancing parties in Sri Sailam and Helebid have been published with the permission of Archaeological Survey of India, New Delhi.

This work, it is hoped, will prove of great service not only to students of history of Sanskrit literature but also for the regeneration of a people's theatre, according to national traditions. The threads of the topic of this work are woven in such a manner as to present a systematic account of the presentation of Sanskrit plays for the use of scholars and the public. It suggests the model on which a national theatre in India can be planned.

I am beholden to late Pt. Madan Mohan Malaviya, Dr. S. Radhakrishnan, Dr. Amar Nath Jha, Mahamahopadhyaya, Dr. Gopi Nath Kaviraj and Dr. P.V. Kane, Prof. S.C. Mukerjee, Dr. P.L. Vaidya, Dr. Satkari Mukerjee, Prof. V.V. Mirashi, Dr. Bhagwan Das, who helped me in the initial stages of my work by their encouragement and assistance. My grateful thanks are due to Dr. Suniti Kumar Chatterji, Dr. Sampurnanand, M. Ananthasayanam Iyangar, Dr. Moti Chandra, Dr. V.S. Agrawala, Prof. K.A. Subramania Iyer, Mrs. Rukmini Devi Arundale, Pt. Baldeva Upadhyaya and Dr. R.N. Dandekar, my dearest friend and co-worker and eminent scholar of Sanskrit and Ancient Indian Culture for kindly agreeing to the dedication of this volume in his name.

My heartfelt thanks go to Dr. Ludo Rocher, W. Norman Brown Professor of South Asian Studies, Department of South Asia Regional Studies, University of Pennsylvania, Philadelphia, author of more than hundred high level books and research papers, for his contributing an appreciative foreword to this book.

New Delhi CHANDRA BHAN GUPTA
June 20, 1990

List of Illustrations

Fig. 1: Nataraja, Tanjore (Courtesy: Archaeological Survey of India, New Delhi) *frontispiece*

Fig. 2: Diagram showing the seating arrangement in a Palace Theatre according to *ŚR* 20

Fig. 3: Temple Theatre (Plan of Vaḍakkunnāthan Kuṭṭampalam, Trichur (Courtesy: Archaeological Survey of India, New Delhi) 21

Fig. 4: Vikṛṣṭa Nāṭyagṛha 26

Fig. 5: Aerial view of Nāṭamandira, Konarak 28

Fig. 6: Caturasra Nāṭyagṛha 29

Fig. 7: Diagram of seating arrangement of spectators in the auditorium as mentioned in the *Nāṭyaśāstra* 30

Fig. 8: Tryasra Nāṭyagṛha 31

Fig. 9: Darbar Hall General View, Belur Temple (Courtesy: Archaeological Survey of India, New Delhi) 34

Fig. 10: Dancing Party from Fort Wall, Sri Sailam (Courtesy: Archaeological Survey of India, New Delhi) 84

Fig. 11: Music and dancing party of Harsaleshwar Temple, Halebid (Courtesy: Archaeological Survey of India, New Delhi) 85

Fig. 12: Diagram of seating arrangement of musicians in an orchestra on the Raṅgaśirṣa as mentioned in the *Nāṭyaśāstra* 86

Fig. 13: Scene from *Abhijñānaśākuntalam* directed by Mrs. Vijaya Mehta (Courtesy: Saṅgeet Nāṭak Akademi, New Delhi) 136

Fig. 14: The Sūtradhāra in Bhāsa's *Madhyamavyāyoga*(Courtesy: National School of Drama and Asian Theatre Institute, New Delhi) 137

Fig. 15: Scene from *Mudrārākṣasa* directed by B.V. Karanth (Courtesy: National School of Drama and Asian Theatre Institute, New Delhi) 137

Abbreviations

Abh. Bh.	Abhinavabhāratī
ABORI	Annals of Bhandarkar Oriental Research Institute
AD	Abhinayadarpaṇa
AR	Anargharāghava
AS	Arthaśāstra
BP	Bhāvaprakāśana
CSS	Calcutta Sanskrit Series
DR	Daśarūpa
GOS	Gaekwad Oriental Series
IHQ	Indian Historical Quarterly
JBRS	Journal of the Bihar Research Society
JOR	Journal of Oriental Research
JRAS	Journal of Royal Asiatic Society of Great Britain and Ireland
JUB	Journal of the University of Bombay
Kar. M.	Karpūramañjarī
KM	Kāvyamālā
KP	Kāvyaprakāśa
KSS	Kāśī Sanskrit Series
Māl	Mālavikāgnimitra
MM	Mālatīmādhava
Mṛch	Mṛcchakaṭika
MS	Mānasāraśilpaśāstra
ND	Nāṭyadarpaṇa
NLR	Nāṭakalakṣaṇaratnakośa
NS	Nāṭyaśāstra
NSP	Nirṇaya Sagar Press
PD	Priyadarśikā
POS	Poona Oriental Series
PR	Pratāparudrīya
Pra. Y.	Pratijñayaugandharāyaṇa
PTS	Pāli Text Society
Rat	Ratnāvalī
RS	Rasārṇavasudhākara
Śāk	Abhijñānaśākuntala
SD	Sāhityadarpaṇa

CHAPTER ONE

The Origin of the Indian Drama

THE INDIAN TRADITION

The earliest authority in India on the presentation of drama on the stage is the *Nāṭyaśāstra* of Bharata. The character of the traditional account of the origin of the Indian drama given in the *Nāṭyaśāstra* forces on us the conclusion that all exact knowledge about it had been lost by the time the *Nāṭyaśāstra* was written.

Gods, according to the account preserved in the *Nāṭyaśāstra*, entreated Brahmā to produce something to play (*krīḍanīyaka*) which could be seen and also heard, a fifth Veda, that would benefit all castes (*sārvavārṇika*). Accordingly he took recitation (*pāṭhya*) from the *Ṛgveda*, song (*gīta*) from the *Sāmaveda*, the art of acting (*abhinaya*) from the *Yajurveda*, and sentiment (*rasa*) from the *Atharvaveda* and asked Bharata to make known to mankind the new *Nāṭyaveda* thus produced and bring into practice the precepts with the help of his sons and disciples, and the *gandharvas* and *apsarās*, as the actors and actresses at the 'banner festival of Indra'. This enraged the *asuras* from whom mischief was apprehended. Indra, therefore, took the banner and attacked them with the staff. That is why his banner is called *jarjara* and it is given as a mark of Indra's protection for all stage productions. The *asuras* had to accept the assurance that the drama was a representation of facts of a general nature and would not be deliberately applied to anybody. The *Nāṭyaśāstra* refers to two other dramas enacted in very early times on two subjects the 'Churning of Nectar from the sea' and the 'burning of three cities'.[1]

The traditional account of the origin of drama as furnished by the *Abhinayadarpaṇa* is as follows:

> In the beginning Brahma gave the *Nāṭyaveda* to Bhārata. Bharata, with groups of *gandharvas* and *apsaras*, performed *nāṭya*, *nṛtta* and *nṛtya* before Śiva. Śiva, remembering his own majestic dance had Bharata instructed in the art by his attendants (*gaṇas*). And before this, out of his love for Bharata, he gave the latter instruction in *lāsya* through Pārvatī, and in *tāṇḍava* through Taṇḍu. Then sages spoke of

[1] *NS-KM*, I. 11, 12, 14, 17, 20b–25; IV. 1–10; *KSS*, I. 11, 12, 14, 17, 54b–60; IV. 1–11; *GOS*, I. 11, 12, 14, 17, 54–59a; IV. 1–11.

it to mortals. Pārvatī, on the other hand, instructed Uṣā, daughter of Bāṇāsura in *lāsya*. The latter taught the art to the milkmaids of Dvārakā, and they taught it to women of Saurāṣtra who, in their turn, taught the same to women of other countries. In this manner this art was traditionally handed down and came to stay in the world.[1]

With regard to the origin of the *Nāṭyaveda*, the *Bhāvaprakāśana* records two stories. The first is that at the end of the *kalpa*. Maheśvara created Brahmā and Viṣṇu, and Brahmā created the world. Nandikeśvara came to Brahmā and taught the *Nāṭyaveda* and its application to him. He said: "the *Nāṭyaveda* may be enacted by Bharata" and disappeared. Brahmā and other gods were pleased and the *Tripuradāharūpaka* was played.

According to the second account, disgusted with the worries of ruling his kingdom, Manu approached Sūryadeva (sun god) for consolatory advice. Sūryadeva said that in days of yore Brahmā disgusted with his work for mankind went to the Lord of Lords for relief. He was advised to go to Śiva. Śiva asked his pupil Nandikeśvara to teach the *Nāṭaveda* to Brahmā. Nandikeśvara taught Brahmā the *Nāṭyaveda* and its method of representation. He came back to his abode and meditated for a while. Then there appeared before him a *muni* with five disciples. They were taught the *Nāṭyaveda*. They put the *Nāṭyaveda* on the stage and thus pleased Brahmā who gave them a boon. Sūryadeva advised Manu to pray to Brahmā for relief from the troubles experienced by him in sustaining the earth. Then Manu went to Brahmā who knowing his difficulty ordered Bharata to go with Manu to Bhāratavarṣa. Accordingly Bharata came to Ayodhyā with Manu.[2]

GENESIS OF INDIAN DRAMA

The earliest representation of plays on the stage appears to be associated with the religious observances of the people. In Greece, for example, the drama derived its origin from the hymns which were sung at the festivals of Bacchus. In the *Ṛgveda* we come across certain hymns in the form of dialogues (*saṁvāda sūktas*)[3] some of which seem to contain dramatic flavour consisting, as they do, of conversation, speech and repartee. The *Vājasaneyi Saṁhitā* of the *Śukla Yajurveda* makes mention of the word

[1] *AD*, 2–7a.

[2] *BP*, III, pp. 55, 56.

[3] *Ṛgveda*, I. 170, 171, 179; III. 33; IV. 18, 42; V. 11; VII. 33; VIII. 100; X. 10, 28, 51–53, 86, 95, 108.

śailūṣa which means an actor. It says that a *sūta* was to be employed for *nṛtta* and a *śailūṣa* for song.[1] The *Sāmaveda* with the hymns set to tune clearly shows that the art of music was fully developed in the vedic Age.[2] Vedic sacrifices were essentially a mimesis. In the *Kauṣītakī Brāhmaṇa* sacrificial priests are described as dancing. In the same *Brāhmaṇa, saṅgīta* (which comprehends music, dance and playing on instruments) forms a part of *yajña-yāgādi.*[3] At the Mahāvratastoma rite young maidens danced.[4]

The *Rāmāyaṇa* refers to *naṭa, nartaka, nāṭaka,* dances and theatrical acts in cities and palaces. Bharata, son of Daśaratha, who was upset by bad dreams at his maternal uncle's house, was cheered up with songs, dances and joyous *nāṭakas.* We hear of festivals and concourses (*samājas*) where actors (*naṭas*) and dancers (*nartakas*) delighted themselves.[5] The *Mahābhārata,* like the *Rāmāyaṇa,* refers to dramatic terms like *naṭa, nartaka, gāyakas* and *sūtradhāra.*[6]

The *Harivaṁśa* which is a supplement to and a continuation of the *Mahābhārata* makes explicit reference to the drama, we learn from it of actors who produced a drama out of the *Rāmāyaṇa* legend. It makes direct mention of a dramatic treatment (*nāṭakīvṛtam*) of the *Rāmāyaṇa.* We are informed that "the renowned actor represents in a drama "the birth of the immeasurable Viṣṇu" for the purpose of fulfilling his wish to slay the prince of the *rākṣasas*". Lomapāda and Daśaratha, in the drama, caused the great *muni* Ṛṣyaśṛṅga to be brought by Sauta and courtesans. Rāma, Lakṣmaṇa, Bharata and Śatrughna, Ṛṣyaśṛṅga and Sauta were personated by characteristically dressed actors.[7]

In some of the *purāṇas* also we come across references to the representation of plays. In the *Śrīmadbhāgavata Purāṇa,* reference is made to actors.[8] In the *Mārkaṇḍeya Purāṇa,* we find Ṛtadhvaja, son of king Sakrajit, fond of dramatic performance and passing his days delightfully in the cultivation of poetry, music and drama.[9]

Elaborate Buddhistic evidence about the early existence of drama is available. The *Brahma-Jālasutta* of the *Dīghanikāya* contains a list of

[1] *Vājasaneyi Saṁhitā,* XXX. 6.
[2] *Nirukta,* 12. 4.
[3] *Kauṣītaki Brāhmaṇa,* XVII. 8; XXIX. 5.
[4] *Kāṭhakam,* XXXIV. 5.
[5] *Rāmāyaṇa,* II. 69. 4; II. 67. 15.
[6] *Mahābhārata,* I. 51. 15.
[7] *Harivaṁśa,* II. 88–93.
[8] *Śrīmadbhāgavata Purāṇa,* I. 11. 20.
[9] *Mārkaṇḍeya Purāṇa,* XX, 4b and 6a.

terms denoting various amusements and performances.[1] In the *Avadānaśataka* there is a clear mention of a *rūpaka* being enacted on the stage.[2]

The *Arthaśāstra* supplies us with a good deal of information on the maintenance and working of the *nāṭakamaṇḍalīs*. In one place we find that if any *nāṭakamaṇḍalī* came from another country to present a play on the stage, it was required to pay five *paṇas* (a particular coin equal in value to 80 cowries) to the king. In another place it is stated that the king's duty was to provide teachers for women, who acted on the stage, to teach them such arts as singing, dancing, acting, writing, painting, playing on instruments, particularly *vīṇā, veṇu* and *mṛdaṅga*, preparing garlands, ornamenting the body with different materials, and to spend on the above-mentioned items from the treasury of the *rājamaṇḍala* (government). The sons of *gaṇikas* (courtesans) and the principal *naṭas* were appointed head *ācāryas* (teachers) for all other stage-players.

In the *Arthaśāstra* it is also mentioned that the king used to employ *naṭas*, dancers, singers, instrumentalists, story-tellers, actors and *aindrajālikas* (jugglers) as spies who would try to reach the enemy-king. Salaries for the different categories of stage-players were fixed. A *kuśīlava* (*naṭa*) was to be paid 350 *paṇas* yearly, while those who were conversant with playing on high class instruments were given 700 *paṇas* yearly.[3] This shows that the stage-craft was highly developed at the time of the *Arthaśāstra*.

Vātsyāyana in his *Kāmasūtra* mentions writers on dramatic art of remote ages whose works are lost save in stray quotations. He describes the recreations of citizens (*nāgaraka*) and refers to the doings of *pīṭhamarda, viṭa, vidūṣaka, kuśīlavas* etc. *Naṭas* appointed by the king were to play *nāṭakas* in the temples of Sarasvatī on the days of *parva*. *Naṭas* who came from outside the state to stage plays were treated in the same manner as the *naṭas* of the place.[4]

By the time of the *Sūtras*, literature on the practice of the histrionic art must have grown in bulk so as to have created the necessity of codifying laws governing them. Pāṇini mentions *naṭasūtras* to show that acting had sufficiently developed and formulation of principles of dancing and acting in the form of *sūtras* was necessary.[5]

In the *Mahābhāṣya* we find more effective evidence of the existence of

[1] *Dighanikāya*, I. 1. 13.
[2] *Avadānaśataka*, II. 24. 75.
[3] *AS*, I. 2. 27.
[4] *Kāmasūtra*, IV. 27–30.
[5] Pāṇini, IV. 3. 110; IV. 3. 111; IV. 3. 129.

plays when it makes mention of two regular plays, the *Kaṁsavadha* and the *Balibandha* being acted on the stage. We have phrases in the *Mahābhāṣya* such as "they cause the death of Kaṁsa", 'they cause the binding of Bali'. The phrase "*rasiko naṭaḥ*" in the *Mahābhāṣya* indicates that the theory of *rasa* was well known in the days of Patañjali.[1]

Coming to the classical period, we find distinct evidence of the representation of plays available with the discovery of the manuscripts on palm-leaves among the Central Asian finds. One of the plays, *Śāriputra-prakaraṇa* was found to be written by Aśvaghoṣa, but no mention of the names of the authors of the other two fragments could be discovered there.

Mahāmahopādhaya Gaṇapati Śāstrī of Travancore discovered thirteen dramas with similarity of expression and construction and ascribed them to Bhāsa. These were also found to be the earliest complete specimens of dramatic composition available. From these it is evident that a long series of dramas were produced and enacted before him.

THEORIES

The question of the origin of Sanskrit plays has been of much interest to scholars. In this respect various theories have been propounded. It has been held that the drama (from Greek '*draiein*'—to imitate or represent and 'Sanskrit *avasthānukṛtirnāṭyam*'[2] the imitation of the circumstances is *nāṭya*) originated in Greece. E. Windisch[3] is the exponent of this theory. He relies for his evidence on the *Mṛcchakaṭika* which he held to be the oldest Indian drama. Attic comedies were available about the third century BC and according to Windisch the *Mṛcchakaṭika* was written about the same time. But we know now that the Sanskrit drama had taken a settled form long before the origin of the *Mṛcchakaṭika*.

The oldest Sanskrit dramas known to us are of an entirely different kind and have no similarity with the Greek drama. Development of a story, shortening of knots and generally the entire characterization of the Sanskrit drama is different from that found in Greece. The conflict in the Sanskrit drama as opposed to the Greek is not based on the character of the person appearing and no correct gradation and climax of the opposition is met with in the former. In its outer form also the

[1] *Mahābhāṣya*, II, pp. 36, 394.

[2] *DR*, I. 7.

[3] A.B. Keith, *Sanskrit Drama*, p. 57; Windisch, *Der Griechische Einfluss im indischen Drama*.

Sanskrit drama is different from the Greek influence. Sanskrit and several Prākṛta dialects are employed in the Sanskrit dramas. Moreover, there is no internal connection whatsoever between the Greek and the Sanskrit dramas. The Greek tragedy belongs to the classical type and the Sanskrit drama is by universal assent admitted to be romantic.

It has been suggested that '*yavanikāpatanam*' in a Sanskrit play has a significant derivative relation to the word '*yavana*', a name which the Indians gave to the Greeks. While dealing with the question of the origin of *yavanikā* in Chapter Four of this book it will be shown that it was not in the least borrowed from Greece.

Bloch[1] believes that he has found support for the Greek hypothesis in the arrangement of the theatre in the Sītābeṅgā cave. He sees in it the imitation of a Greek theatre. But the points of resemblance are extremely meagre as there is no arrangement here of proscenium or orchestra as in the Greek theatre.

To conclude, there is nothing in Indian plays to correspond to the high shoes and limitation in the number of characters that might appear, at the same time, on the stage or the observance of the unities, especially those of time and place. In these respects Indian plays are more analogous to those of Elizabethan England. No importance can be attached to the parallelism between the *vidūṣaka* who is a brāhmaṇa and the confidential slave of the Greek stage. Thus they belong to two opposite schools, totally alien to each other in composition, taste and sentiment. Dr. Horace H. Wilson[2] declares emphatically "Whatever may be the merits or defects of the Hindu drama, it may be safely asserted that they do not spring from the same parent, but are unmixedly its own." Thus the theory of Greek origin is entirely without any foundation and we can say without hesitation that the Sanskrit drama had an indigenous origin entirely free from any foreign influence.

The argument put forward by Mahāmahopādhyāya Haraprasāda Śāstrī[3] in support of the Maypole theory is that the first Indian play is stated to have been produced at the Indradhvaja festival in which a pole plays a prominent part as the object of worship. This suggested to him the Maypole dance of Europe. He therefore held that the origin of the Indian drama was to be connected with the ceremonies associated with spring festivities coming after the end of the dreary and lifeless winter. Unhappily for this theory, the Indradhvaja festival comes at the end of

[1]*ASI-AR 1903–4*, pp. 123–32.
[2]Wilson, *Select Specimens of the Theatre of the Hindus*, I. XI.
[3]*Journal and Proceedings of the Asiatic Society of Bengal*, pp. 351–361.

the rains and indicates Indra's victory over clouds represented as demons.

Dr. Ridgeway's[1] theory of the 'cult of the dead' and Keith's[2] 'vegetation spirit' theory are equally unfounded. Dr. Ridgeway says that there is a feeling of respect for the departed heroes. But Sanskrit dramas are mostly erotic in sentiment and descriptions of the heroic sentiment end with the hero's satisfaction in getting the heroine. As to the 'vegetation spirit' theory, Keith himself could not maintain the view.

Dr. Pischel[3] advances the 'puppet show' theory saying that puppet dance first originated in India. Puppets are mentioned in Sanskrit literature frequently.[4] The stage manager in Indian plays is called *sūtradhāra* (string-holder). This has suggested to Dr. Pischel the theory that the Indian play was in origin a puppet show. The theory falls flat when we realize that naturally men must have acquired the art of acting, dancing and speaking in a dramaturgic form before making a show on the stage through puppets. Moreover this theory is wrongly based on the word *sūtradhāra*, for the word means a person who in brief and in the form of aphorism describes the plot, hero and sentiments employed in the drama.[5]

Prof. Lüders[6] is the exponent of the 'shadow play' theory. Ancient India had also shadow plays wherein moving shadows thrown upon a curtain from behind formed the action of the plot. The shadow Sītā introduced in the *Uttararāmacarita*[7] acquired a new theatrical value from this point of view. But we find no reference of *chāyānāṭaka* in dramaturgic works. Hence this theory cannot be regarded as explaining the origin of the Indian drama.

Legendary traditions thus indicate that the genesis of the drama lie in the Vedas where all its ingredients, song, dance dialogue and some sort of acting as well are found, though a hint is found even in *Nāṭyaśāstra* to the effect that the Indian drama was originally connected with pre-Vedic religion. It is mentioned in *Nāṭyaśāstra* that one who witnesses carefully its performance, attains the same blessed goal which masters of Vedic knowledge and performers of sacrifices or givers of gifts will attain in

[1]Ridgeway, *The Dramas and Dramatic Dances of Non-European Races*, p. 211; *Journal of Royal Asiatic Society of Great Britain and Ireland*, 1916, pp. 821–29

[2]Keith, op. cit., pp. 37–38.

[3]Ibid., p. 52; Pischel, *Die Heimat des Puppenspiels*.

[4]*Mahābhārata*, V. 39. 1; *Bālarāmāyaṇa*, V, p. 251.

[5]*BP*, X. p. 288, ll. 7–8.

[6]Keith, op. cit., p. 53; Lüders, Sitzungsberichte der Konigl, Akademie der Wissenschaften zu Berlin, 1916, pp. 698.

[7]*URC*, III.

the end.[1] But according to the availability of records it is said here that the Indian drama has its origin in the Vedas, their *aṅgas* and *upāṅgas*.[2] They also bring out the fact that the Sanskrit drama was introduced to provide a source of pleasure to people of all castes. The Vedic ritual contained in itself the germs of the drama as is the case with practically every form of primitive worship. The ritual did not consist merely of the singing of songs or recitations in honour of gods; it involved a complete round of ceremonies in some of which was undoubtedly present an element of dramatic art. Performers of rites assumed for the time being personalities other than their own. In a sense, therefore, it may be said that the Indian drama has its origin in the Vedic period. However, there is not even the slightest evidence that the essential synthesis and development of plot which constitute a true drama were made in the Vedic Age. On the contrary there is every reason to believe that it was through the use of the epic recitation that the latent possibilities of the drama were made patent. From a study of the *Arthaśāstra* and the *Kāmasūtra* it becomes evident that in their times the science of stage-craft was highly developed and that the *naṭas* were employed by kings for amusement and for state work. In the *Mahābhāṣya* there is effective evidence on the existence of a drama and it may be concluded safely that the Indian drama attained its full form by the time of Patañjali. Bharata and the commentary of Abhinavagupta remain the principal authorities on the ancient stage. Distinct evidence for the presentation of plays is available in the dramas of Aśvaghoṣa and Bhāsa.

It has been seen clearly that the different theories such as 'Greek' theory, 'Maypole' theory, theory of the 'cult of the dead', 'vegetation spirit' theory and theories of 'puppet and shadow play' are not tenable and cannot explain the origin of the Sanskrit drama as a whole but deal with its individual aspects only.

Thus it can be asserted that the Indian drama is a product of centuries; it was an organism that was continually in a process of evolution, assimilating into itself many new and foreign factors and yet preserving its own peculiar individuality.

[1]*NS-GOS*, XXXVII. 25–27.
[2]Ibid., XXXVI. 49.

CHAPTER TWO

Sanskrit Plays

SIGNIFICANCE

According to Bharata, when the peculiarities of life in a society are connected with certain gestures or when the actions of gods, *ṛṣis* and kings are represented on the stage it is a dramatic play.[1] This fact is corroborated by the *Daśarūpa*, the *Rasārṇavasudhākara* and the *Sāhityadarpaṇa*. According to the *Daśarūpa*, the drama is the imitation of situations. It is a show because it is seen. It is a representation due to the assumption of parts by actors.[2] According to the *Sāhityadarpaṇa*, poetry is of two sorts—poetry to be seen and heard, and poetry to be heard only. Of these, 'visible poetry' is that which can be represented, and this is called *rūpaka*, from the artificial assumption of forms (*rūpa*) by the actors[3]. In the *Rasārṇavasudhākara* the term *rūpaka* is applied to a play on the analogy of *rūpaka* or metaphor, because in a play we assume a non-distinction between characters and the actors representing them.[4] The *Nāṭakalakṣaṇaratnakośa* defines a play as a performance which can be dramatised by gestures.[5] In a commentary on the *Anargharāghava*, the drama is defined as the representation by gestures of the condition of people as affected by their pleasurable and unpleasurable feelings.[6]

In *dṛśya kāvyas* the audience enjoys something more than the words uttered by actors and actresses on a stage. This something consists of the emotion and its intensity expressed in their intonations, the presentation of their characteristic features under the stress of different emotions, the "temperament" of actors putting an original significance into the lifeless words of the drama, the dress and the decoration of the stage producing an illusion about actual life in different periods and countries.

OBJECT

Abhinaya or acting is the representation of high and low characters on

[1] *NS-KM*, XVIII. 10–13; *KSS*. XX. 10–13; *GOS*, XVIII. 10–13.
[2] *DR*, I. 7.
[3] *SD*, VI, *sūtras* 1–2.
[4] *RS*, III, p. 209, ll. 1–5.
[5] *NLR*, ll. 8–9, p. 1.
[6] *AR*, I, commentary, p. 9. Here *śloka* is attributed to Bharata.

the stage under suitable guises. The successful drama should contain suggestiveness in order to conform to the highly cultivated *dhvani* (suggestion) theory of the Sanskrit critics the finer the suggestion, the higher the enjoyment.[1]

A representation is to reflect the life of the world as in a mirror. Bharata lays down that all arts and sciences are to be met with there.[2] The purpose of a play like that of all poetry is to please and "to instruct in a pleasing manner in the style of a loving wife", as Mammaṭa puts it.[3] The aim of combined pleasure and instruction is to be achieved by inspiring various sentiments (*rasas*) in the audience while the actors imitate the different situations of life in the midst of diverse actions. Bharata says that a plot which has 64 divisions and sub-divisions should get nourishment from the *rasas*. Bharata instructs the dramatist to bring the incidents of the plot together, each in its own place, solely with reference to the *rasa* appropriate to each.[4] He further says that the essentials of a play, other than *rasa* and *bhāva*, are to subserve them. Of these two, *bhāvas* are there only to nourish and develop *rasa*. The elements that help us in realizing the main import of a play brought by means of acting are called *bhāvas*. The *bhāvas* secure for us (*bhāvayanti*) the sentiments (*rasān*) which are the very soul of a play.[5] Each of the essentials of a play will be taken separately and it will be shown that they are all used in the Sanskrit play only to subserve the *rasas*.

While giving the etymology of *abhinaya*, Bharata says that *abhinaya* is certainly the most prominent of all, as that is indispensable in helping us to visualise the main import of play. *Abhinaya* has four aspects: the *sātvika* (temperament), the *vācika* (words), the *āṅgika* (gestures) and the *āhārya* (dresses and make-up). On examination it is found that each of these aspects subserves the highest dramatic end of the development and manifestation of *rasa*.[6]

Bharata emphasizes dramatic realism and idealism under the heading *dharmī*. *Lokadharmī* stands for realism in drama and *nāṭyadharmī* for idealism. As the drama is a representation of the world, Bharata justly emphasizes propriety in the presentation of life on the stage. Each act

[1] *KP*, I. 3; *Dhvanyāloka, śloka* I, p. 9.

[2] *NS-KM*, I. 77b-82; *KSS*, I. 108–114a; *GOS*, I. 112–118a.

[3] *KP*, I. 2, p. 6.

[4] *NS-KM*, XIX. 52b–53a, 98b–99a; *KSS*, XXI. 58, 106.

[5] *NS-KM*, VI. 10, 35; VII, p. 69 prose; *KSS*, VI. 10, 34; VII, p. 69 prose; *GOS*, VI. 10, 38; VII, p. 343 prose.

[6] *NS-KM* and *KSS*, VIII. 6–9; *GOS*, VIII. 7–10.

performed, word uttered and garment worn must all be in agreement with what is actually found in life. Thus the representation of life on the stage by the dramatist is realistic. It is *lokadharmī*.[1]

It is the duty of the dramatist to see that his truths are imaginative truths, not actual truths, that his representations are ideal and not photographic. The exhaustive treatment of selection and reticence, dialogue, music, dancing and the minute turns of gesture and expression and other devices on the stage make-up adopted by the artist to idealise facts and help the onlooker to imagine things of his experience and things outside it—all these come within the scope of the *nāṭyadharmī* (conventional). Moreover, if anything used by people, appears in a play as endowed with a corporal form and speech, we have what is called *nāṭyadharmī*.[2]

Thus the drama is the result of the direct intellectual observation of life by the playwright and his artistic imagination. The end of all these means is manifestly the realization of emotional pleasure by the spectators.

Bharata insists on the dramatist making his characters employ the speech, dress, manners and conduct that are theirs. Local usages regarding costumes, languages, manners and professions differ in the different countries of the world. They are the *pravṛtti* or local colour in drama.[3]

The mental disposition of particular personages in particular situations is their *vṛtti*: There are four *vṛttis*: *bhāratī* that which is brought out in words; *sātvatī*, that which is disclosed in conduct, *kaiśikī*, that which consists of words and acts of mildness and delicacy and *ārabhatī*, that which consists of vigorous, strong or even violent words and actions. Bharata details the *rasas* enjoyed by the spectator in each of these forms of *vṛtti* and says that *vṛttis* are the constituent elements of all dramas and that the ten kinds of dramatic composition are considered to have proceeded from these.[4]

Bharata deals elaborately with what ought to be the effect of the stage representation on the spectator. The penetrating onlooker must be made to forget himself and his own identity in his absorption in what happens on the stage. Involuntary expressions of appreciation must come from his lips and he must jump to heights of joy or shed tears in uncontrollable sorrow.[5]

[1]*NS-KM*, XIII. 50–52; *KSS*, XIV. 69–71; *GOS*, XIII. 70–72.

[2]*NS-KM*, XIII. 53–62; *KSS*, XIV. 72–81; *GOS*, XIII. 73–85.

[3]*NS-KM*, XIII. 25b, c and prose, p. 147; *KSS*, XIV. 36b, c and prose, p. 165; *GOS*, XIII. 37 and prose, pp. 205–7.

[4]*NS-KM*, XVIII. 4–9a; *KSS*, XX. 4–9a; *GOS*, XVIII. 4–9a; *ND*, I, III, 103, pp. 11, 152.

[5]*NS-KM* and *KSS*, XXVII, 1–18a.

According to Bharata, music—vocal and instrumental—is a powerful aid in the realization of *rasa* by the spectator. He tells us how music aids the spectator's realization of *rasa* and serves to concentrate his attention on the representation of a play on the stage.[1]

Bharata also deals with the acoustic and other arrangements of the theatre and says that there should be nothing in the theatre to hinder the spectators' sight and hearing, and to obstruct in their maximum enjoyment of the emotional pleasure.[2]

As everything employed in a Sanskrit play points to the arousing of *rasa* in the spectator, it becomes essential for us to understand the nature, process and essence of *rasa* very clearly.

Bharata describes the nature of *rasa* as follows. What are known in ordinary language as causes, effects and auxiliaries of the latent emotion of love and the like come to be spoken of as excitants, ensuants and variants respectively, when found in drama and poetry, and when the latent emotion comes to be manifested by these, it is known as *rasa*.[3] There are different theories regarding the psychological nature of *rasa*.

Bhaṭṭa-Lollaṭa holds the theory of production (*utpattivāda*) which is allied to the Mīmāṁsā school of philosophy. According to it, the sentiment is generated in the presonated character and secondarily recognized in the personating actor. The *naṭa* imitates the original hero and becomes the source of charm to the audience. This theory is open to objection as Bhaṭṭa-Lollaṭa fails to recognize that the sentiment must be in the spectator, otherwise he cannot enjoy it.

Śrī-Śaṅkuka's theory which is based on inference is called *anumitivāda* and is affiliated to the Nyāya school. According to this doctrine *rasa* is inferred to exist in the actor, though not really present in him. The emotion, thus inferred, and then sensed by the audience, adds to itself a peculiar charm and fully develops into a sentiment in the spectator. In this theory the actor is identified with the original hero in the same way as the idea of a 'horse' that one has in regard to the picture of a horse (*citraturaganyāya*). The objection to this view is that it is not inference but perception and feeling that add charm.

Bhatta-Nāyaka's theory is based on the threefold potency of a piece of poetry and is related to the Sāṅkhya philosophy. According to him, the sentiment is due neither to production (*utpatti*), nor apprehension (*pratīti*). "What happens is that in poetry and drama words are endowed

[1]*NS-KM*, XXXVI. 16a; *KSS*, XXXVI. 20a.
[2]*NS-KM*, II. 24; *KSS*, II. 21; *GOS*, II. 24.
[3]*NS-KM*, VI, prose, p. 62; *KSS*, VI, prose, p. 71; *GOS*, VI, prose, pp. 274–89.

with a peculiar presentative potency, distinct from direct denotation (and indirect indication)—which tends to generalize the excitants ensuants and variants, and thereby presents to consciousness the 'latent emotion', which thereupon comes to be relished by a process of delectation abounding in enlightenment and bliss, due to the plentitude of the quality of harmony (*sattva*)". According to this view the relishing of *rasa* is the outcome of the purely verbal process of '*generalized* presentation'. This is open to the objection that it makes the unwarrantable assumption of what is called verbal process.

Finally, we come to the view of Abhinavagupta who holds that a new potentiality like '*bhojakatva*' (power of enjoyment) as enunciated by Bhaṭṭa-Nāyaka is not necessary. Its work can be done by suggestion (*vyañjanā*). Abhinavagupta's theory is *rasa-abhivyaktivāda* (theory of the manifestation of *rasa*). The sentiments already exist in the form of *saṁskāras* (predispositions) in the minds of the cultured (*sahṛdaya*) spectators. It is aroused by the witnessing of a dramatic performance, or on hearing a poem. The actions of Arjuna will excite the heroic sentiment.

The explanation offered by Abhinavagupta is as follows:

> In the mind of such spectators as are proficient in the art of feeling emotion, a particular emotion is already present in the form of a 'predisposition'; thus lying latent, it becomes patently mainfested by such agencies as the feminine figure and such other objects which, in ordinary parlance are known as 'causes', 'effects' and 'auxiliaries; but in poetry and drama, they renounce these names by reason of their being endowed with the faculty of exciting and so forth, and, on this account, come to be known by the extraordinary names of 'excitants', 'ensuants' and 'variants': These excitants and the rest are recognised in their most generalized forms, not partaking of any restrictions due to either the affirmation or negation of any of these specific relationships that are involved in such conceptions as 'this is mine' or 'this is my enemy's', or 'this belongs to a disinterested person' (where specific relationship is affirmed) or 'this is not mine,' 'this is not my enemy's', 'this does not belong to a disinterested person' (whose specific relationship is denied). Though the said emotion actually subsists in the particular spectator himself, yet by reason of the generalized form in which it is presented, the man loses, for the moment, all consciousness of his personality and has it merged in the universal, and thus representing the mental condition of all men of poetic sensibility, he apprehend the said emotion. As it becomes mainfested in its most generalized

> form, it has no existence apart from its own apprehension. In fact its essence consists in its being relished, and it lasts as long as the excitants, ensuants and variants continue to exist. It is relished in the same manner as a mixed beverage, and when it is relished, it appears as if it were moving before the eyes, entering the inmost recesses of the heart, inspiriting the entire body, and throwing into the background everything else; it makes one feel the rapturous bliss of Brahman; the emotion thus manifested becomes the source of transcendent charm and is spoken as *rasa*.[1]

Thus Sanskrit rhetoricians approach the aesthetic pleasure from the point of view of the reader or spectator, while European writers of poetics view it from the poet's standpoint.

A distinction is drawn between sentiment (*rasa*) and emotion (*bhāva*). Emotion may be both pleasant and unpleasant but a sentiment is always pleasurable and unique. There is no unpleasantness in a sentiment as it is aroused through a process of generalization (*sādhāraṇīkaraṇa*). This explains why the pathetic (*karuṇa*) and repulsive (*bībhatsa*) sentiments find place in the scheme of *rasa*. They are unpleasant as emotion (*bhāva*) but when generalized become pure and pleasurable (*ānandamaya*). In this connection and against the above, Rāmacandra and Guṇacandra, authors of the *Nāṭyadarpaṇa*, observe that some *rasas* do produce pain while others produce pleasure. As *rasas* producing pain, they mention the pathetic (*karuṇa*), furious (*raudra*), repulsive (*bībhatsa*) and terrific (*bhayānak*). They assert that the statement that all scenes, whether of pathos or of horror, invariably cause pleasure is against experience. If pleasure is experienced in all scenes, a spectator should not be alarmed—for being alarmed is not consistent with the feeling of pleasure experienced in witnessing a scene of horror. But the spectator gets alarmed on seeing the scenes of Draupadī's or Sītā's misery. In reply to the question why people go to witness *duḥkhātmaka* dramas (whose essence is sorrow), they say that it is owing to the skill of the poet or the actor.[2]

But the analogy given by Rāmacandra and Guṇacandra does not make any appeal. According to Abhinavagupta, aesthetic pleasure has no reference to the actual feelings common in the world of realities but to dormant mental conditions awakened under certain circumstances. A particular *rasa* is pleasurable not exclusively because of its nature.

[1]*KP*, prose, pp. 87–95. For translation of the passage see Translation of *Kāvyaprakāśa* by Gaṅgānātha Jhā.

[2]*ND*, 109 and prose, pp. 158–59.

The erotic sentiment (*śṛṅgāra*) is not pleasurable because it is *śṛṅgāra* but because the reader or the spectator has his mind rid of distractions.[1] We agree with Madhusūdana Sarasvatī who opines in this connection that the tears caused by a pathetic situation were to the original character no doubt tears of worldly sorrow (*laukika*) but to the spectator they were tears only of joy and absolutely transcendental (*alaukika*) in their essence.[2]

The Sanskrit dramas in their preludes state that the object of their presentation is the pleasure of the audience. Thus in the *prelude* of the *Abhijñānaśākuntala*, the manager explains the object of the presentation of the play to the *naṭī* clearly; 'Lady, I tell you the real truth until the wise are satisfied with the representation, I do not consider my skill in representation to be perfect. The heart of man although well instructed has not confidence in itself.'[3] In the *Pāravatīpariṇaya*, the *sūtradhāra* tells the *naṭī* that a play is presented for the pleasure of the cultured.[4] In the *Dhūrtaviṭasaṁvāda*, the object of presentation is said to be the pleasure of the wise and the good.[5] In the *Mālavikāgnimitra*, it is stated that the presentation is for the gratification of all, though their tastes differ in various ways.[6] Thus the object of presentation of plays is to bring satisfaction to the audience by evolving in their minds *rasa*, the transcendental pleasure.

OCCASIONS FOR ENACTMENT

Legendary tradition about the origin of the drama tells us that the practical exhibition of a drama entitled *Fall of Asuras* was arranged for on the occasion of the Indradhvaja festival, the sons and disciples of Bharata and *gandharvas* and *apsarās* being the actors.[7] The first play was enacted on the occasion of the religious festival, the Indradhvaja; which comes at the end of the rains and in the beginning of autumn. According to the *Abhinayadarpaṇa, nāṭya* and *nṛtta* should be witnessed particularly at the time of a festival. Those who desire good luck should cause *nṛtta* to be performed on such occasions as coronation, celebration by a king, a festival, a procession with an image of a god, a marriage ceremony,

[1]*Abh. Bh*, pp. 289–90. *NS-GOS*, I, *Abh. Bh*, pp. 300–12.
[2]*Bhagavadbhaktirasāyana*, III. 5–6, pp. 129–30.
[3]*Śāk.* prelude, 2, p. 6.
[4]*Pārvatīpariṇaya*, 1. 5, p. 2.
[5]*Dhūrtaviṭasaṁvāda*, prelude, p. 1.
[6]*Mal*, I. 4, p. 7.
[7]*NS-KM*, I. 20b–25; *KSS*, I. 54b–60; *GOS*, I. 54–59a.

reception of a friend, entry into a new town or house and the birth of a son, for *nṛtta* is auspicious.[1]

From a close study of the introductory scenes in dramas it is evident that the plays were enacted on different occasions according to their nature. They were not only enacted at the annual fairs of temples and festivals in different seasons but were also performed at the pleasure of the poet's patron or before a learned assembly or the village people.

In the prelude of the *Uttararāmacarita* the *sūtradhāra* says "Let me address the respectable gentlemen assembled today at the fair of the divine *Kālapriyanātha*. Let it be known to your honours—there is, as you know well, an illustrious scion of the Kaśyapa's race, bearing the distinctive title of 'Śrīkaṇṭha,' versed in grammar, *mīmāṁsā* and logic, *Bhavabhūti* by name and son of Jātukarṇī, a Brāhmaṇa, whom the Goddess of Speech follows like one enslaved. The *Uttararāmacarita*, a play composed by him, will now be represented."[2] In the prelude of the *Anargharāghava* the *sūtradhāra* states that an actor named Kalahakandala enacted a drama in the *yātrā*[3] in honour of god Puruṣottama.[4]

In the *Mālavikāgnimitra*, the *sūtradhāra* says: "I am asked by the learned audience that I should represent on the occasion of the spring festival the play *Mālavikāgnimitra*, the plot of which has been composed by *Kālidāsa*. Please therefore begin music."[5] In the *Ratnāvalī*, the *sūtradhāra* says: "Enough of prolixity. To-day, on the occasion of the spring festival, being called with great respect by the multitude of kings, who are dependent on the lotus-like feet of our king, the illustrious Śrī-Harṣa, and who have come here from regions of the various directions, I was thus addressed: 'Our master, Śrī-Harṣa has composed a *nāṭikā* entitled *Ratnāvalī*, graced with a noval arrangement of the plot. We have heard about it from hear-say but have not seen it acted.' Out of respect, therefore, for that very king, the gladdener of the hearts of all people, and with a mind to favour us, the same should be enacted on the stage by you with proper acting."[6] In the Dūtāṅgada, the *sūtradhāra* tells us that the *Dūtāṅgada*, a shadow play, may be enacted during the spring festival in the procession of Śrīkumārapāladeva.[7]

[1]*AD*, 12b–14.

[2]*URC*, prelude, p. 3.

[3]*Yātrā* literally means a 'procession', and also a 'pilgrimage'. In the whole of Northern India *yātrās* are taken out in honour of a deity and they occupy a unique position in Bengal. Huge crowds of all sects of people move in a procession, sing and dance to the glorification of the deity in a temple, street or courtyard.

[4]*AR*, prelude, p. 6.

[5]*Māl*, prelude, p. 2.

[6]*Rat*, prelude, p. 5.

[7]*Dūtāṅgada*, p. 2.

In the *Vikramorvaśīya*, the *sūtradhāra* says, "Oh Māriṣa! this assembly has very often witnessed the plays of former poets. I shall, therefore, bring on the stage to-day a new play known as the *Vikramorvaśīya*. Let the company of actors be told that they should be very careful about their respective parts. Actor: As you command, Sir. *Sūtradhāra*: I shall now announce to the honourable gentlemen here with a bow. Either out of curiosity for us, your humble petitioners, or out of respect for the excellent hero of the plot, you will please listen with attentive minds to this play of Kālidāsa."[1] In the *Prabodhacandrodaya*, the *sūtradhāra* says: "We want to enact the play with the action in which the quietistic sentiment plays an important part. You should enact the drama, the *Prabodhacandrodaya*, in front of the king, Kīrtivarma. The king wishes to see the play with his associates. The king, who has entered the path of *Śāntapatha* for his own pleasure, has ordered me to enact this drama. Therefore, instruct the *naṭas* to dress themselves according to the theme."[2] The *sūtradhāra* in the *Kundamālā* says, "I have been commanded by the audience that I should stage *Kundamālā*, the work of the revered poet Diṅnāga, resident of Arātālapura. So having called the noble lady (wife) rendering co-operation in the performance of this dramatic composition I betake myself to the stage."[3] In the *Kirātārjunīyavyāyoga* (military spectacle) it is stated that the drama was enacted at the pleasure of the king.[4]

Certain plays were enacted only for the amusement of the village people. The *Mahānāṭaka* is the best and the only preserved drama which was improvised by village artists.[5] We find explanation for this when we consider that these are also the prominent features of the *yātrās* of the modern days.

The view of Wilson and some other European scholars with regard to the occasion of the enactment of Sanskrit plays is as follows:

> The dramatic entertainments of the Hindus essentially differed from those of Modern Europe in the infrequency of their representation. They seem to have been enacted only on solemn or public occasions. In this respect they resembled the dramatic performances of the Athenians, which took place at distant intervals, and especially at the spring and autumnal festivals of Bacchus.[6]

[1] *Vik*, prelude, p. 3.

[2] *Prabodhacandrodaya*, prologue, pp. 13–14.

[3] *Kundamālā*, prelude, p. 7.

[4] *Kirātārjunīyavyāyoga*, prologue, p. 1.

[5] *Mahānāṭaka*, 1.5.

[6] Wilson, *Select Specimens of the Theatre of the Hindus*, I. XIII-XIV

But in this connection our view is different from that of the European scholars. Though the occasions mentioned by the authorities on Sanskrit dramaturgy are of infrequent occurrence, the mention of the theatre for general people and regular troupe of actors and actresses and also the reflection from the preludes of dramas as to their enactment at the will of the poet's patron at any time of the year, shows that they were kept in regular occupation by more frequent representation than what is generally considered.

PLACES FOR PERFORMANCE

The theatre is a place specially designed and equipped for the presentation of plays. The various terms used in Sanskrit for the theatre are *nāṭyagṛha, nāṭyamaṇḍapa, prekṣāgṛha* or *prekṣāgāra*. The drama and the theatre point to each other's mutual existence and a dramatic work becomes most impressive when it is enacted on the stage. They constitute a very important chapter in the social and cultural history of a nation. The *Mṛcchakaṭika* gives a more graphic description of the ancient Indian society than any other work of that time.

The ancient Indian kings had pleasure gardens, theatres and music halls attached to their spacious palaces, generally for the entertainment of their queens. Playwrights and regularly appointed professors and actors were patronised by them. Histrionics, music and dancing were a part of the education of the high-born ladies. In the *Mālavikāgnimitra*, Gaṇadāsa and Haradatta were appointed professors and Mālavikā was taught not only dancing but also histrionics.[1] In the *Śilparatna*[2], the *Kāvyamīmāṁsā*[3] and the *Saṅgītamakaranda*[4] there is reference to a palace theatre. From the seating arrangement of the theatre described in the *Saṅgītaratnākara* it is clear that it belonged to a king. The audience consisted of men of education, culture and artistic sense, such as kings, queens, ministers, court-poets and courtiers.

From an account given in the *Saṅgītaratnākara* the following information is available: The music hall was decorated in a unique manner. It was furnished with flowers, flags and jewelled pillars. The president, generally the king, took his seat on a beautiful lion throne in the middle of the auditorium. To his left, court ladies of the harem were seated, but the chief queens were provided seats to his right. Behind these chief

[1]*Māl*, II. 8.
[2]*ŚR*, I. 39, 35–36a, p. 199.
[3]*Kāvyamīmāṁsā*, prose, pp. 54–55.
[4]*Saṅgītamakaranda*, I. 2–7.

queens, seats for the chief treasury officers were arranged. Close thereto, honoured astronomers, astrologers, physicians, psychologists, humorous poets and people conversant with tradition were seated. To the right of the chief queens were the seats for ministers and military officers of high rank. Fashionable men and women were seated in such a manner as to surround the ladies of the court. Just behind the king youthful and beautiful women guards, wearing twinkling bracelets and holding beautiful chowries, were to occupy their places. Forward guards were seated to the left, having in front the vocal singers, conversationalists, bards and experts in panegyric. Seats for members of the royal family were provided in the surrounding places. Then there were seats for dexterous guards holding canes. Armed bodyguards used to stand in the four corners of the theatre. In the above manner the audience was provided seats and thus the king used to see the performance. In this type of ancient theatre[1], a diagram of which is given herein, (Fig. 1) there appears to be no place for the general public. This is apparently a theatre in the palace itself.

In the *Mānasāraśilpaśāstra*, there is a reference to the seating arrangement in a temple theatre as also in a palace theatre. Theatres are said to have been built in continuation of the open courtyard, linking the tank or shed in the temple and the palace. In the theatre the divine and royal thrones and seats made of wood, stone and brick were arranged in compartments partitioned by low sliding walls.[2]

Most of the celebrated temples in India had *nāṭamandiras* where dancers and actors propitiated the god or goddess through the representation of their art. The name *nāṭamandira* is significant as pointing to the existence of temple theatres. Paid women dancers were employed in all rich temples and dramas in praise of a deity were represented in festivals. The *Uttararāmacarita* was enacted at the annual *yātrā* in honour of Kālapriyanātha.[3] In some of the temples even now dances are prominent items of the daily programme after the evening offerings to the gods. *Devadāsīs* dance in temples in Jagannāthapurī and south India even these days. In ancient India places, halls or yards, were specially provided in temples for dancing, music and recitations. In the Kailāśa temple at Ellora caves a *nāṭamandira* hall is easily noticeable. Primarily these *nāṭamandiras* were used as recreation resorts for priests, *sādhūs*, religious and learned folk. These temple theatres are called *kūṭṭampalams* in

[1]*ŚR*, VII. 1351–1361a.
[2]*MS*, XLVII. 1–17, pp. 308–9.
[3]*URC*, prelude, p. 3.

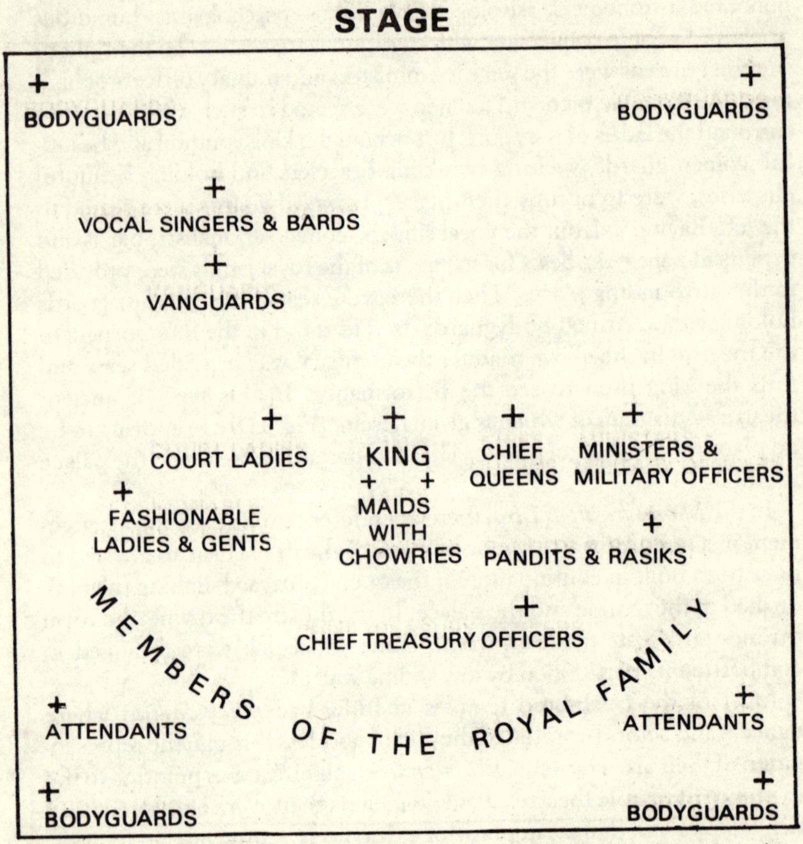

Fig. 2: Diagram showing the seating arrangement in a Palace Theatre according to *ŚR*

Kerala. A sample of this *kūṭṭampalam* is preserved in the Trivandrum Museum (Fig. 2).

Plays were presented to the general public in open courtyards and on improvised stages. People used to pay money to see a dramatic show. On the other hand, the *Nāṭyaśāstra* mentions all kinds of charities as also allowing people to enjoy a dramatic show without payment is praised highly.[1] The stage was temporarily built and thus, evidently, its paraphernalia was very simple. There was preponderance of singing and dancing and of the comic element. The *Mahānāṭaka* is the only available

[1]*NS-GOS*, XXXVII. 28.

TEMPLE THEATRE

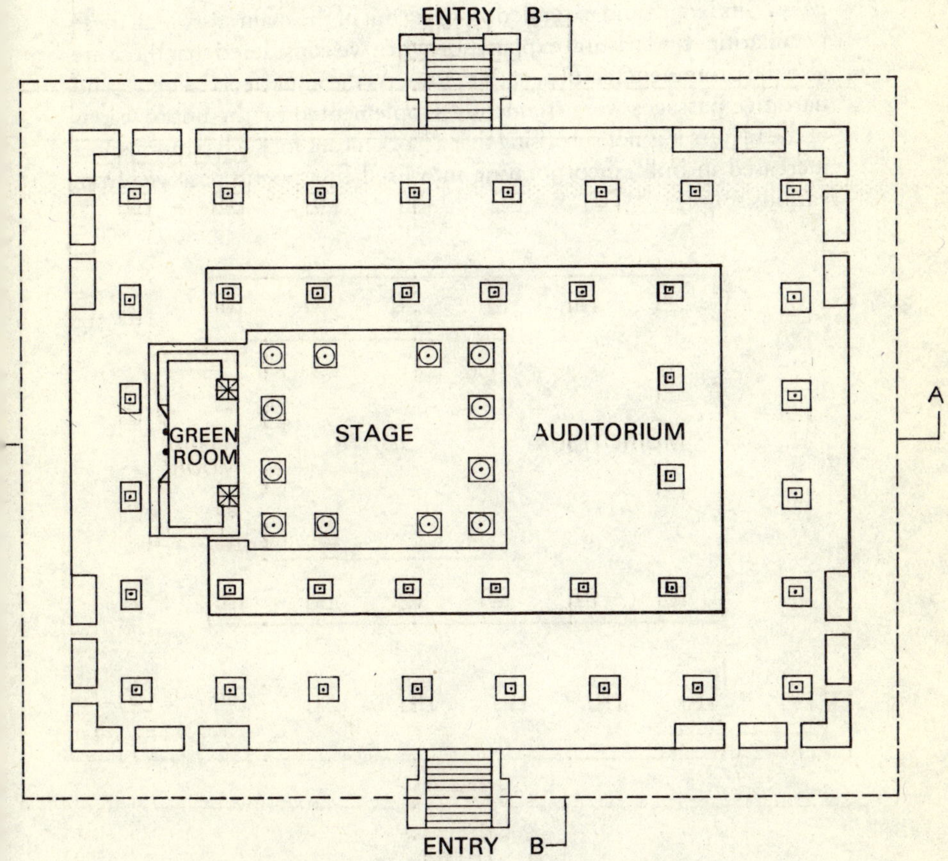

Fig. 3: Plan of Vaḍakkunnāthan Kūṭṭampalam, Trichur
(Courtesy: Archaeological Survey of India, New Delhi)

drama of the species. The general plot-setting is given by the poet with some excellent pieces of poetry. Dialogue is improvised by the actors and actresses. It is easily understood because the subjects are taken from the *Rāmāyaṇa*, the *Mahābhārata* or the *purāṇas*. The religious or mythological theme of the *Mahānāṭaka*, its epic or narrative character, the imperfect nature of its dialogues, its descriptive passages interspersed with elaborate and vivid stage directions, its charms like *vaitālika vākyas*, its length and extended working out of the main story—all these peculiarities find natural explanation when we considered that these are also the prominent features of the *yātrās*. As the imperfect dialogues and narrative passages were frequently supplemented by the improvisions of the players it is not surprising that a work meant for such performances increased in bulk, incorporating into itself fine poetic passages from various sources.'

CHAPTER THREE

Construction of the Theatre

TYPES AND MEASUREMENTS

A detailed account of the interior arrangement of the theatre is given by Bharata. Later authorities also furnish details which show that the main features described by Bharata were adhered to in later times.

According to the *Nāṭyaśāstra*, the *Śilparatna* and the *Bhāvaprakāśana*, the play-house as made ready for performance may be of three types. The *Viṣṇudharmottara*[1] states that the theatre might be of two types, rectangular and square. The square theatres, according to it, should be 32 × 32 *hastas* (cubits) in area.

In Sanskrit texts dealing with architecture, dimensions of all kinds of buildings are comparative and suggestive and can be altered to suit the requirements of the various kinds of structures. The *Śilparatna* says that the play-house may be of two or rather three types, divided into four equal parts, either by drawing lines lengthwise or breadthwise externally or from top to bottom, every part or two parts being separated by pillars for the audience and the fourth part, left for the stage proper.[2]

The architectural details of the *nāṭyamaṇḍapa* are very clearly laid down in the *Nāṭyaśāstra*. There are three types of play-house—*vikṛṣṭa* (rectangular), *caturasra* (square) and *tryasra* (triangular).

The *Bhāvaprakāśana* reads *vṛtta* in place of *vikṛṣṭa*,[3] but no structural details are given there. One has therefore to rely on the three types given in the *Nāṭyaśāstra*—*vikṛṣṭa*, *caturasra* and *tryasra*.[4] The *vikṛṣṭa* is rectangular theatre according to Abhinavagupta.[5]

He notes two views about the varieties of theatres. According to one opinion, *vikṛṣṭa* is *jyeṣṭha*, *caturasra* is *madhya* and *tryasra* is *avara*. The other divides each of the first type into *jyeṣṭha*, *madhya* and *avara*, thus getting nine types which when measured in *hastas* and *daṇḍas* would be eighteen. Abhinavagupta accepts this opinion and propounds clearly

[1] *VD*, III. 20. 4.

[2] *ŚR*, I. 39, 60–67, pp. 201–2.

[3] *BP*, X, p. 295, ll. 9–18.

[4] *NS-KM*, II. 8–14; *KSS*, II. 7–11; *GOS*, II. 7–14. In *GOS* and *KM* editions, verses 13 and 14 are repeated. The repeated verses in *GOS* are numbered as 25 and 26 while in *KM* they are not numbered but written between verses 24 and 25.

[5] *Abh. Bh*, I, p. 50.

his view about the nine divisions of the theatre. But we should accept the three types of the theatre as they are referred to at various places and are actually defined in the *Nāṭyaśāstra*. The only question which arises is that at one place the *Nāṭyaśāstra* states that *jyeṣṭha* is 108 *hastas*, *madhya* is 64 *hastas* and *kanīya* is 32 *hastas*, and at another place 64 × 32 *hastas* is said to be the measurement of the *vikṛṣṭa* type and 32 × 32 *hastas* of the *caturasra* type. Thus no clear indication about the measurement of the *avara* type is available. It is therefore difficult to establish any connection between the two statements. So, to harmonise the statements, it can be said that there were nine varieties, or even eighteen varieties of theatres taking the *hasta* and the *daṇḍa* measurements into consideration as stated by Abhinavagupta. Though Abhinavagupta himself feels that so many divisions have no purpose to serve, yet he refers to them only to maintain a particular standpoint.[1]

From the *Nāṭyaśāstra* one can find that the *jyeṣṭha* type is specially meant for gods, *madhya* for kings and *avara* for ordinary people. Abhinavagupta says that the *jyeṣṭha* theatre may be used for dramas where gods are heroes, as in *Ḍima*, the *madhya* when kings are heroes, as in *Prakaraṇa*, and the *avara* when ordinary men are heroes as in *Bhāna* and *Prahasana*.[2]

When we consider the verse of the *Nāṭyaśāstra* '*Pramānaṁ Eṣāṁ nirdiṣṭam hastadaṇḍasamāśrayam*'[3] we find that measurement for the building of theatre was dependent upon the conception of *hasta* and *daṇḍa*. What are these measurements? The *Naṭyaśāstra* accepts that the smallest measure is *aṇu* (atom). The table of measurement according to this authority is as follows. Eight *aṇus* make one *raja* (cardust), eight *rajas* one *bāla* (hairend), eight *bālas* one *likṣā* (*nit*), eight *likṣās* one *yūkā* (*louse*), eight *yūkās* one yava (barley), eight *yavas* one *aṅgula*, 24 *aṅgulas* one *hasta*, four *hastas* one *daṇḍa*.[4] This list substantially agrees with the one given in the *Arthaśāstra* of Kauṭilya.

From the *Mānasāraśilpaśāstra* we find that *aṅgula* (finger breadth) and the *hasta* (cubit) measures are in fact of the same category. The finger breadth, equivalent to three-fourths of an inch, is perhaps the earliest unit of measure. It has its own defects, namely, the finger of two persons is hardly of equal breadth and the length of the finger of a person is liable to change owing to various natural causes. Apparently with a view to avoid these defects the finger breadth is ascertained by the measure of certain other objects, atom, cardust, hairend, *nit*, louse and barley grain.

[1]*Abh. Bh.*, I, pp. 50–51. [2]Ibid., pp. 51–52.
[3]*NS-KM*, II. 10a; *KSS*, II. 9a; *GOS*, II. 9a.
[4]*NS-KM*, II. 15–19; *KSS*, II. 12–16; *GOS*, II. 15–19.

The largest finger breadth is stated to be equal to eight barley grains, the intermediate of seven barley grains and the smallest of six barley grains.[1] The *aṅgula* measure is practically the same in almost all Sanskirt works, such as the *Arthaśāstra*,[2] bearing on the subject.

The measuring tape should be made of *kārpāsa*, *vādara*, *valkala* or *muñja* and must have no joints. Wise people should employ such thread as cannot be broken. The type should be handled carefully.[3]

In constructing a play-house it is necessary, according to Bharata, that the soil should be first examined. It must be even, steady, hard and black or white. The whole field must be ploughed and bones, nails, skulls and such other things taken out. Then in the *Puṣya* constellation it must be measured with a white string. After the foundation walls have been constructed the pillars may be erected in the Rohiṇī or the Śravaṇa constellation. Emphasis is thus laid on the selection of hard land, on its purification from bones and bushes and on fixing definite boundaries with a thread, so that the prescribed measurements are adhered to.[4]

The standard theatre (*nāṭyaveśman*) is a rectangular building, 64 cubits in length and 32 cubits in breadth, marked out into two equal divisions, the auditorium (*raṅgamaṇḍala*) and the stage (*raṅgabhūmi*). The stage is divided into two equal parts—the front and the rear, the latter being the green room. The front part is again divided into two equal parts. Of these two parts the one behind is the head of the stage (*raṅgaśīrṣa*) and the front part is the stage proper where the play is acted. On both sides of the stage proper, two *mattavāraṇis*, equal in measure to the stage, are constructed. It is clear from the diagram of the rectangular theatre that the auditorium is thus 32 × 32 cubits, the front stage 8 × 16 cubits, the back stage 8 × 32 cubits and the green room 16 × 32 cubits[5] (Fig. 3). Abhinavagupta gives two views on the measurements of the stage proper. According to one view, it was 16 cubits in length and 8 cubits in breadth, and according to the other, it was 8 cubits in length and 16 cubits in breadth.[6]

The *caturasra* type of theatre is 32 cubits in length and 32 cubits in

[1]*MS*, II. 20–32, pp. 4–5.

[2]*AS*, I. 2, 20.

[3]*NS-KM*, II. 30b–34; *KSS*, II. 28b–32; *GOS*, II. 31–34. Here in *GOS* numbering is wrong: 31, 32, 33 are repeated.

[4]*NS-KM*, II. 27–30a; *KSS*, II. 24–28a, 46a; *GOS*, II. 29–33a, 48a. Here in *GOS* numbering is wrong. The numbers 31, 32, 33 are repeated but the verses are different.

[5]*NS-KM*, II. 36–37, 57–58, 74b; *KSS*, II. 34b–36a, 64b–66a, 69–70, 86b; *GOS*, II. 36b–38a, 66b–68a, 71, 72, 90a.

[6]*Abh. Bh*, I, p. 58.

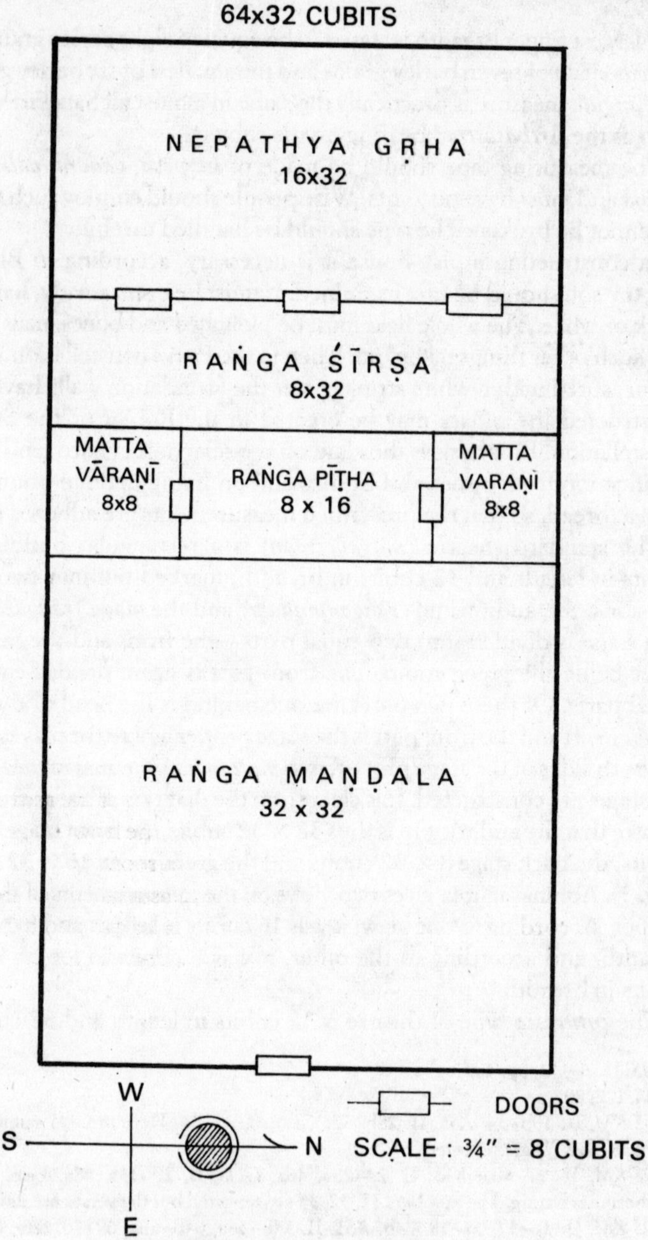

Fig. 4: Vikṛṣṭa Nāṭyagṛha.

breadth.[1] Abhinavagupta quotes Śaṅkuka's opinion on the divisions of the *caturasra* theatre. He states that the whole field 32 × 32 cubits should be divided lengthwise and breadthwise into eight equal parts, thus making 64 squares as is done in a chess-board. The *raṅgapīṭha* should be in the four inner squares. In this type the *mattavāraṇīs* will be 8 × 8 cubits each and the *raṅgańśīrṣa* 8 × 8 cubits (or 8 × 32 cubits as there are no walls on the breadth line). The size of the *nepathyagṛha* is 4 × 32 cubits and that of the auditorium 12 × 32 cubits. This type is also shown in the diagram of the *caturasra* theatre (Fig. 5).[2]

The *tryasra* theatre is in the form of an equilateral triangle. It is divided into eight parts on each side and from each dividing point lines are drawn parallel to those on the side of the equilateral triangle. Thus 64 triangles are formed. In four triangles in the middle the *raṅgapīṭha* is constructed. Behind the *raṅgapīṭha* is placed the *raṅgaśīrṣa* in five triangles (or thirteen triangles in the absence of walls) and the *nepathyagṛha* in fifteen triangles. Each of the *mattavāraṇīs* is constructed in eight triangles. The remaining triangles are reserved for the audience. This is illustrated in the diagram of the *tryasra* type (Fig. 7).[3] But no exact measurement of this type of theatre is available in the *Nāṭyaśāstra* or the *Abhinavabhāratī*.

RAṄGAPĪṬHA AND DECORATION

The height of the theatre invariably depended on the type of the play to be presented in it. Theatres were constructed in two storeys having the shape of a mountain cave with a few windows to ensure excellent accoustic effects. What does the word *dvibhūmi* occurring in '*Kāryaḥ śailaguhākāro dvibhūmirnāṭyamaṇḍapaḥ*'[4] indicate? Various opinions are cited by Abhinavagupta about the interpretation of this word. According to one view, it was the higher and lower portions of the *raṅgapīṭha*. The second view is that there is another wall round the *mattavārṇīs* just as there are two walls with an intermediate passage for circumambulation in a temple. According to the other view there was another *maṇḍapa* on the terrace, while still another view took it as *advibhūmi*. Then Abhinavagupta states and supports the view of Upādhyāya thus: From the *raṅgapīṭha*, from where the seats for the audience commence to the exit, *bhūmis* should be made, each one higher than the preceding one, the last

[1]*NS-KM*, II. 75–77, 84b–89; *KSS*, II. 87–89, 96b–101; *GOŚ*, II. 90b–93a, 100–105a.
[2]*Abh. Bh*, I, p. 66.
[3]*NS-KM*, II. 90–93a; *KSS*, II. 102–4; *GOS*, II. 105b–8.
[4]*NS-KM*, II. 69b; *KSS*, II. 81b: *GOS*, II. 84a.

Fig. 5: Aerial view of Nāṭamandira, Konarak.

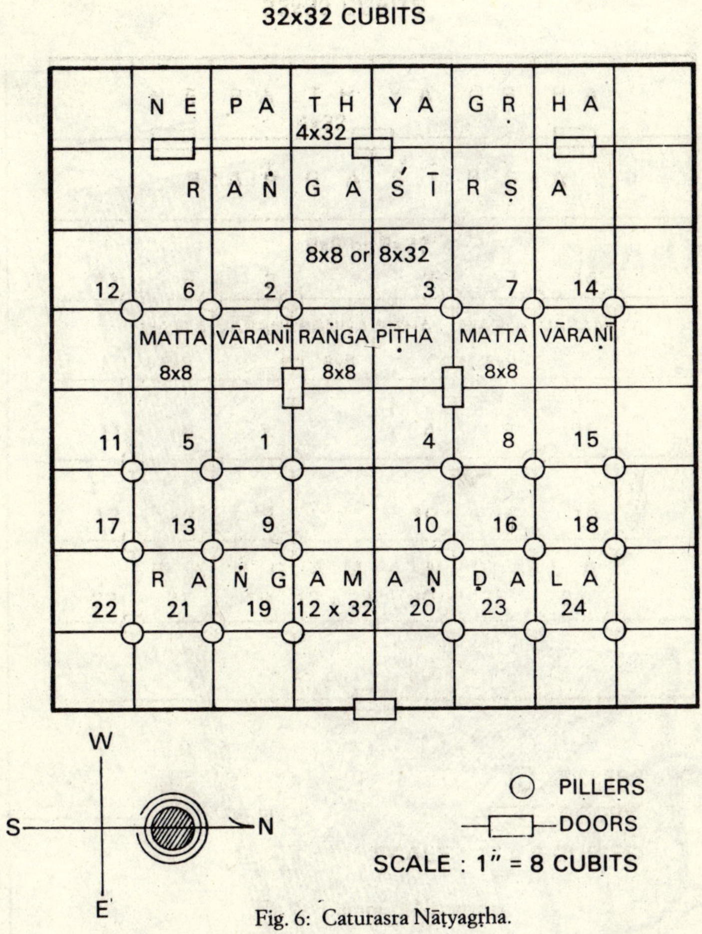

Fig. 6: Caturasra Nāṭyagṛha.

having a height equal to the height of the *raṅgapīṭha*, so that the rows of the spectators may not obstruct one others' view.[1]

In our opinion *dvibhūmi* used with *nāṭyamaṇḍapa* refers to a double-storeyed stage. The upper storey must have been used for the presentation of the dramatic actions of celestial regions and the lower one for that of the terrestrial ones. The stage was often a two-storeyed building. Scenes

[1] *Abh. Bh*, I, pp. 64–65.

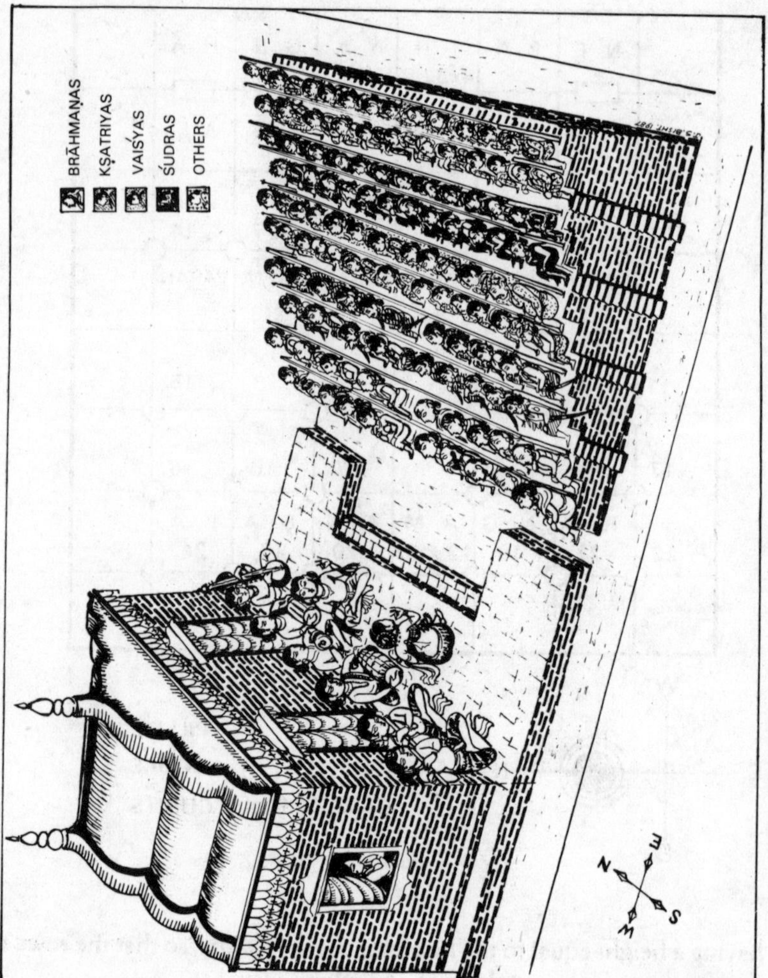

Fig. 7: Diagram of seating arrangement of spectators in the auditorium as mentioned in the *Nāṭyaśāstra.*

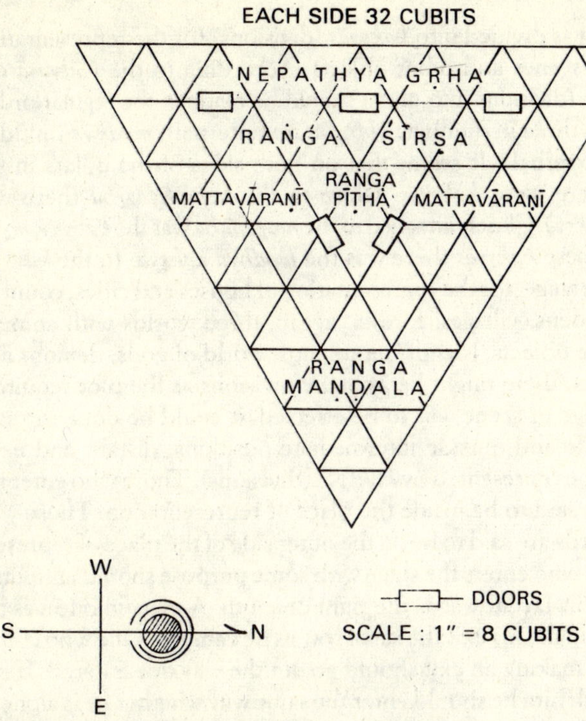

Fig. 8: Tryasra Nāṭyagṛha

like climbing up and down could be easily enacted on the stage with the aid of the *bhūmis*.

The terrace in the *Ratnāvalī* suggests that the stage had an upper storey. Yaugandharāyaṇa says: "I conjecture His Majesty has started for the palace to witness the merriment of the citizens heightened by the Madana festival. (looking up). Ah! How now? The king has ascended the palace."[1]

In the *Mṛcchakaṭika* we have the following (enter Sthāvaraka fettered in a palace): "Shall I let myself down from here. I shall throw myself down from the gate room of the palace—terrace, through the worn-out lattice". Further on Saṁsthānaka says: "Now I shall climb the second storey of my palace—terrace and look on my handiwork" (he does so and sees the crowd; he gets down and approaches the crowd).[2]

[1]*Rat*, I, pp. 9–10.
[2]*Mṛch*, X, pp. 230–33.

The stage was divided into *kakṣyās* (divisions) for the representation of change in scenes and other objects. According to the *Nāṭyaśāstra*, *kakṣyāvibhāga* (divisions into parts) should be made in the regular order. *Kakṣyās* were three in number: *obhyantara* (internal), *madhya* (middle) and *bāhya* (external). It seems that on both sides of the pillars in the *raṅgaśīrṣa* there were *kakṣyās*. Close to the *nepathyagṛha* there was *abhyantara kakṣyā*. Closely attached to the *raṅgapīṭha* was the *bāhya kakṣyā*. In between these *kakṣyās* there was the *madhya kakṣyā*. In the *kakṣyā-vibhāga* of the stage, for the representation of houses and cities, country-side with gardens, villages, forests, ocean, three worlds with animate and inanimate objects, islands, mountains, world of gods, demons and nether regions, there might be as many divisions as the plot required. When a change of scene was to be effected, it could be done through *kakṣyās*. Inside and outside intermediate positions, distant and near, places could be represented by *kakṣyās* (divisions). Those who enter the stage first are said to be inside the place of representation. Those who enter afterwards are said to be on the outer side of the place of representation. A man who enters the stage with some purpose should announce himself with his face towards the right or south. A man who leaves the scene should make his exit the same way as he came in. One who comes in again after making an exit should go out the way one entered. If any body goes with him he should enter the same way whether he is alone or accompanied by that person. A person walks along with another of equal rank and is followed by others of lower rank.[1]

To indicate change of scene, directions such as '*iti parikrāmati*', '*iti parikramya*' are found in Sanskrit plays. In presenting a change an actor would walk on the stage and take rounds as required by distance.

We may take the *Mṛcchakaṭika* as an example to illustrate the use of *kakṣyās* on the stage.

In the *Mṛcchakaṭika* Cārudatta and Maitreya after attending a music concert come to their house. Maitreya says: "Well, here is our house, Vardhamānaka, open the door."

Vardhamānaka says: "I hear the voice of the noble Maitreya. The noble Cārudatta has come. So I will open the door for him." (He does so). Entering the house they both go to sleep.

Now Śarvilaka enters the stage and looks at the sky joyfully: "Why, the moon is setting". He feels the wall, finds it deteriorated. He measures and surveys the wall with his sacred thread. A snake bites him. He binds his finger with his sacred thread and acts the manifest effect of poison.

[1]*NS-KM*, XIII. 1–25a; *KSS*, XIV. 1–35; *GOS*, XIII. 1–36b.

Dvitīyaḥ pūrvaraṅgavidhau pariśiṣṭanṛttalakṣyatayā.'

He resumes his work shoving in a dummy man at first. With that he enters the house and looking before him says: "I see there are two persons sleeping here. All right, I shall open the door as a defensive measure. But hark, the door squeeks as the house is very old. Let me go in search of water. Now where can water be found?" (He goes about in search, brings water and sprinkles it on the door and enters the house and takes ornaments).

Radanikā (entering) "Oh, alas, Vardhamānaka is sleeping in the outer rooms." Śarvilaka wants to kill Radanikā, leaves here because of her being a woman and escapes.

She wakes Maitreya and Cārudatta.

From the above incident one can anticipate the existence of a door on the stage, but in reality there was none. It was all done with gestures. Only Maitreya and Cārudatta enter one *kakṣyā* from another *kakṣyā*. Then Śarvilaka searches for water and brings it.[1] Of course, as described in the *Nāṭyaśāstra* he must have come the same way through which he might have gone out. Vardhamānaka is said to be sleeping in the outer room when really he might have been sleeping in another *kakṣyā*.

Further, in the same drama a court scene is represented. Śodhanaka, a court peon, enters and says: "Officials of the court have commanded me, Śodhanaka, go to the court and lay the seats. I shall just go to the hall of justice to keep it ready." (He walks a few steps and looks before him). "Here is the hall of justice. I will enter". (He enters and sweeps it and spreads a carpet). "I have swept the hall of justice and laid the seats. So I shall just go back to the officials to tell them about it." (He walks a few steps and looks before him). "What? It is that bad man, the king's brother-in-law, who is coming this way. So I shall avoid his sight and go in another direction." (He stands away: Now enters Saṁsthānaka, gorgeously dressed. Saṁsthānaka walks a few steps and looks before him). "Here it is the hall of justice. I shall enter." (He enters and looks round). "Why, the seats have been placed. The court officials will come in a moment. I shall take my seat here in this grassy quadrangle and wait." (He does so. Śodhanaka walks in another direction and looks before him). "Here come the officials of the court, I will approach them." (He approaches them).

(Enters the judge accompanied by the mayor, the clerk and others). Śodhanaka: "Please come your Lordship, come this way, please." (They walk a few steps). "Here is the hall of justice. May your Lordship enter." (They all enter).

[1]*Mṛcb*, III, pp. 69–77.

Fig. 9: Darbar Hall General View, Belur Temple

Judge: "Good Śodhanaka, go out and see if there are any petitioners."

Śodhanaka goes out and Saṁsthānaka places his complaint before the judge.

Cārudatta and Vasantasenā's mother are called. And the petition is considered.[1]

From the above it is quite clear that the carpet is spread in the court and the seats are arranged. This is one division (*kakṣyā*). Saṁsthānaka waits for the officials to come outside the court hall. He is in another division of the stage (*dvitīyā kakṣyā*). The judge, accompanied by the mayor, the clerk and others, enters. The judge is naturally in front of them all and then others enter according to their rank. The servant who goes out to call Cārudatta and Vasantasena's mother might have brought them the same way as he had gone.

The use of *kakṣyās* can be shown with reference to other dramas also. Thus from the testimony of the *Nāṭyaśāstra* and the actual incidents in the *Mṛcchakaṭika*, we find that the stage could be used to represent a place where persons sleep and court scenes are enacted and that it was divided into as many apartments (*kakṣyās*) as the plot required.

Theatres were decorated with all the oriental splendour, colour and brilliance. The front portion of the stage used to be built of wood and richly decorated with wooden carvings. Garlands were hung on it and ornamental arches added to its grace. The *maṇḍapa* had windows. The woodwork was polished and the walls whitewashed before pictures were painted on them. The woodwork and *ūha* (an additional moulding—uppermost portion of a column), *pratyūha* (a supporting member, lowermost portion of a column), *sañjavana* (quadrangle), *vyāla* (an arch marked with leograph), *Śālabhañjikā* (an image or figure made of *śāla* wood i.e. statuettes), *nirvyūha* (a cross circle), *kuhara* (interior window), *vedikā* (pedestal), *yantra* (an architectural member of the bedstead, a band), *jāla* (a latticed window), *gavākṣa* (windows resembling the cow's eye), *pīṭha* (pedestal, a pavement) *dharaṇī* (a kind of tree of which pillars are constructed), Kapotālī (a dovecot, crown work, fillet) and *kuṭṭima* (a pavement) and *stambha* (column). Thus it is decorated with various columns. After the woodwork, come the walls. The column, *nāgadanta* (a kind of window resembling the hood of a cobra), *vātāyana* (window), *kona* (a class of building), *pratidvāra* (moulding of the base or column of a door), *dvāra* (door, gate), should not come opposite a door leading to

[1]*Mṛch*, IX.

the *raṅgapīṭha*.[1] Dr. A.K. Coomaraswamy notes some changes of meaning in the terms quoted above. He thinks that *nirvyūha* means 'storey', *vedikā*, 'a railing' and *gavākṣa* 'an ordinary carved window'.[2]

RAṄGAŚĪRṢA, GREEN ROOM AND MATTAVĀRAṆĪS

In the *vikṛṣṭa* type of theatre the back stage (i.e. *raṅgaśīrṣa*) is 8 × 32 cubits and in the *caturasra* type it is 8 × 8 cubits. As there are no walls breadthwise it may also be imagined to be 8 × 32 cubits. The exact measurements of *tryasra* type are not available.

The *raṅgaśīrṣa* is built of six pieces of wood and furnished with two doors leading into the green room. It is smooth and even like a mirror and decorated with jewels. Its surface is not like the back of a tortoise or the back of a fish. The intermediate space is filled with very fine black earth, having the lustre of a pure mirror and studded with emeralds, sapphires, corals and other precious stones, arranged in various designs on the four sides.[3]

The *raṅgaśīrṣa* is constructed with six planks. According to Abhinavagupta, attached to the wall of the *nepathyagṛha* and *raṅgaśīrsa*, two pillars should be erected, each at a distance of eight cubits from the other. By their side two other pillars, with a mutual distance of four cubits are raised. They will thus be four and with the upper and lower planks, will make the total six. At this place two doors one for the exit from and the other for entry into the *nepathyagṛha* are constructed.

Portions of the back stage (*raṅgaśīrṣa*), as Abhinavagupta points out, seem to have been reserved as a place of rest for actors, for maintaining the secrecy of the entrance and exit and for purposes such as prompting, securing some stage effect and storing stage paraphernalia.[4]

It can be proved easily that the *raṅgapīṭha* and the *raṅgaśīrṣa* were two different portions. Scholars, except Manomohan Ghosh, hold that *raṅgapīṭha* and *raṅgaśīrṣa* were two distinct parts of the theatre. The *Nāṭyaśāstra* testifies to this. Again the terms *raṅgapīṭha* and *raṅgaśīrṣa* are suggestive of the whole theatre being regarded as one construction. According to Abhinavagupta, there is a curtain between the *raṅgapīṭha*

[1]*NS-KM*, II. 64–74; *KSS*, II. 76–86; *GOS*, II. 78–90a. The meanings of architectural terms have been taken from the *Dictionary of Hindu Architecture* by P.K. Acharya and the *Sanskrit-English Dictionary* by Monier-Williams.

[2]*Indian Historical Quarterly*, vol. IX, p. 594.

[3]*NS-KM*, II. 57b–62a; *KSS*, II. 69b–74a; *GOS*, II. 71b–76a.

[4]*Abh. Bh*, I, pp. 62–63.

and the *raṅgaśīrṣa*. The *raṅgaśīrṣa* was of a level higher than the *raṅgapīṭha* in the *vikṛṣṭa* type of theatre and of the same level in the *caturasra*. The *raṅgapīṭha* and the *raṅgaśīrṣa* were situated in two different parts of the theatre as they were used for different purposes. The *raṅgapīṭha* is meant for the actual representation of the plot whereas the *raṅgaśīrṣa* is left as a place of retirement for actors.

The *raṅgaśīrṣa* was also used for accommodating the orchestra. In the *Nāṭyaśāstra* it has been laid down that the musicians should sit in the *raṅgaśīrṣa*.[1]

The green room (*nepathyagṛha*) is a part of the main building. Behind the curtain are the quarters of the actors (*nepathyagṛha*). In the *vikṛṣṭa* type of theatre the green room is 16 × 32 cubits and in the *caturasra* type it is 4 × 32 cubits. No measurements are available regarding the *tryasra* type.

The green room is fairly spacious to enable the several characters to attend to their 'make-up'. The *nepathyagṛha* is a place from where sounds are raised to indicate uproar and confusion; here also are uttered the voices of gods and other persons whose presence on the stage is not desirable. In the *Mṛcchakaṭika* when Śarvilaka boards the cart with Madanikā and starts on his journey, a voice from behind the curtain is heard, "who hears? who hears?" The chief of the police issues these commands. "Here is the cowherd boy named Āryaka, whom a prophecy has declared to be a prospective king. King Pālaka, alarmed on account of his faith in the prophecy, has removed him from his hamlet and has put him in prison. Be diligent, therefore, in your respective posts."[2] In the above passage the confusion and alarm which could not be represented on the stage were reported from the green room. Then, again, in the *Ratnāvalī* the magician's art which could not be shown on the stage was described through uproar behind the scenes: "Here in the upper apartment, fire has broken out all of a sudden, imparting to the mansions the beauty of golden turrets by its masses of flames; its intense heat is indicated by its scorching the top of the trees in the garden; the pleasure-mountain looks dark like a watery cloud with smoke descending on it; the women-folk are distressed by the heat. Moreover, this fire has sprung up to give veracity, as it were, to the rumour about the queen's being burnt, which was formerly circulated in Lāvaṇaka."[3]

The *Nāṭyaśāstra* prescribes that on both the sides of the *raṅgapīṭha*, two *mattavāraṇīs* are to be constructed. Both of them are higher than

[1] *NS-KM*, XXXIV, prose, p. 429; *KSS*, XXXIII, prose, p. 449.
[2] *Mṛch*, IV.
[3] *Rat*, IV, 14–15.

the *raṅgapīṭha* by one and a half cubit. A *mattavāraṇī* has four columns. Here it may be noted that the plinth of the auditorium (*raṅgamaṇḍala*)[1] should be equal in height to that of the two *mattavāraṇīs*. In the *vikṛṣṭa* and the *caturasra* types of theatre the *mattavāraṇīs* are to be 8 × 32 cubits each.[2]

Abhinavagupta says that *mattavāraṇīs* in *vikṛṣṭa* theatre may be eight cubits square. He holds out two distinct interpretations. According to one, the *mattavāraṇīs* are one and a half cubit higher than the *raṅgapīṭha*, and according to the other, the *raṅgapīṭha* and *mattavāraṇīs* are of the same height. Abhinavagupta seems to believe that *mattavāraṇīs* were used as *kakṣyās*.[3]

Scholars have interpreted the term *mattavāraṇīs* differently. Dr. P.K. Acharya considers the *mattavāraṇīs* as part of the pillars supporting the stage. On the two sides of the stage, over the four pillars is erected on entablature (*mattavāraṇa*) one and a half cubits or two feet and three inches high. This is the total height of the stage pavilion (*raṅgamaṇḍapas* as stated by the commentator). But neither the height of the platform nor of the pillar is mentioned. The actual height of the stage is unspecified.

Some scholars think that *mattavāraṇīs* performed the same functions as the wings of modern theatres. But if we follow the *Nāṭyaśāstra* faithfully we find that *mattavāraṇīs* were higher than the *raṅgapīṭha* and that they were some special portions of the *raṅgapīṭha* because action was performed on these *mattavāraṇīs*. At one place Abhinavagupta refers to the size of the *raṅgapīṭha* as 8 × 32 cubits which, it seems, includes the *mattavāraṇīs* also. In *svāṅgas* or folk theatres of northern India we find even today that there is a structure on both sides of the stage which is supported by wooden pillars from where some special and exciting speeches are made and scenes shown. The *mattavāraṇīs* could be used as *kakṣyās* if they were really used in this manner. The *kakṣyās* could be built low or high according to the requirement of the plot.

PILLARS AND SEATING ARRANGEMENTS

In connection with the *caturasra* theatre the *Nāṭyaśāstra* describes the

[1]J. Grosset's edition of the *NS* reads *raṅgamaṇḍala* but other editions of *NS* read *raṅgamaṇḍapa* instead. In our opinion the correct reading seems to be *raṅgamaṇḍala*. Mankad seems not to be right when he says that "these two *mattavāranis* and *raṅgapīṭha* should be higher (than the auditorium) by one and a half cubit." (D.R. Mankad, *Ancient Indian Theatre*).

[2]*NS-KM*, II. 87–88a; *KSS*, II. 64b–65, 99–100a; *GOS*, II. 66b–67, 102b–103.

[3]*Abh. Bh.* I, pp. 61–62.

arrangement of pillars as follows: On the *raṅgapīṭha* there must be ten columns strong enough to bear the burden of the *maṇḍapa*.[1] According to Abhinavagupta who states the view of Śaṅkuka, four columns, nos. 1, 2, 3 and 4, should be raised at the four corners of the *raṅgapīṭha*. From the pillars in the *āgneya* (south-east) and *nairṛta* (south-west) directions, two pillars, nos. 5 and 6, each at a distance of four cubits towards the south, should be erected. Two more pillars, nos. 7 and 8, each at a distance of four cubits towards the north should be placed from the pillars in the *vāyava* (north-west) and *aiśāna* (north-east) directions. And from the pillars in *āgneya* and *aiśāna* directions, two pillars, nos. 9 and 10, each at a distance of four cubits towards the east, should be placed. Thus there are ten pillars to support the *raṅgapīṭha*.

In the auditorium (*raṅgamaṇḍala*) at first six columns and then eight columns are erected.[2] According to Śaṅkuka, Abhinavagupta explains: From the pillars nos. 5 and 6, two pillars nos. 11 and 12 are placed at a distance of four cubits towards the south, at a distance of eight cubits from each other. From the pillars, nos. 7 and 8, two pillars, nos. 14 and 15, should be placed at a distance of four cubits towards the north but they should also be at a distance of eight cubits from each other. Then from the pillars, nos. 5 and 8, two pillars, nos. 13 and 16, should be placed each at a distance of four cubits towards the east. These are the first six pillars supporting the auditorium.

From pillars nos. 11 and 15, two others, nos. 17 and 18, are placed to the east, each at a distance of four cubits. These pillars are also stated to be at a distance of four cubits from the southern and northern walls. Then at a distance of four cubits, half-way from the eastern wall on both sides, two pillars nos. 19 and 20 may be placed. And from these pillars, nos. 19 and 20 pillars nos. 21 and 22, 23 and 24 should be placed, each at a distance of four cubits apart. Thus the next eight pillars should be arranged in the auditorium (Fig. 5).[3] The positions of pillars are marked in the diagram of the *caturasra nāṭyagṛha*.

This is the arrangement of columns according to Śaṅkuka and others. Abhinavagupta, following *vārttikakāra* and Upādhyāya, has explained the arrangement in a different way to signify that the last eight columns should be in the *nepathyagṛha*. But this view is not found in the *Nāṭya-śāstra* and is, therefore rejected.

[1] *NS-KM*, II. 78–79a; *KSS*, II. 90–91a; *GOS*, II. 93b–94.
[2] *NS-KM*, II. 81b–82; *KSS*, II. 93b–94; *GOS*, II. 97–98a.
[3] *Abh. Bh*, I, pp. 66–67.

The auditorium in the *vikṛṣṭa* theatre was 32 × 32 cubits in the *caturasra* 12 × 32 cubits and in the *tryasra* according to the measurement of the theatre. People of different castes were to sit at places indicated by columns of various colours. Brāhmaṇas had the front seats indicated by a white column. Kṣatriyas occupied seats indicated by a red column. Behind them sat Vaiśyas and Śūdras, the former to the north-east and the latter to the north-west, their seats being indicated by yellow and blue columns.[1] There were other columns too, perhaps, to accommodate those who were not included in the four castes. Galleries were to be erected one behind the other. Seats in the auditorium were to be arranged in the form of a staircase to ensure visibility. They were to be made of wood and bricks and were to be one and a half feet (one *hasta* or cubit) above the ground. On these the spectators sat.

Thus, as the *Nāṭyaśāstra* prescribes different places for the castes and for various strata of society, it became clear that the theatres, in ancient India though constructed as a temporary structure, were planned for the general public.

DOORS AND ROOF

According to the *Nāṭyaśāstra*, the *vikṛṣṭa* theatre has two doors leading to the green room from the *raṅgaśīrṣa*. Between these doors sat players of musical instruments. In the *caturasra* type a door leads to the *raṅgapīṭha*. The first door is for people to enter the theatre. The second door is in front of the auditorium. In the *tryasra* type there is one door at the back of the *raṅgapīṭha* and another in one corner for the entry of the audience.[2]

Abhinavagupta cites two views about the construction of doors in a theatre. According to one view, there are only three doors, two from the *nepathyagṛha* leading to the *raṅgaśīrṣa* and one in the auditorium for the entrance of spectators. According to the other, there are four doors; two in the *nepathyagṛha* wall, one by which the *naṭa* enters with his wife '*bhāryāmādāya naṭaparivāraḥ praviśati*' and one in the auditorium. Here Abhinavagupta takes '*ekadvāram*' as a collective use for two doors. Thus there are four doors in the *nāṭyagṛha*. Others again hold that the theatre had six doors. They believe that two more doors existed on the southern and northern sides of the *raṅgapīṭha* leading towards the

[1]*NS-KM*, II. 48–54; *KSS*, II. 47b–54; *GOS*, II. 49b–56a.

[2]*NS-KM*, II. 57b–58a, 84b–86a, 91–92a; *KSS*, II. 69b–70a, 96b–98a, 103–104a; *GOS*, II. 71b–72a, 100–101, 106b–107.

mattavāraṇīs (Figs. 3, 5, 7).[1] The positions of doors are indicated in the diagrams of all the three types of theatre.

In order to know the directions in the theatre hall it has been mentioned in the *Abhinavabhāratī* that in the representation of drama that direction should be regarded as the east where the orchestra is situated by the side of the door leading to the green room.

The question has been asked if Indian theatres had roofs or they were open-air theatres as in Greece. In this connection we note that in the *Nāṭyaśāstra* there is only one reference to theatres without roofs. But the theatres in which plays were performed must have had roofs.[2] There are indications in the *Nāṭyaśāstra* which prove the existence of roofs. In the section on arrangement of columns the *Nāṭyaśāstra* says that the columns should be *śaktā maṇḍapadhāraṇe* and *dṛḍhānmaṇḍapadhāraṇe* both expressions meaning "capable of supporting the roof". Bharata further praises a *śailaguhākāra* theatre, which too suggests the existence of roof. Abhinavagupta, emphasising that the theatre should not be too wide or too narrow, explains its properties of resounding (*anuraṇana*). This again presupposes a roof. The *Nāṭyaśāstra* itself frequently uses the term *nāṭya-maṇḍapa* for the theatre. Thus there were theatres of both kinds—open-air theatres and those with roofs.

Now the question arises whether the structure of the theatre in ancient India was of a temporary or a permanent type.

Bharata's description of theatres, their construction, size and shape, the position of the stage, orchestra and auditorium, indicates that theatres were of a permanent nature. The existence of such a word as *prekṣāgṛha* or *pekkhāghara* also supports this view.[3] Further the *Nāṭyaśāstra* states that the play-house should have the form of a mountain cave and should be two-storeyed.[4] The ruins of a cave found in the Rāmagarh hills which seems to have been used for the performance of plays or recitation of poems also support the view that the theatre was of a permanent nature.[5] The *Meghadūta* also refers to *Śilāveśma*.[6] There is, however, no historical record of a permanent theatre in ancient India. As the above-mentioned cave or the *śilāveśma* could have been a *nṛtyaśālā* and not a *nāṭyaśālā* and as it might have been used as a pleasure house by kings, one cannot say definitely that the theatre was of a permanent nature. It is certain that there were public theatres of a temporary nature in ancient India. I cannot agree with Prof. Macdonell when be says: "There were no special theatres

[1] *Abh. Bh*, I, pp. 69–70.
[2] Ibid., p. 54.
[3] *Māl*, I, p. 21.
[4] *NS-KM*, II. 69b; *KSS*, II. 81b; *GOS*, II. 84a.
[5] *ASI-AR 1903–4*, p. 123.
[6] *Meghadūta*, I. 25.

in the Indian Middle Ages, and plays seem to have been performed in the concert-room (*saṅgītaśālā*) of royal palaces".[1] The above remark of the learned professor seems to be based on a superficial study of the problem and on insufficient data.

[1]Macdonell, *A History of Sanskrit Literature*, p. 352.

CHAPTER FOUR

Scenic Representation

THE CURTAIN

In the scenic representation the curtain plays an important role. The word *yavanikā* or *javanikā* occurs in the *Nāṭyaśāstra* in connection with the arrangement of musical instruments required in the presentation of plays on the stage. In the preliminaries (*pūrvaraṅga*) for the presentation of Sanskrit plays a great deal of musical practice is done: the arrangement of musical instruments, fixing the position of musicians, examining of musical instruments, setting of wind and stringed instruments to vocal music, and the entrance of dancing girls. All these are to be done behind the screen (i.e. *yavanikā* or *javanikā*).[1] We have said earlier that musicians sit in the *raṅgaśīrṣa*, between the two doors leading to the *nepathyagṛha*. Thus the curtain cannot be behind the *raṅgaśīrṣa* but in front of it. So it appears there is a curtain between the *raṅgaśīrṣa* and the *raṅgapīṭha*. After the musical instruments are arranged and tuned, the curtain is drawn aside and dances and recitals are given with the playing of musical instruments and a *dhruvā* song in praise of gods is sung.

The *Nāṭyaśāstra* has a phrase from which it is clear that the curtain is drawn aside on two sides and not pulled up by pulleys after the *dhruvā* song. After the curtains are drawn aside, the actors, who are instrumental in bringing about the sentiments, enter the stage.[2] This indicates that when the curtain which between the *raṅgapīṭha* and the *raṅgaśīrṣa* is drawn aside, musicians become visible to the audience. In the *Kuṭṭanīmata* which refers to the performance of the *Ratnāvalī* the following occurs. The king with *vidūṣaka* is on the *raṅgapīṭha*. Two maids enter and dance for a while, deliver a message to the queen and go behind the *javanikā*. Then the queen enters with her maid after the *tiraskariṇī* (curtain) is drawn aside.[3] Here the word *apanītā* is quite clearly mentioned in the text and it proves that the curtain is drawn aside according to the requirement of the stage. But in no case can it be actually removed.

Abhinavagupta says that the *yavanikā* is hung between the *raṅgapīṭha*

[1]*NS-KM*, *KSS*, and *GOS*, V. 11–21.

[2]*NS-KM*, XII. 2b–3a; *KSS*, XIII. 3; *GOS*, XII. 3.

[3]*Kuṭṭanīmata—KM*, 886–87, p. 107; Bombay, 909–10, pp. 358–59.

and the *raṅgaśīrṣa.*[1] With the help of this curtain also phrases such as *apaṭikṣepeṇa*[2] (with a toss of the curtain) can be explained. The common view is that the curtain is parted in the middle. Dr S.K. De does not agree with this view and takes the stage direction for hurried entrance *apaṭikṣepeṇa praviśati* in the sense of 'enters without a toss of the curtain'.[3] But the real sense of this phrase is lost if we accept Dr. De's view. Mankad[4] opines that the character of parting the curtain from the middle given by European scholars to *paṭi* in explaining stage direction *apaṭikṣepeṇa* has no ground. But this statement seems to be incorrect.

Our viewpoint becomes clear when the stage directions *nepathye* and *apaṭikṣepeṇa* so often found in Sanskrit dramas, are explained in connection with each other? In the second act of the *Mṛcchakaṭika* (Mathura is shouting from behind the scenes) Saṁvāha enters with a toss of the curtain in a flurry. In the same act Karṇapūraka enters in high glee, dressed in gorgeous dress with a toss of the curtain. In act VI Āryaka enters with a toss of the curtain excited and with a chain on one leg he walks about. In act VIII the monk enters with a toss of the curtain. In act X the executioners say (Turning towards the *nepathyagṛhra*). "This way, this way, Sir, come here, child, come" (enters Maitreya with Rohasena).[5]

Voices are heard behind the scenes. In the *Pratijñāyaugandharāyaṇa* the soldier says: "The page has gone to the tavern and is drinking liquor. Well, you may go. (Stepping round). Here is the liquor shop. I will just call him. He, page! page!" (voice behind the scene). "Now who is calling me on the high road, page, page?" Soldier: "Here comes the page, his eyes as red as china roses, full of liquor laughing aloud and drunk. I won't stand in his way." (Stands aside). (Enters the page as described).[6]

In *Avimāraka* the stage-manager looks towards the dressing room and in the same drama, the nurse speaks to a maid behind the scenes.[7]

From these examples, it is clear that there is a curtain between the *raṅgaśīrṣa* and the *raṅgapīṭha* as without it *apaṭikṣepeṇa* cannot be explained. As there is a wall between the *raṅgaśīrṣa* and the *nepathyagṛha*, it is not easy for a nurse to talk to a maid. So it is quite possible that the maid is in the *raṅgaśīrṣa* behind the curtain and not in the *nepathyagṛha.*

[1]*Abh. Bh*, I. p. 212; II, p. 130.

[2]*Halāyudha*, 2, 154. He gives *apaṭi* as a synonym of *paṭī* or *javanikā*.

[3]S.K. De's "The Curtain in Ancient Indian Theatre", *Bhāratīya Vidyā*, vol. IX, 1948.

[4]D.R. Mankad, *Ancient Indian Theatre*, p. 18.

[5]*Mṛch*, II, pp. 46, 62; VI, p. 142; VIII, p. 190; X, p. 227.

[6]*Pra. Y*, IV, prose, pp. 94–95.

[7]*Avimāraka*, I, prose, pp. 109–10; III, pp. 137–38.

Uproar and the voice of gods which are made only in the green room can be heard distinctly by spectators in the auditorium. The purpose of the *nepathyagṛha*, *raṅgaśīrṣa* and *raṅgapīṭha* has to be very clearly understood. It has been seen in chapter 3 that the *nepathyagṛha* was meant for the make-up and for the representation of uproars, and the *raṅgaśīrṣa* for musicians and prompters, as also for affording rest to actors who had done their part or were to appear on the stage very soon. Whenever the orchestra is required, the curtain is drawn aside and music is on: whenever ordinary scenes go on, the curtain is down. The actual action of the drama takes place on the stage (*raṅgapīṭha*).

The ancient Indian theatre, it appears, had no drop-curtain. This can be explained from the peculiar ending of Sanskrit dramas. Sanskrit dramas never ended abruptly as is often the case is modern dramas. The acts, in all Sanskrit dramas, end usually with some description of the time of the day or with some other quiet suggestion to the characters on the stage to make for their exit. This peculiar termination of dramas is due to the absence of the drop-curtain.

Let us examine the *Vikramorvaśīya* from this point of view. At the end of act I the king looks up in the direction of Urvaśī and describes her in the following words. "This celestial damsel, while flying into the sky, violently tears away my heart, as the female swan, before soaring into the sky, draws off a film from a lotus stalk the tip of which has been already cut off." At the end of act II, the king, looking up, describes the time which is past mid-day as follows: "Tired of the heat the peacock sits in the cool basin round the root of a tree; the bee, having forced open the flower-buds of *karṇikāra*, lies therein; the duck, leaving the hot weather, resorts to the lotus-plant growing on the brink, and the encaged parrot in the pleasure-house, being exhausted, calls for water." At the end of act III the king makes a request to Urvaśī, "Formerly, when I had not achieved my object, the night seemed to me to increase a hundred fold; if it increases similarly now when I am in your company, I shall be blessed." At the end of act IV, on a question by Urvaśī as to how he desires to go, the king says: "Oh, you gifted with a sportive gait, bear me home on a new cloud made into a balloon, with streamers in the form of flashes of lightning and beautified by fresh painting in the form of the rainbow." At the end of act V, there is the benedictory stanza: "May there be always, for the welfare of the good, a union of the goddesses of wealth and learning who are opposed to each other—a union which is difficult to be found in one place."[1]

[1]*Vik*, ending of 1–5 acts, pp. 16–17, 50–51, 74–75, 98–99 and 122.

From this analysis it is clear that the acts ended not with any dramatic incident so as to require the fall of the curtain, but with the description of some kind or other. And there is a definite instruction after every act that the actors go out. If there were any drop-curtain, there was no need of the actors leaving the stage; they could as well be on the stage while the curtain came down.

But now how to explain scenes where an actor enters seated or any situation is said to be set on the stage as soon as a new act begins? Let us take scenes from different dramas. In the *Mṛcchakaṭika*, in act II, the scene opens with Vasantasenā, seated, deeply in love, and also Madanikā.

In act IV, a female servant enters. Servant: "Madam's mother has told me to go to madam. Here is madam with her gaze fixed on a painting. I would just approach." (She advances a few steps.) The scene opens with Vasantasenā who is in the manner described earlier and Madanikā. In act V Cārudatta enters, seated and full of amorous thoughts.[1] In the drama *Avimāraka*, Avimāraka enters seated.[2] Such instances can be produced from many other dramas. Instructions such as '*praviśati āsanasthaḥ*' and the examples quoted above help us to arrive at the inference that there was some sort of a curtain which was withdrawn to present the actors to the audience at the appropriate moment, thus pointing towards existence of the drop-curtain. But it may also be quite possible that actors used to come and sit on the stage. It could then be said that an actor entered seated.

S.M. Tagore in his *The Eight Principal Rasas of the Hindus* refers to the drop-curtain. He says: "The scene which hangs before the audience before the commencement of the play, or which drops in the intervals between the scenes is called *yabanikā*. As in every act and its subdivisions, scenes are changed, so the drop-scene should also change. In classical times two comely girls appeared and removed the two wings of every scene."[3]

While describing the Jogīmārā and Sītābeṅgā caves, Bloch[4] refers to certain holes on two sides of the caves and presumes that they had been provided to facilitate the use of curtains.

But there is no reference to the drop-curtain in the *Nāṭyaśāstra* or *Abhinavabhāratī*. On the contrary *The Eight Principal Rasas of the Hindus* which hints at the drop-curtain is a modern work and the injunction 'such and such actor enters seated' can be represented without the

[1] *Mṛch*, II, p. 42; IV, p. 84; V, p. 111. [2] *Avimāraka*, II, p. 121.
[3] *The Eight Principal Rasas of the Hindus*, pp. 58–59.
[4] Bloch, *ASI-AR 1903–4*, p. 123.

use of the drop-curtain. Further as Bloch's interpretation of the drop-curtains in the Sītābeṅgā and Jogīmārā caves is not conclusively proved and we have already seen that the ending of acts in Sanskrit dramas does not require any drop-scene, we conclude that no drop-curtain was used in presentation of Sanskrit plays.

The theory of a transverse curtain propounded by Wilson is not supported by facts. He superficially remarks: "It seems possible, also, that curtains were suspended transversely, so as to divide the stage into different portions, open equally to the audience but screening one set of actors from the other, as if the one were within, and the other outside a house or chamber."[1]

A.K. Coomaraswamy thinks there was no drop-curtain. He remarks: "As for the curtain, of course, there were two curtains, neither of them a drop-curtain, but one over each door way leading from the *nepathyagṛha* on to and from the stage, just as in the Chinese theatre even today, where anyone who cares may see the actor entering with a toss of the curtain."[2] But it is not clear from where A.K. Coomaraswamy got the idea of the two curtains in Indian plays. Probably this theory of his is based on mere conjecture or to anticipate certain types of curtains on the stage doors in order to explain stage directions—*paṭikṣepeṇa* or *apaṭikṣepeṇa*.

Thus from the above analysis we arrive at the conclusion that the ancient Indian theatre had only one curtain and that it was placed between the *raṅgaśīrṣa* and the *raṅgapīṭha*.

Apart from this one curtain there were probably some other minor curtains used to partition the *kakṣyās*. These types of curtains could be termed as *citra-yavanikā*[3] flexible curtains to be used anywhere on the stage. Some scenes must have been screened from the audience by curtains and exposed when necessary, for example, the scenes in the *Abhijñānaśākuntala* such as Kanva's garden, the *rājasabhā* of Duṣyanta, the street scene where the fisherman is caught, the scene half-way up in heaven showing Marica's *āśrama*, the king's garden and the king painting the portrait of Śakuntalā. These are different parts of scenes. They must have been kept ready and shown with the help of *kakṣyās* partitioned by minor curtains. But this can only be a probability and we are not sure of such scenic representation in ancient India.

[1]Wilson, *Select Specimens of the Theatre of the Hindus*, I. 58.

[2]A.K. Coomaraswamy, 'Hindu Theatre', *Indian Historical Quarterly*, vol. IX, Calcutta, 1933, p. 594.

[3]The word *citra-yavanikā* is used in act VI of *Mālatīmādhava* of Bhavabhūti. It is quite likely that such curtains must be of variegated colours Bhavabhūti has also suggested how they were used.

ORIGIN OF THE CURTAIN

Now the question arises whether the curtain was imported from outside (i.e. Greece) or it was of Indian origin. Let us consider the terms *yavanikā javanikā* and *yamanikā* to get a correct idea about the curtain of the ancient Indian stage. The Kāvyamālā edition of the *Nāṭyaśāstra* has the reading *javanikā* while the texts of the Kāśī Sanskrit Series, the Gaekwad Oriental Series and also the *Abhinavabhāratī* have the reading *yavanikā*.[1] The edition of Grosset (1898) has the form *javanikā*, but in one of the passages the reading is *yavanikā*. The form *yamanikā* is found in some manuscripts of Sanskrit plays and poems. Dr. De has tried to show that *yamanikā*[2] is as much a recognized form of the word for curtain as *javanikā* or *yavanikā*.

According to Apte's dictionary the meaning of *yavanikā* and *javanikā* is the same i.e. 'curtain'.[3] On this point we may note that *javanikā* is the Prākṛta form of *yavanikā*.[4] Let us now take up the word *javanikā* and look to its etymological meaning. *Javana* means going fast and it is derived from the root '*ju*' by Bhaṭṭoji Dīkṣita in his *Siddhāntakaumudī*. Pāṇini has the following *sūtra* '*jucaṅkramyadandramyasṛgṛdhijvalaśucalaṣapatapadaḥju iti Sautro dhāturgatau vegeca, javanaḥ*[5] which shows that the word *javana* was derived from the root '*ju*'. The feminine form of *javana* is *javanī* or *javanikā*. It may mean a curtain which was to be drawn with force. In the *Amarakoṣa* the meaning of *javanikā* is given as a curtain or *kanāta*, as in the following '*pratisīra javanikā syāttiraskariṇī ca sā*'[6]. As to the word *yavanikā* it can be derived from the root '*yuñ bandhane*'[7], '*yuñ, yunāti, badhnāti āvṛṇnoti vā anayā iti*'[8] i.e. any thing by which something is covered from the sight of the spectators, i.e. curtain. The word *yamanikā*[9] is derived from the root *yam* 'to stop or restrain' signifying a covering or curtain and the word *yamanī*, from which *yamanikā* is directly derived, is traceable as far back as the *Vājasaneyi Saṁhitā*.[10] Thus as the words

[1] *NS-KM*, *KSS*, and *GOS*, V. 11–12.

[2] S.K. De, "The Curtain in Ancient Indian Theatre", *Bhāratīya Vidyā*, vol. IX, 1948.

[3] V.S. Apte, *The Practical Sanskrit-English Dictionary*, pp. 450, 782.

[4] The word *yavanikā* is not included as a synonym of the curtain by old Indian lexicographers.

[5] *Siddhāntakaumudī*, p. 594; Pāṇini, 3.2.150.

[6] *Amarakośa*, II. 120, p. 152.

[7] *Siddhāntakaumudī*, 1480, Dhātupāṭha.

[8] *Commentary to Kuṭṭanīmata*, edited by T.M. Tripathi, p. 359.

[9] Bohtlingk and Roth summarily dismiss the form *yamanika* as a scribal mistake for *yavanikā* and Sten Konow take it as merely secondary.

[10] *Vājasaneyi Saṁhitā*, XIV. 22.

javanikā, *yavanikā* and *yamanikā* all can be derived to mean curtain it can be asserted that the curtain which was used on the ancient Indian stage had an indigenous origin and growth.

Critics hold that *yavanikā* points to the Greek origin of the curtain as being derived from Ionia or Greek. If the curtain was borrowed from Greece, *yavanikā* could have had no special application to the curtain of the theatre for there was no curtain in the Greek drama. Windisch contends that the curtain was called Greek because it took the place of the painted scenery at the back of the Greek stage. Keith remarks: "Behind the Indian stage is the painted curtain (*paṭī, apaṭī tiraskariṇī, pratisīrā*) to which the name *yavanikā* (*prākṛta javaṇikā*) is given, denoting merely that the material is foreign and forbidding any conclusion as to the Greek origin of the curtain itself or the theatre.[1] Dr. De does not agree with the view of Dr. Keith and says that there is no evidence to support this presumption.[2]

On account of the mention of *yavanas* and *yavanīs* and their supposed connection with *yavanikā* it has been put forward that the Sanskrit drama had Greek influence on it. The *Mālavikāgnimitra* speaks of *yavanas* having attacked the army of king Puṣpamitra when he crossed the Indus.[3] In the *Abhijñāśākuntala* women *yavana* attendants, who carried bows in their hands, are represented as constituting some of the king's bodyguards.[4] Now as to the word *yavana* it is not universally accepted as meaning only Greek. Keith says: "It applies to anything connected with the Hellenized Persian Empire, Egypt, Syria, Bactria and it, therefore, cannot be rigidly limited to what is Greek. As applied to the curtain it is an adjective, (*paṭī, apaṭī*) as foreign, possibly as Lévi suggests, Persian tapestry brought to India by Greek ships and merchants.[5] As to the employment of *yavanī* girls in Sanskrit dramas as bodyguards of kings, Greek drama offers no parallel. It is probable the *yavanī* women used to draw aside the dissected curtain.

Thus we can assert that the word *yavanikā* which has *javanikā* for its Prākṛta form and probably *yamanikā* as its variant was of purely Indian origin. It is however, quite probable that material imported from Greece might have been used to make curtains.

[1]Keith, *Sanskrit Drama*, pp. 61, 359.
[2]S.K. De, "The Curtain in Ancient Indian Theatre", *Bhāratīya Vidyā*, vol. IX, 1948.
[3]*Māl*, V. p. 102.
[4]*Śāk*, II, p. 42.
[5]Keith, *Sanskrit Drama*, p. 61; Lévi, *le Theatre Indien*, I. 348.

EMPLOYMENT OF PAINTING

Painting played a significant role in the secular and religious life of India. The *Viṣṇudharmottara* gives a long account of how the sage Nārāyaṇa in order to put the *apsarās* to shame created the most beautiful nymph Urvaśī by drawing her outline with mango juice.[1] In the above legend the origin of the art of painting is seen in the outlining of a human figure for the purpose of creating a living human form. A similar notion is to be found in the *Svapnavāsavadattā* where king Udayana and princess Vāsavadattā, with whom he had eloped, are united in marriage by their parents by drawing the portraits of the two on aboard. Nurse: "Thus saith the queen: Vāsavadattā has passed away. To me and to Mahāsena you are as dear as our Gopāla and Pālaka, for from the very first we intended you to be our son-in-law. That is why you were brought to Ujjain. Under the pretext of learning the lute we gave her to you, with no ritual fire as witness. In your impetuosity you carried her off without celebrating the auspicious nuptial rites. So we had portraits painted of you and of Vāsavadattā on a panel, and therewith celebrated the marriage. We send you the portraits and hope they will give you satisfaction."[2] This instance proves that the artist draws from his memory when visualising a portrait.

The modelling capacity of the outline is also described in the *Viddhaśālabhañjikā*.[3]

The *Viṣṇudharmottara* holds the rules for painting as valid for sculpture also, which may either be hollow or massive. Hollow figures must have stood, among other places, on the stage, where images of gods, demons, *yakṣas*, elephants, horses, deer and birds made of clay, wood, cloth, leather or iron were placed.[4]

There were various types of paintings on walls, boards and canvas.[5] When a picture is on canvas or board, it is known as *paṭa*. In *Pañcadaśī* we read the principles of painting a picture on *paṭa*. We are told of its four stages: (1) *dhauta*—to be washed, (2) *ghaṭṭita*—rubbed with rice, (3) *lañchita*—decorated with the help of ink, (4) *rañjita*—painted with colours proper.[6] In the *Āryamañju-śrīmūla-kalpa* we get a description of a *paṭa*. A picture (*paṭa*) should be painted on new white cloth, having fringes. It should be two cubits long and one cubit broad. It may be

[1] *VD*, I. 1–19.

[2] *Svapnavāsavadatta*, VI, prose, pp. 50–51.

[3] *Viddhaśālabhañjikā*, I. 33, 35, 36, 39, pp. 28–34. Poona edn., 1886.

[4] *VD*, III. 43. 27b–39.

[5] *ŚR*, I. 46. 26–34, p. 247.

[6] *Pañcadaśī*, VI. 1–3.

painted on cloth, *ātasya* or the bark of a tree, which must be true and devoid of any string. It should be painted on a cloth which is not silken. Other articles on which pictures can be painted have also been described.[1] Pictures on canvas were sometimes in the shape of rolls, exhibiting continuous representation. Such a roll was spread out by a spy of Cāṇakya before the people in Candanadāsa's house and was exhibited by him with songs in the *Mudrārākṣasa*: "Spy:—listen, noble sir. Employed by your noble self to note the doings of others, I entered the house of the jeweller-banker Candanadāsa, roaming with this Yama's canvas which cannot excite suspicion. There opening out the canvas I began singing songs."[2]

Wall paintings have been referred to in the *Nāṭyaśāstra*. After white washing the walls, pictures were painted on them. They were generally of men and women. Nooses of creepers were employed. Incidents from many aspects of life were drawn.[3] Decoration on the stage has been referred to in chapter three.

Let us now analyse some of the important dramas with regard to the technique and details of the art of painting in ancient India. In the *Ratnāvalī*, Sāgarikā enters with a picture board and brush. She is love sick and is engaged in painting. Susaṅgatā comes and with gentle step stands behind her and sees with joy, "how, now; she has painted our master. Noble, Sāgarikā noble: or rather, how can a royal swan find pleasure except in a tank full of lotuses? Susaṅgatā comes and forcibly take the boards. Susaṅgatā: O friend, who is this that is drawn by you here? Sāgarikā: Friend, god Anaṅga. Susaṅgatā: (smiling) Oh, your skill. But how is it then that the picture depicts him along? So I too will draw and make him have Rati by his side (takes the brush and pretending to portray Rati, paints Sāgarikā)."[4] From the above it is quite clear that paintings on board, i.e., *paṭa* with human figures, were prevalent in ancient India.

In the *Mṛcchakaṭika* Vasantasenā is seen with her gaze fixed on a portrait. The scene actually opens with this incident. "Vasantasenā: Madanikā, is this portrait of the noble Cārudatta faithful to the original? Madanikā it must be. Vasantasenā: How can you know it? Madanikā: Since Madam's gaze is fastened on it with so much affection. Vasantasenā afterwards says to Madanikā: Just keep this picture in my bedroom, girl, and come quickly with a fan. Madanikā: As you command me, Madam (takes away the picture)."[5]

[1] *Āryamañju-śrīmūlakalpa*, I, p. 131.
[2] *Mudrārākṣasa*, I, p. 68.
[3] *NṢ-KM*, II. 71b–74a; *KSS*, II. 83b–86a; *GOS*, II. 87–89.
[4] *Rat*, II. pp. 30–33.
[5] *Mṛch*, IV. pp. 84, 87.

In act I of the *Mālavikāgnimitra* Vakulāvalikā and Kaumudikā describe the circumstances in which the king saw Mālavikā. "Vakulāvalikā, listen, the queen had gone to the painting hall and was setting a picture of the teacher on which the colours were still fresh: in the meantime the king came.

Kaumudikā: What then?

Vakulāvalikā: 'Then after the customary salutation, the king sat down on the same seat with the queen, and observing Mālavikā quite close to the painted queen in the midst of her attendants, he asked the queen.' This conversation shows that picture halls and paintings were very much in vogue.

Then in act IV there is the portrait of the king, which Vakulāvalikā shows to Mālavikā.[1]

In act VI of the *Abhijñānaśākuntala* there is a portrait of Śakuntalā on a board drawn by the king himself. Its graceful and lovely presentation is described here. "*Vidūṣaka*: Excellent, my friend. The depiction of natural state has become charming by reason of that sweet and beautiful attitude. My eye stumbles, as it were, in the prominences and depressions in the picture. I believe that out of the three ladies painted in the portrait she—who with the end of her hair dropping flowers by reason of the fillet being slackened, with a face on which drops have collected, and with the arms greatly drooping, has been drawn as if a little tired by the side of the mango-tree, with its new grown leaves fresh with watering—is Śakuntalā. So the other two are her companions. King: you are discerning. In it there is a proof of my passion for her. On the edge of the sketch is seen the black impression of the perspired fingers; and this drop of tear fallen on her cheek is observable by reason of the swelling of the paint."[2]

In the *Uttararāmacarita* the painter is said to have portrayed the life of Rāmacandra up to Sītā's purification on the wall. Lakṣmaṇa: "Victory to your highness: Sir, that painter has, according to your instructions, portrayed your life on this wall. You can see it." (They rise and move about.) Sītā: "(marking with attention) Who are these stationed above in a compact line that seem to praise my lord?" Lakṣmaṇa: "These are the well-known Jṛmbhaka missiles with their mysterious charms." Lakṣmaṇa: "Here is the account of the events that occurred at Mithilā." Sītā: "Oh, here is my lord painted." Lakṣmaṇa: "Behold, lady, behold, here is your father with Śatānanda, son of Gotama, the priest of the Janaka family, honouring Vaśiṣṭha and others." The scenes of Sītā's marriage,

[1]*Māl*, pp. 5, 72–73.

[2]*Śāk*, VI. 14–15 and prose, pp. 151, 158–59.

departure to the forest from Ayodhyā, meeting with Guha at Sṛngavera, Bhagīrathī with flowing waters, penance groves on the bank of mountain brooks, Prasravaṇa at Janasthāna with the river Godāvarī, Pañcavaṭī, the fight between Jaṭāyu and Rāvaṇa, lake Pampā, and of the countless achievements of Rāma and of the noble monkey and *rākṣasas*, represented on the wall, were lively and full of vigour.[1]

In connection with painting we have analysed the following dramas: the *Svapnavāsavadattā*, the *Mudrārākṣasa*, the *Ratnāvalī*, the *Abhijñānaśākuntala*, the *Uttararāmacarita* and we come to the conclusion that wall paintings, pictures on board and canvas were popular. In the *Ratnāvalī* and the *Abhijñānaśākuntala* pictures on board are found and in the *Mudrārākṣasa* pictures on canvas and the *Uttararāmacarita* wall paintings are referred to. Many portraits and landscapes painted by artists of the royal and the servant class alike are mentioned in almost all the dramas referred to above.

It is certain now that there was at least one curtain between the *raṅgapīṭha* and the *raṅgaśīrṣa* and possibly there were other minor curtains to partition the *kakṣyās*. When paintings on canvas were popular curtains could easily be available. The colour of the curtain, according to some authorities, must necessarily be in harmony with the dominant sentiment of the play, in accordance with the classification of sentiments already given, but others permit the use of the red in every case.[2] Then the walls between the *raṅgaśīrṣa* and *nepathyagṛha* might have been painted to represent the most interesting scenes of the play. Pillars and ceilings of the theatre might also be painted as we find paintings in the Ajantā caves.

TIME OF PRESENTATION

From the *Nāṭyaśāstra* it is clear that plays were performed in the morning, afternoon and in the first part (*prahara*) of the night and also in the fourth part (*prahara*). That which is pleasing to the ear and which speaks about religion, which is pure or mixed should be represented in the morning. That which is magnificent, full of *sattva* qualities and sounds of musical instruments should be represented in the afternoon. That in which the *kaiśikī* style is employed and in which the erotic sentiment predominates and which is full of vocal and instrumental music should be represented in the first part of the night. That which is full of important events and in which the pathetic sentiment predominates should be represented in

[1] *URC*, prose, pp. 15, 17, 18
[2] S.M. Tagore, *The Eight Principal Rasas of the Hindus*, pp. 58–59.

the fourth part of the night. Plays were not allowed to be presented at midnight, midday and at dinner time.[1] But if the king ordered plays could be staged without restrictions of time and space.

The time of the perfomance is not in many cases stated, but in a number of plays such as the *Mālatīmādhava*[2] and the *Karṇasundarī*[3] it is found that it is assumed to be the time when the sun is rising. According to Nīlakaṇṭha, people avoided to see *naṭas* in the morning.[4] It is clear that people did not like to see plays in the morning at least during his lifetime.

In the *Kirātārjunīya-vyāyoga*[5] and in the *Rukmiṇīharaṇa*,[6] the plays are stated to have been presented when the moon is rising. In the former drama the *sthāpaka* says it is night fall which is essentially beautiful. This also happens in the *Rukmiṇīharaṇa*. The *Harivaṁśa* makes mention of a dramatic treatment (*nāṭakīvṛttam*) of the *Rāmāyaṇa* and the *Mahābhārata* performed in first part of the night.[7] The *Nāṭakalakṣaṇaranakośa* tells us that a play is to be presented when the moon is rising.[8]

In most cases dramatic performances were held generally in the afternoon and they lasted for nearly four or five hours. While in a Greek theatre often three tragedies and a comedy were enacted the same day, in India one single, well sustained and systematically evolved drama was presented. Indian seasons allowed the necessary light throughout the day, for as a rule few plays were produced during the rainy season. The use of torches on the stage was not unknown. In the *Mṛcchakaṭika*, Cārudatta tells Maitreya: "So let it be. I shall accompany her myself Well, then let the torches be lighted so that we may go with confidence on the king's path."[9]

From the testimony of the *Nāṭyaśāstra* and plays in general it is evident that plays were performed in daytime and when the moon was rising. While scenic effect could be very easily produced at night, it is interesting to find how such effect was produced by day also. From a study of the occasions for the performance of the drama in chapter two we found that plays were generally enacted at annual fairs in temples, at the pleasure of the poet's patron and at festivals rural or urban, public or private. On these occasions, except the dramas which were played at the pleasure of

[1] *NS-KM*, XXVII. 80–84; *KSS*, XXVII, 89–93.
[2] *MM*, prologue, p. 4.
[3] *Karṇasundarī*, 1. 4, pp. 1–2.
[4] *Mṛch*, X, commentary of Pṛthvīdhara, p. 249.
[5] *Kirātārjunīya-Vyāyoga*, I-5: p. 2.
[6] *Rukmiṇīharaṇa*, prologue, p. 37.
[7] *Harivaṁśa*, II. 93.
[8] *NLR*, 2186; p. 91.
[9] *Mṛch*, I, prose, p. 40.

the poet's patron or king etc., there must have been holidays when people used to gather to witness plays by day. Reflections of mirrors might have been used just as lights were used at night. Sanskrit dramas had critical audience as is clear from many preludes of dramas. Bhavabhūti and Kālidāsa must have been understood by the learned people. Imagination played a great part in Sanskrit plays as in Shakespearian plays. The miracle of fire shown by the juggler in the *Ratnāvalī* must have been left to the imagination of the audience.[1]

There was a time-limit for a play. The Sanskrit play was to be finished in a fixed time. From the testimony of the *Nāṭyaśāstra*, we understand that a play was judged by a critic (*prāśnika*) from the point of view of the accuracy of timing (*naḍikāsiddhi*) since the time when the *jarjara* was placed in a dramatic performance by the manager (*sūtradhāra*).[2]

[1]*Rat*, IV, pp. 103–6.
[2]*NS-KM*, XXVII. 39; *KSS*, XXVII, 40.

CHAPTER FIVE

Paraphernalia

SIGNIFICANCE OF ĀHĀRYĀBHINAYA

The Sanskrit word *abhinaya* is made up of the prefix *abhi*, towards, and the root *ni*, to carry. Thus it means 'representing' or 'carrying' a play to the spectators. *Abhinaya* is known to be fourfold: *āhārya* (dresses and make-up) *āṅgika* (gestures), *vācika* (words) and *sātvika* (temperament).[1] In this chapter we shall deal with *āhāryabhinaya* (costumes and make-up) reserving the other kinds of *abhinaya* for a letter treatment.

In ancient India stage outfit and scenic arrangement were not so elaborate as in modern times. Some sort of scenery and stage machinery are referred to by Bharata. Mechanical contrivances, probably a sort of crane and pulley, worked from the sides (*mattavāraṇīs*), seem to have been used on the stage. Bharata carefully notices the process of stage carpentary (*dārukarma*) and speaks of machines (*yantras*) aiding movements to and from the stage. Lattices and windows are described mechanically constructed for the purpose.[2] In the *Mṛcchakaṭika* when Madanikā is sent to bring a fan and when she begins to talk with Śarvilaka, Vasantasenā says: "Madanikā has tarried long. Where can she be? (She peeps outside through a latticed window.) What? She is standing there talking to a man."[3]

The presence of several deities seated in aerial vehicles is a noteworthy feature of some of the Sanskrit plays. Now when these celestial characters are actually present on the stage and imitate aerial motions, the direction is precise, viz., 'Thus they act' (*nāṭayanti*). In act VI of the *Uttararāmacarita* a pair of resplendent *vidyādharas* in an aerial vehicle enters the stage.[4] In act VI of the *Abhijñānaśākuntala*, Sānumatī, a nymph, enters the stage in a celestial car to see the doings of the king and remains there practically up to the end of the act.[5]

As to how these actions and vehicles should be represented in the play is all described in *āhāryābhinaya*. In *āhāryābhinaya* are included

[1]*NS-KM* and *KSS*, VIII. 6–9; *GOS*, VIII. 7–0; *VD*, III. 27.1.
[2]*NS-KM*, II. 64–74; *KSS*, II. 76–86; *GOS*, II. 78–90a.
[3]*Mṛch*, IV, p. 87.
[4]*URC*, VI, p. 140.
[5]*Śak*, VI, pp. 143–69.

subjects such as the preparation and use of dresses and ornaments, painting of the persons of men and women, arrangement of hair and depiction of scenes. Writers on dramaturgy have treated these under four heads i.e., *pusta*—model work, *alaṅkāra*—decoration (ornaments, garlands and dresses), *aṅgaracanā*—painting the limbs (colouring, hair and beard) and *sañjīva*—living creatures (construction of stage animals).[1] In *pusta* is described how items are prepared for representing different scenes. In *alaṅkāra* the occasion when a man or a woman should wear a particular kind of ornament or dress is stated. The kind of painting a person should use on his or her body in the representation of a particular character, the kind of hair women should wear, methods of dressing the hair in different countries and use of moustaches—all these are discussed in *aṅgaracanā*. Under *sañjīva* we are told how animate objects other than human beings, should be prepared for the stage if their presence was needed in connection with the performance.

PUSTA

Pusta (model work), according to the dictionary of Monier-Williams, means 'binding'.[2] An object prepared after binding different things together is called *pusta*. The *Nāṭyaśāstra* distinguishes three forms of *pusta*: *sandhima* (joined), *vyājima* (indicating) and *veṣṭita* (wrapped).[3] Different articles are joined together with the help of bamboos covered with mat, skin or cloth to make a *sandhima*. Rocks, carriages, chariots, aerial cars, horses and elephants are thus represented on the stage. When objects are made to work by mechanical means the term *vyājima* is used. According to Abhinavagupta things on the stage were made to move by pulling a thread from behind the curtain.[4] For example, if the movement of an aerial car, animals or a chariot is to be shown, it would be done by preparing frames of objects with pieces of bamboo and then by covering them with painted cloth, palm-products (*talīya*), mats (*kaliñja*), *bheṇḍa*, bees-wax, lac and sheets of mica and be pulled from behind the curtain. Certain other things used on the stage were prepared by wrapping cloth only (*veṣṭita*) or by movements only, if we read *ceṣṭita* instead of *veṣṭita*.

[1]*NS-KM*, XXI. 1–4; *KSS*, XXIII. 1–5; *VD*, III. 27. 2–3a.

[2]Monier-Williams, *Sanskrit-English Dictionary*, p. 640.

[3]*NS-KM*, XXI. 5–8. *KSS*, XXIII. 6–9.

[4]*Vyājaḥ sūtrasyā karṣādirūpaḥ kṣepastena nirvṛtto vyājimaḥ*. *Abh. Bh*, XXI, pp. 11–12. (MSS Saraswati Bhawan Library, Banaras).

Avaloka on the *Daśarūpa* speaks of elephants being made in this way in *Udayanacarita.*[1] In the *Pratijñāyaugandharāyana*, Yaugandharāyaṇa says to Śālaka: "That, too, is a sign of an intelligent man. Well, a report has reached us that Pradyota intends to hoodwink our king by setting up a blue elephant. I only hope our master's judgment has not already been led astray. But oh, how fearful Pradyota must be of the king of the Vatsas. The inefficiency of the vast army is manifest."[2] To the *vyājima pusta* belongs the earthen toy-cart in the *Mṛcchakaṭika*[3] and the moving chariot in the *Abhijñānaśākuntala.*[4] Puppets could be made to move about or dance by mechanical arrangements. A puppet impersonating Sītā is actually introduced in the *Bālarāmāyaṇa.*[5]

According to Abhinavagupta, when Bharata speaks of his having been instructed by Brahmā to direct the dramatic performance because of his being a sage with one hundred sons, of his having been given an umbrella, crown and throne etc., by different gods, of the appointment of certain divine beings to guard over certain parts of the theatre or certain actors and of the creation of fairies, he simply means to tell the requirements of the stage and the way to manage it.[6]

Here it will not be out of place to describe the seats for characters on the stage, as these are essential for the representation of different beings in a play. Gods, kings and chief queens used to sit on thrones (lion-seat). Seats of cane were assigned to ministers, priests and their wives. The commanders of the army, crown princes and the wives of the king other than the chief queen occupied seats called *muṇḍāsana* i.e. a chair without arms. Wooden seats were meant for Brāhmaṇas. Woollen seats or carpets (*kālīna*) were used by princes. Women of the household occupied seats of wood or skin. The seats for ascetics were according to the rules of the orders they belonged to. Generally those observing vows, *brahmacārīs* or *ṛṣis* used to sit on *muṇḍāsana* or cane seat. Other characters used to sit on the ground. These rules for seats were observed among people in general or in the royal court. In one's own house one can take any seat according to one's liking.[7]

Different kinds of weapons were used in the presentation of plays. The *Nāṭyaśāstra* prescribes that weapons and armours should be proportionate to the stature of actors and actresses. Bharata has given the length

[1]Avaloka on *DR*, II. 58a. [2]*Pra. Y*, pp. 58–59.
[3]*Mṛch*, VI, pp. 137, 139. [4]*Śāk*, 1. 6–9 and prose, pp. 10–13.
[5]*Bālarāmāyaṇa*, V, pp. 239, 242–51.
[6]*NS-KM*, I. 26–29a; *KSS*, I. 61–64; *GOS*, I. 59b–62; *Abh. Bh*, pp. 27–28.
[7]*NS-KM*, XII. 179–89; *KSS*, XIII. 205–17; *GOS*, XII. 214–26.

and breadth of different weapons in *tālas* or *aṅgulas* (measurements). *Tāla* is a short span, measured by the thumb and middle finger. Bharata speaks of five varieties of spears: *prāsa, śūla, tomara, kunta* and *bhiṇḍi*. The handle of the *prāsa* was twenty *aṅgulas* in length and its pointed blade was six *aṅgulas*. The *śūla* and *tomara* were each eight *tālas* in length, while the *kunta* (javelin) was often *tālas* and the *bhiṇḍi* of twelve *tālas*. Out of these five kinds of spears, the *prāsa*, *śula* and *tomara* were hurled at the opponent while the *kunta* and *bhiṇḍi* were not. The *śataghnī* and *śakti* were also among weapons thrown at the opponent. Their length is stated to be eight *tālas*. The bow (*dhanu*) should be eight *tālas* in length and two cubits in breadth at the time of drawing. The *śara* (arrow) should be four *tālas* in length. The *gadā* (mace) and *vajra* should be of the same size as the *śara*. Bharata has further stated that there are three varieties of swords. Of these, the *asi* was forty *aṅgulas* in lẹngth, the *kaṁpana* made of thin pointed *pattara* twenty *aṅgulas* and one '*śabala*', the smallest, sixteen *aṅgulas*. The *kheṭaka*, a kind of shield, is thirty *aṅgulas*. The *cakra* (disc) should be twelve *aṅgulas* and the *paṭṭisa* is of the same size as the *prāsa*. The *daṇḍa* should be twenty *aṅgulas*. The *kaṇaya* should be made of bamboos. The *carma* (shield) is sixteen *aṅgulas* and is for use by both hands. The *jarjara* should be made of wooden logs with knots, and the *chatra* (umbrella), *cāmara* (chowrie), *dhvaja* (banner staff), *bhṛṅgāra* (water-jar) should be of the same size as those made for ordinary use. The weapons must not be made of hard or heavy materials such as stone or iron, but of stiff blades of grass, bamboo, lac, skin, cloth and earth. Gestures could very well serve the purpose of hard blows and cuts. The *Nāṭyaśāstra* prescribes that no missile should be released on the stage and no weapon should pierce or strike any one. They are to be used only to make a gesture of an attack and should simply touch a spot.[1] The lightness of weapons made them convenient for being taken from one court theatre to another by troupes. The basic conception was to create an illusion rather than to represent real things. Various kinds of weapons described in Sanskrit dramas can easily be represented by means of bamboos covered with cloth according to the shape and size of the weapon.

Statues as those used in the *Pratimānāṭaka*[2] and *Vīṇāghoṣavatī* in the *Pratijñāyaugandharāyaṇa*[3] could be more of earth and wood and lac. Extensive use is made of lac to effect colourful representations. In the *Bālacarita*, the discus, bow, club, conch and sword have been given

[1] *NS-KM*, XXI. 130b–39; 170–80; *KSS*, XXIII. 154–63, 194–203, 212–214a.
[2] *Pratimānāṭaka*, III, p. 277.
[3] *Pra. Y*, I, pp. 63–64.

human form.[1] Actors personating the five weapons must have appeared on the stage adorned with different masks.

ALAṄKĀRA

The second kind of *āhāryābhinaya* is *alaṅkāra* i.e., decoration of persons appearing on the stage. There are three kinds of *alaṅkāra* (decoration): (1) ornaments made of coral, diamond, silver and gold; (2) garlands made out of different kinds of flowers and wreathes and (3) costumes.[2]

Kings and women of distinction freely used ornaments of all sorts for the head, ear, nose, neck, waist, wrist and ankle. They were not, however, genuine and were made of copper, mica or wax, sparkling from a distance and presenting the effect of verisimilitude. The *Nāṭyaśāstra* describes the ornaments of men and women according to the country and caste and in due consideration of place and time. It has prescribed four kinds of ornaments according to the method of wearing them. They are: *āvedhya*, *bandhanīya*, *prakṣepya* and *āropya*. *Āvedhya* includes the *kuṇḍla* (ear-rings) and other ornaments for the ear which are fixed in holes pierced in the skin. *Bandhanīya* includes *aṅgada* (arm-band) and girdles and *prakṣepya* includes *nūpura* (anklets) and such other ornaments. *Āropya* refers to *hemasūtra* (gold chains) and necklaces that are to be worn round the neck.[3]

Bharata prescribes the following ornaments for men: *cūḍāmaṇi* (crest-jewel) and *mukuṭa* (crown) for the head; *kuṇḍala* (ear-ring), *mocaka* (ear-pendant) and *kila* (ear-top) for the ear; *muktāvalī*, (pearl necklace), *harṣaka* (a snake-shaped ornament) and *sūtra* (gold thread) for the neck; *vāṭikā* and *aṅgulīmudrā* (finger-ring) for the fingers; *hastavī* and the *valaya* (bangle) for the forearm; *rucika* (bracelet) and *uccitika* for the wrist; *keyūra* (armlet) and *aṅgada* (arm-band) for the upper arm; *trisara* (three-stringed necklace) and *hāra* (necklace) for the neck and chest; *tarala* and *sūtraka* (golden thread) for the waist; and suspended jewelled necklaces and flower-garlands for the entire body.[4]

Ornaments for women are also described by Bharata. Women wore *pādapātra* on the *janghā* (shanks); *aṅgulīyaka* (toe-rings) on the toes and *tilaka* on the big toes. *Nūpura*, *kiṅkiṇī*, *ratnajāla* (jewel-net) and ringing *kaṭaka* ornaments are worn round the ankle. An additional decoration

[1]*Bālacarita*, I, p. 522 and V, pp. 550–51.
[2]*NS-KM*, XXI. 9; *KSS*, XXIII. 10; *VD*, III. 27. 5b–7a.
[3]*NS-KM*, XXI. 11–13; *KSS*, XXIII. 12–14.
[4]*NS-KM*, XXI. 14–19a; *KSS*, XXIII. 15–21a.

of the feet will be the lac-dye applied on them in various patterns to impart to them the natural colour of Aśoka blossoms. Ornaments named *kāncī* with a net of pearls, *mekhalā raśanā* and *kalāpa* are worn round the waist. There is only one string in *kañcī*, eight strings in *mekhalā*, 16 in *raśanā* and 25 in *kalāpa*. *Hāras* were found to be of 8, 16, 32, 64, 100 strings. Women used to wear *hāras* of different jewels on their bosom and round the neck. They are: *muktāvalī* (pearl-necklace), *vyālapaṅkti* (snake-ground), *ratnamālikā* (jewel string), *ratnāvalī* (jewel necklace) and *sūtraka* (neck-chain). Different kinds of ornaments mixed with jewels were worn by ladies on the bosom or the back. On the fingers they used to wear rings. *Śaṅkakalāpī* (*hastidanti cuḍiyān*), *kaṭaka*, *patrapuraka*, *kharjura*, *aṁsopitika* ornaments were worn by women on the wrists. *Aṅgada* (arm-band) and *valaya* (bangle) were used on the upper arm. The *varjura* and the *svecchitika* are ornaments of the fore arm. *Tilaka* and *patralekhā* adorned their temples. *Karṇika*, *karṇavalaya*, *karṇamudrā* entwining the ear, *dāntapātra* set with jewels, *karṇapura* and *karṇotkīlaka* (ear-top) were prescribed for the ears. Bunches of flowers tied to the hair dangled above their eyebrows. They used *śikhāpāsa*, *śikhājāla*, *khaṇḍapātra*, *cūdāmaṇi* (crest jewel), *makarikā*, *muktājāla* (pearl-net), *gavākṣa* and *śīrṣajāla* (hair-net) as ornaments for the head. Bharata has not mentioned any ornament for the nose. It appears the reference to such ornaments is lost or ornaments for the nose came into vogue in later times. Ornaments are to be worn according to emotions and sentiments and having a consideration of tradition, measurements of the wearer and physical form.[1]

The *Abhinayadarpaṇa* says bells should be made of bronze, copper or silver; they should be sweet in tone, well-shaped, dainty and tied with an indigo string with a knot between each pair of bells. Dancers should have 100 or 200 bells on each foot, or 100 for the right foot and 200 for the left.[2]

The use of some of these ornaments is referred to in Sanskrit dramas. For instance in the *Svapnavāsavadattā*, *karṇacūlikā*, an ear ornaments,[3] and in the *Ratnāvalī*, *nūpura*, anklets, *kiṅkiṇi-cakravāla* and *kalaka* are mentioned.[4]

Various sets of ornaments are prescribed for various roles. *Vidyādharīs* use pearl-studded *śikhāpuṭas* and *śikhaṇḍas*. *Yakṣīs* and *apsarās* wear ornaments studded with gems. *Yakṣīs* use only one *śikhā* (top-knot).

[1]*NS-KM*, XXI. 19b–35; *KSS*, XXIII. 21b–43.
[2]*AD*, 29–30.
[3]*Svapnavāsavadattā*, p. 13.
[4]*Rat*, I. 16; II. 2 and prose, p. 45.

Nāgīs use ornaments of the type usually worn by the divine women and have creeper of pearls and gems with points. The dresses of *siddha* women are decorated with pearls and emeralds. *Padmamaṇi* is the ornament for *gandharvis*. Ornaments for *rakṣasīs* have *indranīlamaṇi. Vaiḍūrya* and pearls go to make up the jewellery of goddesses. Dresses adorned with flowers, jewels and ornamented with *vaiḍūrya* are worn by monkey women of divine origin. Women belonging to the south use *kumbhīpadaka* and *vartalāṭika*. The ornaments of prostitutes vary according to their country. In *vipralambha śṛṅgāra* women wear white dress only and do not use any ornaments.[1]

Over-ornamentation on the stage is discouraged. Gold ornaments are disallowed but ornaments of lac or mica are commended. If an actor or actress is loaded with heavy ornaments he or she is liable to be exhausted. The wearers often get fatigued and may even swoon. Instead of solid gold ornaments those filled with lac and not overloaded with jewels are recommended. Gods and men in general are to use ornaments according to the country and circumstances.[2]

Mukuṭas (crowns) are included among ornaments as they are prepared with gold and jewels. They come under the category of *pratiśira* (masks) which are to be used for gods and men according to their habitation, birth and age. *Mukuṭas* are of three kinds: *kirīṭi*, *mastakī* and *pārśvamaulī* (or *pārśvagata*). The *kirīṭi mukuṭa* is the best among the *mukuṭas*. It is fitted to the head like a high-levelled cap. It is made of gold and studded with jewels. The *mastakī mukuṭa* is not as high as the *kirīṭī mukuṭa* but is enough to cover the head. It may also be made of gold and studded with jewels. The *pārśvamaulī mukuṭa* is only as high as the forehead. It does not cover the whole head and is also called *ardhamukuṭa*. It is made of gold. Kings usually wear crowns of the *mastakī* type. It is prescribed that gods should wear the *kirīṭi*, *mastakī* and *pārśvamaulī* crowns according to their status and age. Generals, crown-princes and writers should wear *pārśvamaulī mukuṭas*. Gods in general, *gandharvas*, *pannagas*, *rākṣasas* and *samantas* are to use *pārśvamaulī mukuṭas*. For *vidyādharas*, *siddhas*, *cāraṇas*, *mukuṭas* which could be tied to the hair are prescribed. Ministers, those in charge of harems, merchants and priests are to use *mukuṭas* covered by the foldings of the turbans (*sāfā*). The *Nāṭyaśāstra* further prescribes that *mukuṭas* to be used on the stage should not be made of gold and jewels, for if they are heavy, actors will

[1] *NS-KM*, XXI. 41–55; *KSS*, XXIII. 49–72a.
[2] *NS-KM*, XXI. 36–40; *KSS*, XXIII. 44–48.

perspire, be overwhelmed and swoon. Copper should, therefore, be used in making *mukuṭas*.[1]

It will not be out of place here if we describe briefly how openings in the *paṭī* for the mask, on which various forms of crowns are set, were made. The *paṭī* is to measure 32 *aṅgulas* or can have any measurement according to need and be prepared by using *bilva* paste on cloth. Masks should be made with ashes or husks of paddy being mixed with *bilva*-paste or some loose form of it. After getting the *paṭī* dried up holes should be pierced into it. An opening six *aṅgulas* long and an *aṅgula* wide should be made for the forehead; another opening two *aṅgulas* long and one and a half *aṅgula* wide for the cheeks, two openings each three *aṅgulas* long for the ears mouth and one of twelve *aṅgulas* for the neck.[2]

Ornamentation through garlands is the second kind of *alaṅkāra*. Bharata has named five ways of preparing garlands: *veṣṭita, vitata, saṅghātya, tepita* and *pralaṁbita*.[3] He has not, however, given any details. The *Abhinavabhāratī* gives details about the varieties of the garland. The *veṣṭita* garland is that in which bunches are prepared by folding together green grass, leaves and flowers. Flowers are woven into garlands to make a *vitata*. The *Saṅghātya* is that in which flowers are placed in a row and their stems tied with a thread in such a way that they are not visible. In the *tepita*, bunches of flowers are taken separately and a garland is prepared after tying each of them with a thread. The *pralaṁbita* is a single long garland.[4] The stage and persons appearing on it are to be adorned with any of these garlands as needed by the situation.

Dress for the characters on the stage is the third item in *alaṅkāra*. There was a conventional stage costume prescribed and it was in keeping with the dress in ordinary life. The costume and appearance of the *naṭa* help him in his work. Dress reveals the sex and race, sect or class, social or other position of the character represented. Bharata has mentioned three kinds of dress: *śuddha* (undyed or white), *vicitra* (variegated) and *malina* (dirty). Ascetics wear garments of rags or bark; those in charge of the harem reddish (*kaṣāya*) jackets; warriors gay garments with weapons. *Ābhīrā* maidens wear dark blue clothes; *vidyādharis* white clothes; demon women dark clothes; divine beings blue clothes. Dirty

[1] *NS-KM*, XXI. 115–23: 181–87a; *KSS*, XXIII. 131b–40, 204–10.

[2] *NS-KM*, XXIII. 176–86.

[3] *NS-KM*, XXI. 10; *KSS*, XXIII. 11 and repeated in 114.

[4] *Veṣṭitaṁ tṛṇaveṣṭamayābhimataṁ behumālāveṣṭanakṛtaṁ ca vāvitatyāveṣṭitanyonya-śliṣṭamālāsamūhātmakaṁ vastradhārabhāvenoṁbhitaṁ saṅghātyam vṛttaṁ vāsya cchidrāntaṁ prakṣiptasūtraṁbahupuṣpagucchoṁbhitaṁ vāgrandhibhiṭṛnṃitaṁ vā prālaṁbitaṁ iti jālādi-paryatavyārākaṁ*. (MSS. Saraswati Bhawan Library, Banaras) *Abh. Bh*, XXI, p. 12.

clothes indicate madness, distraction, misery or a journey. A woman whose husband has gone out also wears dirty clothes. Uncoloured or white garb is used for one engaged in worship or solemn religious service or one who is a trader (*prāpaṇika*). Gods, *dānavas*, *gandharvas*, *uragas*, *yakṣas* and *rākṣasas* as well as lovers and kings normally wear gay, variegated clothes. But the costumes of the kings should be white when due to ominous appearance of any star (*nakṣatrotpāta*) they are engaged in any propitiatory rite. Costumes and decorations of the sages, the Jain (*nirgrantha*) and the Buddhist (*śākhya*) monks, the Tridaṇḍis and Brāhmaṇas well-versed in the Vedas (*śrotriya*) should be made according to the traditions of the order and respective society. Generally the dress of men and women varied according to their age and status.[1]

AṄGARACANĀ

Aṅgaracanā (painting of the limbs) is the third aspect of *āhāryābhinaya*. It includes dyeing of the limbs of persons appearing on the stage and their style of dressing the hair and beard.[2]

A keen appreciation of colours is a marked feature of the oriental play, for in the representation of great legendary heroes, divinities and mythical beings, the elements of place, time, age, rank and profession were never lost sight of. As regards painting, the *Viṣṇudharmottara* says the primary colours are of five kinds: white, yellow, black, blue and myrobalan colours.[3] But Bharata in the *Nāṭyaśāstra* speaks only of four primary colours: white (*sita*), blue (*nīla*), yellow (*pīta*) and red (*rakta*). It is for the artist to mix these primary colours. The colouring of things witnessed, says the *Viṣṇudharmottara*, should be true to nature. Great emphasis is laid on the thousandfold mixture of colours left to the imagination of the artist, and on the light and dark shade of every tone. The range of colours must have been wide enough to show in as subtle a manner as possible the local colour of objects.

According to the *Nāṭyaśāstra* there are four fundamental colours: white, blue, red and yellow—from which others are developed. For instance, *pāṇḍuvarṇa* is developed by mixing white and blue; *Kapotavarṇa*

[1] *NS-KM*, XXI. 100b–114; *KSS*, XXIII, 116–31a.

[2] *Keśaracanādirāsamantādhriyate poṣyate kāntiryena tadābharaṇaṁ śikhāvyālādikṣīrakarma pulakādiyojanāparicchedaḥ vicitravastuyogaḥ etadveṣādipralaṁbhena kartavyādvijā ca kravyaṁ deśo anantyādiḥ avasthāratiśokādyāstatreti puruṣeṣvevāṅganānāṁ rūpaparivartanasaṁpādanātmakaṁ varṇavartanā kartavyā nastrīpātreṣviti yāvat.* (MSS. Saraswati Bhawan Library, Banaras) *Abh. Bh.*, XXI, p. 13.

[3] *VD*, III. 27. 7b–26.

by mixing white and blue; *padmavarṇa* by mixing white and red; *harita* by mixing yellow and blue; *kaṣāya* by mixing blue and red; *gaura* by mixing red and yellow. When different colours are to be developed by mixing three or more primary colours, then the strong colour should be taken in one part and the weak colours in two parts each. But when the strong colour is blue, then one part of blue and three parts of other colours should be taken. As blue is very powerful, its dominance would be noticeable in the mixture. After carefully preparing different colours and keeping in view the age, country and caste of the character, the paint should be employed in such a way that the character, whom the *naṭa* represents, should seem natural.[1]

Different colours are suitable for kings of different regions. They are to be either painted lotus colour (*padmavarṇa*), or reddish yellow (*gaura*) or dark blue (*śyāma*). The sages should always be given the colour of plum (*vadara*). Gay persons are to use reddish-yellow (*gaura*). Kirātas, Barbaras, Āndhras, Draviḍas, the people of Kāśī and Kosala, Pulindas and people of the Deccan are to be coloured brown (*asita*), The Śakas, Yavanas, Pallavas, Bāhlikas and people of the North are generally to be reddish-yellow (*gaura*). Pañcālas, Śūrasenas, Māgadhas, Uḍhras, Aṅgas, Vaṅgas and Kaliṅgas are coloured dark blue (*śyāma*) as also Vaiśyas and Śūdras in general. Brāhamaṇs and Kṣatriyas are to be reddish (*rakta*) and Vaiśyas and Śūdras dark blue (*śyāma*). Gods, *yakṣas* and *apsarās* are to be painted reddish yellow (*gaura*); Rudra, Arka (sun), Druhiṇa (Brahman) and Skanda are to have the colour of gold. Soma, Bṛhaspati, Śukra, Varuṇa, clusters of stars, ocean, Himālaya, the Ganges when personified are to be painted white (*śveta*) and *Aṅgārak* red (*rakta*). Buddha and fire are to be painted yellow (*pīta*). Nara, Nārāyaṇa, Somanāga, Vāsuki, the *daityas*, *dānavas*, *rākṣasas*, *guhyakas* and *piśācas*, water and the sky are to be painted dark blue (*śyāma*). The sick and evildoers, those who are oppressed by evil stars or have taken shelter in penance and all family men engaged in toilsome work should be made brown (*asita*). Thus mixtures of paints appropriate to several roles are suggested for people belonging to different provinces, professions and grades of society.[2]

The dress of actors is carefully regulated especially as regards colour which evidently was regarded an important item in the matter of sentiments. Each *rasa* had to be painted in its expressive colour. The erotic (*śṛṅgāra*) was of dark blue (*śyāma*), the comic (*hāsya*), white (*sita*), the

[1]*NS-KM*, XXI. 57–69a; *KSS*, XXIII. 73b–84a.

[2]*NS-KM*, XXI. 69b–92a; *KSS*, XXIII. 84b–105; *ŚR*, I. XLVI. 134–42; pp. 256–57.

pathetic (*karuṇa*), ash-coloured (*kapota*), the furious (*raudra*), red (*rakta*), the heroic (*vīra*), reddish yellow (*gaura*), the terrific (*bhayānaka*), black (*kṛṣṇa*), the marvellous (*adbhuta*), yellow (*pīta*) and the repulsive (*bībhatsa*), blue (*nīla*).[1]

Dressing of hair is another aspect of *aṅgaracanā*. Elaborate instructions on the subject of *keśaracanā* are laid down by the *Nāṭyaśāstra* for different characters. Persons playing the role of ascetic girls are to wear only one braid (*veṇī*) of hair on their head. Maidens of Avantī and Gauda wear ringlets. The latter have the *śikhāpāśa* and the *veṇī* (braid). Women of the North tie their hair high on the head. Otherwise the plaits are usual. Married women, officers of the king and men of foppish nature should have curly hair. The young women of the Abhiras put on two braids on their head, which are covered with a piece of deep blue cloth. *Vidyādharīs*, *yakṣīs*, *apsarās* and *nāgīs* wear pearls and jewels. *Vidyādharīs* tie up their hair in the form of a knot at the top, decorated with strings of many pearls, while *yakṣīs* are to wear simple *śikhā*. The *nāgaīs* are at once recognizable by the snake's hoods over their heads.[2]

Piśācas, mad men, *bhūtas*, ascetics and those who have not fulfilled their vows leave their hair loose. Buddhist monks (*śākya*), experts in Vedic studies (*śrotriya*), Jain monks (*nirgrantha*) and other ascetics are to have their heads shaven clean or should have curly or long hair loosely hanging down. Boys have three tufts and so also servants, if their hair is not cut short. The *Vidūṣaka* (jester) is bald or with the *kākapāda* (crow's foot).[3]

In the *Raghuvaṁśa*, Kālidāsa describes the *alaka* of Indumatī as having ringlets.[4] The three kinds of arrangements of hair in the *Meghadūta* are named as *alaka* (spiral or grizzled locks), *sīmanta* (hair separated in the middle by a straight line) and *cūḍāpāśa* (locks tied at the back).[5]

Beards come under the scope of *aṅgaracanā*. After painting the face and other limbs one should provide beards to persons according to their habitation, activity and age. Four kinds of beards are prescribed by the *Nāṭyaśāstra*. They may be shaven clean (*śuddha*) dark blue (*śyāma*), carefully trimmed (*vicitra*) and bushy (*romaśa*) Some shave their beards and moustaches clean and this is called *śuddha śmaśru*. Some do not take

[1]*NS-KM*, VI. 42–43; *KSS*, VI. 42–43; *GOS*, VI. 47–48.
[2]*NS-KM*, XXIII. 53–56, 64–68, 71a.
[3]*NS-KM*, XXI. 124–27; *KSS*, XXIII. 141–48; *VD*, III. 27. 37b–43.
[4]*Raghuvaṁśa*, VIII. 53.
[5]*Meghadūta*, II. 71; see V.S. Agrawala's article in *Nāgarī Pracāriṇī Patrikā*, Kārtika, 1997 Saṁvat.

care to have them clean and allow them to grow. This is called *romaśa śmaśru* (bushy). Those usually shave themselves but do not get time to do so owing to some work are stated as having *śyāma śmaśru* (dark blue). Fashionable persons get their beard and moustaches trimmed, and they are called *vicitra* (carefully trimmed).

Ministers, priests, ascetics and persons who have consecrated themselves for any ritual should be clean shaven (*śuddha*). Kings, divine persons, *siddhas*, *vidyādharas*, fashionable persons, princes and persons who ordinarily live gayly wear beards carefully trimmed (*vicitra*). Persons in misery and those under religious penances and those who are overtaken by misfortunes wear dark blue beards (*śyāma*). Sages, ascetics and those engaged in sacrifices lasting a long time have bushy beard (*romaśa*).[1]

Dress, ornaments and painting have a vital role in dramas as they are used with deference to the appropriate sentiment intended to be represented according to customs of the provinces and circumstances and after taking into consideration the age and creed of the people.

SAÑJĪVA

Sañjīva (living creatures), the last aspect of *āhāryābhinaya*, signifies the appearance of animals on the stage and deals with the preparation of artificial animal forms for the stage. Animate objects which are generally seen on the earth are of three categories: four-footed, two-footed and with no foot.[2] Lions, tigers, elephants, horses and other wild animals, birds and serpents could be represented on the stage with the help of bamboos, cloth, wool, *kaliñja*, *bheṇḍa* and *abaraka*. It is quite evident that there were contrivances to represent the ingress and egress of carriages as in the case of the *Mṛcchakaṭika*. The artificial elephant in the *Svapnavāsavadattā*, horse, deer and lion in the *Abhijñānaśākuntala* are all examples of the *sañjīva* type of *āhāryābhinaya*.

Those with many arms, many faces and deformed persons, lions, donkeys, camels, elephants and the like should be prepared with earth, wood, man covered with animal's skin according to the ingenuity of the manager of the theatre. The actor should enter with appropriate feeling, concealing his own form with colouring materials and ornaments. Thus the actor should merge himself completely into the character whose role he is playing. If a man represents an animal, he should assume the feeling

[1] *NS-KM*, XXI. 92b–99; *KSS*, XXIII. 106–113a; *VD*, III. 27. 27–32.
[2] *NS-KM*, XXI. 128–30a; *KSS*, XXIII. 151b–153; *VD*, III. 27. 44–45a.

of that animal and act the role with appropriate voice, gait, gestures and efforts.[1]

We refer to the *Ratnāvalī* to illustrate the *sañjīva* type of *āhāryābhinaya*. In Act II the cage of starling (*sārikā*) is opened by a monkey and there is a hubbub.

'Enters Susaṅgatā with the cage of a starling in her hand'. The monkey's plight is described thus:

"(Behind the scenes)—Dragging under him the remaining part of the gold chain round his neck after it had snapped, and with the circle of small bells jingling on account of the wanton movements of the feet, this monkey here, broken loose from his stable, having crossed the gates, is entering the king's palace, frightening the ladies, with his path followed in haste and confusion by stable keepers.

Susaṅgatā: "O! you who are quite at ease, what have you still to do with the picture-board? Here is the wicked monkey fond of rice and curds. He has opened the cage of the starling and run away. Medhāvinī (the sharp-talented bird) has flown away. Come then, let us quickly follow her. She has caught the words of our conversation and might utter them before any body."

Then the bird is described as having flown away. *Vidūṣaka* is repeating the words uttered by the starling.[2]

Thus a monkey and a starling are shown on the stage. A monkey could easily be shown by a man wearing a garment appropriate to a monkey. In some such way a starling also could be presented.

We may therefore assert that though there was no scenery on ancient Indian stage as in modern times, some of the scenes were shown to the audience by preparing the necessary paraphernalia with the help of bamboos, lac, cloth skin, wool, earth, bark of trees, *bhenḍa* and *abaraka*.

[1]*NS-KM*, XXVI. 13b–19a; *KSS*, XXXV. 9–14.
[2]*Rat*, II. 2 and prose pp. 29, 36, 41.

CHAPTER SIX

Accessory Arts

MUSIC AND ORCHESTRA

Vocal music: *saṅgīta* comprises *gīta* (vocal music), *vādya* (instrumental music) and *nartana* (dancing) and depends upon rhythm (*gītaṁ vādyaṁ tathā nṛtyaṁ yatastāle pratiṣṭhitam*).[1] People generally consider *saṅgīta* and *gīta* synonymous but there is a marked difference between the two. While *saṅgīta* is *tauryatṛka*, the union of song, dance and instrumental music triple symphony, *gīta* (vocal music) deals with only one aspect and is a combination of *svaras* (tones of the musical scale or gamut).[2]

According to authorities on the art of music there are also two main distinctions in the theory and practice of *saṅgīta*. They are recognized by the names *mārga* (high style) and *deśī* (popular style). *Mārga saṅgīta* (*gandharva* or celestial music) was employed by the celestial musicians or by sages who knew the theory of sacred music. *Deśī saṅgīta* (terrestrial music) varies from country to country according to the taste of the people of a particular region and is a source of pleasure.[3] The word *mārga* should not be thought to have been derived from the root *mṛg* (to search for) but should be traced back to *mārga* (path) and then the *mārga* music could accord to the ancient path i.e. classical, as opposed to music that is current in different places (*deśī*). The sage, Mataṅga considers that the word *deśī* (popular) applies to all earthly music. Sound (*dhvani*) goes everywhere in every place and comes to the lips in the form of a 'melodious movement' (*varṇa*), giving rise to *deśī* (popular) music. Hence it is called *deśī*.[4]

The sound of music is called *nāda*, intelligible sound, and is said to result from the union of physical breath with the fire of intellect. All music is based upon relations between sounds. According to the Indian theory, the sounds of music are first perceived as relative pitches or intervals and then from the 22 main intervals (*śrutis*) come

[1]*SR*, II. 21.

[2]Kallinātha's commentary on *SR*, I. 11–21.

[3]*SR*, II. 22–24; *Saṅgītapārijāta*, 20–24; *Rāgavibodha*, I. 6–7; *Saṅgītamakarandaḥ*, I. 3.

[4]*Bṛhaddeśī*, II. 11b and 12. *deśe deśe pravṛttosau dḥvanirdeśīti sanjñitaḥ, ākrantaṁ dhvaninā sarvaṁ jagat sthāvarajaṅgamaṁ, dhvanistu dvividhaḥ prokto vyaktāvyaktavibhāgatah, varṇopalambhanād vyakto deśīmukhamupāgatah.*

the seven notes (*svaras*) called *ṣaḍja, ṛṣabha, gāndhāra, madhyama, pañcama, dhaivata* and *niṣāda.*[1]

Śārṅgadeva says: "Sound is first heard as an interval, a *śruti*: but the resonance that immediately follows, conveying itself (without an external aid) an expression to the mind of the hearer, is called a *svara*, a musical note."[2] The sound that generates an expression is a *svara*, a note. The word *svara* (note) denotes that which shines of itself—from *rājr* (to shine) with the word *sva* (self) prefixed to it.[3] The ornaments of the notes consist of *gamakas* (graces). "When in singing, a note rises from its own pitch and moves towards another so that the second sound passes like a shadow over it, it is called a *gamaka* (grace)."[4]

Authorities on music refer each note to the sound of some animal. The cry of an animal tends to be always on the same note. The sound produced by the peacock is at its highest pitch called *ṣaḍja*. *Ṛṣabha* is said to represent the sound of *cātaka* bird. *Gāndhāra* is the bleat of the goat. *Madhyama* is the cry of the heron. *Pañcama* is the note of the cuckoo (*kokila*). *Dhaivata* is the croaking of the frog in the rainy season and *niṣāda* the trumpeting of the elephant.[5]

Bharata divides *svaras* (notes) into four kinds according to the number of *śrutis* between them and this has remained the accepted division ever since. They are *vādī* (sonant), *saṁvādī* (consonant), *anuvādī* (assonant) and *vivādī* (dissonant).[6]

Vādī (sonant) is the king of notes.[7] It is the most important note taken in the *rāga* (*rañjayatīti rāgaḥ* i.e. that which charms is a *rāga*). It is repeated several times in the *rāga* oftener than the rest of the notes. *Vādī* is the predominant expression of the *rāga*: its character determines the mood. It helps one to recognize a *rāga* and indicates the time of singing it. *Saṁvādī* (consonant) is like a minister and is a note less important than *vādī* and more important than the other notes. "The nature of the consonant (*saṁvādī*) is to reinforce the sonant (*vādī*) by which the expressiveness of the mode is engendered."[8] The *saṁvādī* is almost

[1] *Rāgavibodha*, I. 13–14, *Saṅgītapārijāta*, 26–27. *Saṅgītamakarandaḥ*, I. 10–11.

[2] *ŚR*, I. 3, 24–26.

[3] *Bṛhaddeśi*, 63b: *rājṛ dīptāviti dhātoḥ svaśabdapūrvakasya ca*

[4] *Saṅgītasamayasāra*, 1. 47.

[5] *Saṅgītamakarandaḥ*, I. 12–15; *SR*, I. 3. 48; *Bṛhaddeśī* commentary on 63.

[6] *NS-KM*, XXVIII. 22–23, 24 and prose pp. 303–4; *KSS*, XXVIII. 19–20, 21 and prose pp. 317–18; *SR*, I, III. 49–52.

[7] *Saṅgītamakarandaḥ*, 2–7.

[8] *Bṛhaddeśī* commentary on 63; *yad vādisvarena rāgasya rāgatvaṁ janitaṁ tannirvāhakatvaṁ nāma saṁvāditvaṁ*.

always a fifth or a fourth above the *vādī*. This corresponds with an interval of twelve or eight *śrutis*. The notes of a *rāga* excluding the *vādī* and the *saṁvādī* are called *anuvādī* and are said to be the servants in relation to the king and the minister. *Vivādī* (dissonant) notes are like enemies. This note is not natural to a *rāga* but occurs in it sometimes only accidentally. It is very difficult to use a *vivādī* note in a *rāga* without marring its beauty and hence it is left out of the *rāga* and is called the *varjya svara* (abandoned note). Thus the speaking note is called *vādī*, the note which converses with it is *saṁvādī*, that which increases the beauty of the *rāga* is *anuvādī*, but that which clashes with it is *vivādī*.

Our music is traditionally based on the three *grāmas* named *ṣaḍja*, *madhyama* and *gāndhāra*. *Ṣaḍja* and *madhyama grāmas* are found on earth while *gāndhāra* is reserved for heaven. A combination of *svaras* is called *grāma*. The three *svaras* (notes) namely *udātta* (raised), *anudātta* (not raised) and *svarita* (circumflex) of the Veda are not included in the *grāma*. *Ṣaḍja grāma* is the best of all the *grāmas*.[1]

Rāgas (modes) necessarily depend upon two *grāmas* and are mainly produced from *ṣaḍja grāma*. *Rāga* is the basis of melody in our music. The notes which are to convey certain definite emotions or ideas must be carefully selected from the 22 intervals of the *śruti* scale and then grouped to form a mode, a *rāga*. It is defined as an arrangement of sounds, which possesses *varṇa* (melodic movement), furnishes gratification to the senses and is consisted of musical notes.[2] The term *varṇa* (melodic movement) refers to the act of singing and is of four kinds, viz., *sthāyī* (level), repetition of the same sound, *ārohī* ascent, *avarohī* descent, and *sañcārī*, wandering or ascent and descent combined.[3] The twelve notes, seven major and five minor, constitute the octave. The ascent as well as the descent taken in regular order beginning and ending with a particular note of the octave is called *mūrcchanā*.[4] "That which spans (*mūrccha*) the scale of a mode is called *mūrcchanā*."[5]

According to ancient musical theory there are three important notes in the *rāga*. These are the *graha*, the *aṁśa* and the *nyāsa*. The *graha* is the starting note, the *aṁśa* the predominant and the *nyāsa* the ending note.[6] Today singers do not observe the rules regarding the starting or ending

[1]*Saṅgītapārijāta*, 97–98, p. 28; *ŚR*, I. 4. 1–2.

[2]*ŚR*, II. 2. 1–9a, *Rāgavibodha*, I. 1.

[3]*ŚR*, I. 6. 1–3, *Saṅgītapārijāta*, 219–20.

[4]*Saṅgītapārijāta*, 103.

[5]*Bṛhaddeśī*, 94, *mūrchate yena rāgo hi mūrchanetyabhisañjitā. Ārohaṇāvarohaṇakrameṇa svarasaptakaṁ*.

[6]*ŚR*, I. 7. 30a, 32b and 38b.

note of a particular *rāga* but they usually begin and end as they wish. Now *aṁśa* is considered all important and thus is the soul of the *rāga*. Śārṅgadeva identifies the *aṁśa*, the main note, with the sonant, the *vādī*. "Because it is most used during a performance, the *vādī* (sonant) is called *aṁśa* (main note)."[1] This is also supported by Abhinavagupta in the *Abhinavabhāratī*. "The *aṁśa svara* (note) is the same as the *vādī*."[2] All the characteristics of the *rāga* are embodied in its *mūrcchanā* or *ṭhāṭa*.

Music was an indispensable adjunct of Sanskrit plays. Theorists state that each sentiment has its appropriate music and each action its special accompaniment.[3] Usually the Sanskrit drama begins with music and ends with it. During the enactment of plays also, there are various references to the music performed. In the *Ratnāvalī* two maids sing *dvipadīkhaṇḍa* before the king.[4] In the *Mālavikāgnimitra*, Mālavikā sings and acts.[5] In the *Mṛcchakaṭika*, Cārudatta goes to attend a musical concert and while returning explains the beauty of the song of Rebhila to his associate *vidūṣaka*, Maitreya. "Really his song was impassioned, sweet, smooth, clear, and full of emotion, graceful and charming. To tell the truth, I feel that although the musical concert is over, I am as it were still listening, as I walk, to that cadence of the notes of his sweet voice; and to those well-blended notes of the lute, high-pitched when following up with the harmonious swell and fall of the sounds of the syllables (of the song), but low towards the close; - and to the song, sung with due regard to the pitch of sounds, graceful and repeated twice where the *rāga* (passion) required it."[6] In the same manner, examples from other dramas can also be cited to show what a high place music occupied in the presentation of Sanskrit plays.

Dramatic songs pre-eminently were *dhruvās* having *varṇa*, *alaṅkāra*, tempo (*laya*), *jāti* and *pāṇi* in a systematic manner. *Dhruvās* had five classes: *prāveśikī*, *ākṣepikī*, *naiṣkrāmikī*, *prāsādikī* and *antarā* based on occasions and suggesting respectively entrance (*praveśa*), turning aside (*ākṣepa*), departure (*niṣkrāma*), countenance (*prāsāda*) and transition (*antarā*) in the course of the development of plots of different plays.[7]

Prāveśikī dhruvās[8] were sung at the entrance of characters on the stage taking into consideration short dissertations of various sentiments.

Ākṣepikī dhruvā[9] were sung when a new sentiment is brought to rise

[1] *ŚR*, I. 7. 34.
[2] *Abh. Bh.*, on *NS*, *GOC*, XXVIII. 23.
[3] *NS-KM*, XXIX. 12–13; *KSS*, XXIX. 17, 18.
[4] *Rat*, I. 13–15.
[5] *Māl*, II. 4, p. 26.
[6] *Mṛch*, III. 4–5.
[7] *NS*, XXIII. 364.
[8] Ibid., 365.
[9] Ibid., 373.

having subdued the one already present. They were sung on occasions like one's being obstructed, fallen or afflicted with illness.

Naiṣkrāmikī dhruvā[1] songs were sung at the exit of characters to show their going out of the stage.

Prāsādikī dhruvās[2] were sung for bringing solace to the audience after they witnessed something which agitated their feeling very much.

Antarā dhruvās[3] were sung by adopting a quick tempo in place of medium or slow tempo to divert attention of the audience at a time when principal characters become gloomy, absent minded, angry, intoxicated, or falling into a swoon. Thus *dhruvā* is sung mostly from "behind the scenes".

It may be remarked that the *dhruvās*[4] were a sort of "background" music based on the contents of the songs, their metres, language, tempo and *tāla*, suggesting acts and moods of different characters in a play.

The *ṛk*[5], *pāṇikā* (a kind of song or singing *yājñ*) and *gāthā*, and some traditional types of songs which have different measures, are called *dhruvās*.

The dramaturgic works prescribe that the audience should be entertained with music right from the beginning (i.e. *pūrvaraṅga*) to the end (i.e. *bharatavākya*) during the performance of a drama on the stage.

Dhruvās are considered to be the vital life of dramatic performance "*dhruvā hi nāṭyasya prathame prāṇāḥ*" by Rājaśekhara.[6]

The language in the application of *dhruvās* is mainly Śaurasenī Prākṛta. Sometimes it may be Māgadhī Prākṛta.[7] Sanskrit songs have been prescribed in the case of heavenly beings but half-Sanskrit songs are used in the case of human beings.[8] Dr. Raghavan's[9] view does not seem to be correct when he expresses that *dhruvās* were always in Prākṛta and not in Sanskrit.

Prāveśikı dhruvā in *Bālabhārata* is in Sanskrit "*haracūḍā maṇirindus-trijagaddipaśca dinakaro devaḥ* etc.[10] *Nāṭyadarpaṇa* cites an example of *ākṣepikī dhruvā* from *Udātarāghava*. Here the heroic sentiment is introduced by brushing aside the sentiment of love "O, you hermit, halt, where are you going now etc."[11]

[1]Ibid., 366. [2]Ibid., 368.
[3]Ibid., 367, 369–70. [4]Ibid., 392, 400.
[5]*NS*, XXXII. 2 (recitation of *ṛk* stanzas, *sāman* chants).
[6]*Bālabhārata* of Rājaśekhara—*prastāvanā* prose after verse 13.
[7]*NS*, XXXII. 440. [8]Ibid., 441.
[9]*The Journal of the Madras Music Academy*, vol. XXV.
[10]Rājaśekhara's *Bālabhārata, prastāvanā*, verse 13.
[11]*Nāṭyadarpaṇa*, p. 195 (*GOS*, 1929 edition).

The song sung by Mālavikā in the beginning of the second act of *Mālavikāgnimitra* was a *dhruvā* song. Gaṇadāsa, the music teacher of Mālavikā informs the king that the fourth stanza of the *catuṣpadā* (a variety of *dhruvā*) had to be sung by Mālavikā.[1]

The particular *dhruvā* sung by Mālavikā can be of *prāsādikī* type as it was adjusted to *madhya tāla* and was sung to heighten charm of *sṛṅgāra rasa*.

Song sung by Malayavatī in the first act of *Nāgānanda* proves that *dhruvās* were sung on the stage by the main characters of a drama.[2]

Nāṭyadarpaṇa mentions that a *dhruvā* song is, as a rule, the creation of the dramatist himself.

Dāmodaragupta in *Kuṭṭanīmata*[3] describes in detail the performance of the first act of *Ratnāvalī nāṭikā*. Let us analyse the depiction from the point of the *dhruvās*. Here the *sūtradhāra* enters and introduces himself by singing *dvīpādanyasmādapi* etc. (in the prologue). After conversing with the Naṭī he goes out. Dāmodaragupta considers both these actions of the *sūtradhāra*, as *praveśikī dhruvā* and *naiṣkrāmikī dhruvā* respectively. Towards the end of the first act, Vatsarāja, the king sings the two verses "*udayataṭāntaritamiyam*" etc. and "*Devi tvanmukhapaṅkajena śaśinaḥ*" and goes out of the stage along with *vidūṣaka* and others. This is again the *naiṣkrāmikī dhruvā*.

To conclude here, it is obvious from the text of the *Ratnāvalī* that the *dhruvā* songs were composed in Sanskrit and Prākṛta verses. Sometimes *dhruvā* songs were sung from behind the curtain and composed by the artists attached to the dramatic companies in ancient India.

Instrumental music: There are four kinds of musical instruments in our country; stringed instruments; wind instruments, drums and cymbals—bells and gongs. According to the *Nāṭyaśāstra*, *tatam* comes under the category of stringed musical instruments *suṣira* under wind instruments and *avanadham* under instruments of percussion[4] like drums and *ghanam* (solid) instruments (cymbals) which are struck against each other. The materials of which the instruments are made for the most part those that are easily procurable. Large gourds, bamboos, canes, reeds, jackwood, earthen ware, hides of calves, sheep and buffaloes are used.

[1] *Mālavikāgnimitra*, act II, *Devaḥ sarmiṣṭhāyan kṛtirlayamadhya caṭuṣpadā* etc.

[2] *Nāgānanda*, act I, verse 14. "*Utphullakamalakesaraparagauradyute, mama hi Gaurī*" etc.

[3] *Kuṭṭanimata*, verses from 879 to 927 (Bombay edition, 1924).

[4] *NS-KM*, XXVIII. 1–15; XXX. 1, 2; XXXI. 1–4a; *KSS*, XXVIII. 1–14; XXX. 1, 2; XXXI. 1–4.

Ancient Sanskrit treatises and Indian sculpture depict musical instruments in detail. Various kinds of *vīṇās*, drums, pipes, gongs and bells are exhibited in sculptures of Bharhut, Mathura, Amarāvatī, Sanchi, Nagarjunakonda, Konark, the temples of southern India, such as Chidambaram and paintings of Ajanta, Bagh Thanjavur etc.

In ancient plays, orchestra (*kutapa*) served a definite dramatic purposes. The *Nāṭyaśāstra* points out that musicians sit in *raṅgaśīrṣa* in this manner: the *mādaṅgika* facing the east between the two doors of the green room, the *pāṇavika* and the *dārdarika* to his left, *gāyaka* to the south of the *raṅgapīṭha* facing the north, *gāyikā* to his front on the north facing the south, *vaiṇika* to their left and two *vaṁśīkas* to their right. In all the three types of theatres, players of musical instruments occupy a place in the *raṅgaśīrṣa* between the two doors.[1] K.R. Pisharoti is surely wrong when he says: "The arrangement of the Athenian stage is very simple: it consisted of a round orchestra, and a low rectangular *skēnē* with a projecting parascenia and a low platform stage. Between the *skēnē* and the auditorium lies what is termed the proscenium which is understood as the back wall of the stage in front of which the actors act or as pillars in front of the stage between the actors and the audience or as the stage. In these respects this agrees with our theatre, particularly in our having the *mattavāraṇī* and the *ṣaḍ-dāruka*."[2]

Temples have played a great part in the preservation of musical instruments. Dramatic poses as described in the *Nāṭyaśāstra* are found sculptured on the walls of the Naṭarāja temple at Chidambaram showing some musical instruments. At Ajanta also there is a painting representing the dance intended to allure Mahajanaka. The orchestra there comprises of five artistes, two of them playing cymbals, one a pair of drums, another a *mṛdaṅga* and the fifth apparently a guitar. Two women playing the flute are also found in the painting.[3]

In our country there are nearly 400 musical instruments each with a distinct name, shape and quality of tone. The *Nāṭyaśāstra* mentions instruments such as *mṛdaṅga paṇava, dardura, dundubhi, muraja, jhallari, paṭaha, vaṁśa, śaṅkha* and *ḍakkinī*.[4] According to the *Mirror of Gesture* the following accessories are called the outer life of danseuse: the drum, cymbals of a good tone—the flute, chorus, the *droṇa*, lute (*vīṇā*), the

[1] *NS-KM*, XXXIV, prose on p. 429; *KSS*, XXXIII, prose on p. 449.

[2] K.R. Pisharoti, "The Ancient Indian Theatre", *Rajah Sir Annamalai Chettiar Commemoration Volume*, Annamalai University, 1941.

[3] Ajanta cave no. 1.

[4] *NS-KM*, XXXIV. 9–16; *KSS*, XXXIII. 2, 10–17.

bells, and a male singer (*gāyaka*) of renown.[1] In the *Saṅgītamakarandaḥ* ten kinds of *vīṇā* are described and further on various instruments are mentioned.[2] In other treatises on music innumerable other names of instruments are mentioned.

As orchestras (*kutapa*) can be organised with Indian instruments alone in the modern age and as they help the presentation of a particular *rasa* and have a rich variety we can conclude that orchestras were similarly organized in ancient India with the help of four kinds of instruments referred to in the *Nāṭyaśāstra*. An orchestra (*kutapa*) was organised at the Udai Shankar India Culture Centre Almora, in 1941 exclusively with Indian instruments.

HISTRIONICS

Now we come to *āṅgikābhinaya*, gestures or action with limbs. It is expressed in three ways: by *aṅga, pratyaṅga* and *upāṅga*. The head, hands, chest, sides (flanks), waist (hips) and feet are called *aṅgas*. Some writers consider the neck also as an *aṅga*. The shoulder-blades, arms, back, abdomen, thigh (calves) and shanks are called *pratyaṅgas*. Some writers add the wrists, elbows, knees and the neck also to the list of *pratyaṅgas*. The shoulders, eyes, eye-brows, cheeks, nose, jaws, lips, teeth, tongue, chin and face are called *upāṅgas*. Then there are the heels, ankles, toes and fingers. *Aṅgas, pratyaṅgas* and *upāṅgas* are to be used in every dance. When an *aṅga* (major limb) moves, the *pratyaṅga* and *upāṅga* also move.[3]

Detailed are the directions on *āṅgikābhinaya* and here Bharata depended upon older *naṭasūtras*. The different parts of the body are described and motions and gestures and their significance assigned. The head is described as *akaṁpita* when it is moved slowly up and down, *kaṁpita* when the same movement is made quickly.[4] Each motion has a distinct significance. The glance changes according to the sentiment and the pupils move in different ways to express different sentiments and conditions.[5]

A series of rules are found on the motions of seven kinds of the brows[6], six of the nose,[7] six of the cheeks[8], six of the lips[9], seven of the

[1]Coomaraswamy, *The Mirror of Gesture*, p. 35 (1936 edition).

[2]*Saṅgītamakarandaḥ*, IV. 6–12.

[3]*AD*, 42–49a, *NS-KM*, VIII. 11–15; *KSS*, VIII. 11–15; *GOS*, VIII. 12–16.

[4]*NS-KM*, VIII. 16–37a; *KSS*, VIII. 16–37a; *GOS*, VIII. 17–40a.

[5]*NS-KM*, VIII. 38–51; *KSS*, VIII. 38–51; *GOS*, VIII. 41–55.

[6]*NS-KM*, VIII. 112b–122a; *KSS*, VIII. 114–23; *GOS*, VIII. 118b–129a.

[7]*NS-KM*, VIII. 122b–127; *KSS*, VIII. 124–30a; *GOS*, VIII. 129–136a.

[8]*NS-KM*, VIII. 128–32; *KSS*, VIII. 130b–135a; *GOS*, VIII. 136b–141a.

[9]*NS-KM*, VIII. 133–38; *KSS*, VIII. 135b–141a; *GOS*, VIII. 141b–147a.

chin[1] and nine of the neck.[2] Further 24 postures of single hands, 13 of the different combined hands and 64 *nṛtta* hands are described.[3] *Mudrās*, gestures by figures from the most important and powerful means of expression in a dance. Their richness creates a unique dramatic language and their conventionalised meanings and symbolism lend an added charm and glamour to the art of dancing. *Mudrās*, gestures by fingers set forth in the *Nāṭyaśāstra* are said to include the divine actions of celestial dancers and their application to the feelings and aspirations of human beings. We can examine the definition of one or two gestures of the hand to ascertain how they signify different objects. When the four fingers are outstretched parallel to one another and the thumb is bent, the *patākā* (flag) hand is formed. The hand is held against the forehead in this manner to express blows, injuries, oppressions, gladness, or haughtiness. The same posture of the hand with the fingers separated from one another and shaken indicate the glare of heat, torrential rain or shower of flowers. When the posture of *patākā* is kept and the third finger is bent, it is called the *tripatākā* hand and signifies the bringing or giving something, or dismounting or entry.[4] In this manner by stating the definitions of other hands and by describing their significance it can be shown that different things are represented by different gestures of the hand in the presentation of plays.

Further directions are given regarding chest, flanks, abdomen, hips, thighs, legs and feet. As a matter of fact the *Nāṭyaśāstra* deals elaborately with different *cārīs*,[5] *maṇḍalas*[6] and *gatis*.[7] An attempt to set aright the feet, thighs, chest and abdomen is called *cārī*. Where an action is made by taking one step it is called *cārī*. As the *cārīs* connected with different limbs relate to (*vyāyacchante* from *vyā-yaṁ*, stretch out to) one another they constitute a *vyāyāma* system. Where two steps are taken it becomes *karaṇa* and the combination of *karaṇas* is said to be *khaṇḍa*. Three or four *khaṇḍa* make one *maṇḍala*. *Cārī* is employed in dancing, movements, dropping of weapons and in battle. Thus *nāṭya* is dependant on *cārī*. In *nāṭya* no limb moves without the employment of *cārī*. According to the *Nāṭyaśāstra*, *cārīs* are 32 in number and are divided into two classes: earthly (*bhauma*) and heavenly (*ākāśagāmī*). But the *Abhinayadarpaṇa*

[1] *NS-KM*, VIII. 139–144; *KSS*, VIII. 141b–147a; *GOS*, VIII. 147b–153a.
[2] *NS-KM*, VIII. 153b–159; *KSS*, VIII. 164–170a; *GOS*, VIII. 170–176a.
[3] *NS-KM*, IX. 4–16; *KSS*, IX. 4–17; *GOS*, IX. 4–17a.
[4] *NS-KM*, IX. 17b–30; *KSS*, IX. 18–31; *GOS*, IX. 18–32.
[5] *NS-KM*, X. 1–12; *KSS*, XI. 1–13; *GOS*, X. 1–13.
[6] *NS-KM*, XI. 1–5a; *KSS*, XII. 1–5; *GOS*, XI. 1–6.
[7] *NS-KM*, XII. 7b–33; *KSS*, XIII. 8–39; *GOS*, XII. 8–40.

has only eight *cārīs* and they constitute only one class by themselves.[1] *Maṇḍalas*, according to the *Nāṭyaśāstra* are twenty in number and are divided into two classes: earthly (*bhauma*) and heavenly (*ākāśika*), but the *Abhinayadarpaṇa* gives only ten of them and does not classify them at all.[2] The *Nāṭyaśāstra* and the *Abhinayadarpaṇa* have no name common in their *cārīs* and *maṇḍalas*. The *nāṭyācārya* should employ *gati* (gait) having ascertained fully the *sthita* (slow), *madhya* (medium) and *druta laya* (quick tempo). The *gati* (gait) of nobles should be with steadiness, that of the middle class with medium tempo, while the low class should have quick and copious gait. Different kinds of beings walk in different ways and the gait should also vary according to the situation. *Cārīs, maṇḍalas* and *gatis*, according to their relation to one another, are endless in number and variety. The *naṭa* has no room to be original in his gestures, for that is the business of master (*ācāryas*) of the art who know the theory and practice thoroughly. It is the action, not the actor, which is essential to the dramatic art.[3]

An elaborate description of how animate or inanimate objects can be represented through *abhinaya*, particularly *āṅgikābhinaya* is given in one full chapter on special representation (*citrābhinaya*) in the *Nāṭyaśāstra*. It deals with methods of describing through bodily gestures natural phenomena such as dawn, night, twilight, day, the six seasons and the sky, mountains, oceans, stars, moonlight, heat, wind and the mid-day and evening sun, lightning; human beings and animals; objects stationed in heaven such as gods and *bhūtas*; expressions of happiness, anger, jealousy, calamity, misery, fear, intoxication, bravery and the various emotions. Different kinds of poisonous effects could be represented on the stage through bodily gestures. Let us now take some examples to show how these were represented by actors and actresses playing different roles. Cold is indicated by people of lower position by contracting their limbs, trembling, clenching their teeth, moving their lips and making a '*sī, sī*' sound. Darkness is indicated by people slipping and grouping their way with their hands. A person gets into a carriage by raising his eyes and feet and enters a palace by taking longer paces and raising the feet higher. The act of getting into water is done by raising the clothes and if the water is very deep he represents that by outstretching his hands. Joy is represented by one embracing the other's body, by smiling eyes as well as by horripilation (*tathālpakathana*), while anger is indicated by upturned red eyes, biting of lips, deep breathing and

[1] *AD*, 260–73. [2] Ibid., 298–308.
[3] Coomaraswamy, *The Mirror of Gesture*, p. 3 (1917 edition); p. 18 (1936 edition).

trembling limbs.[1] Each and every part of the body is important to signify some emotion or feeling. Deep significance lies in the mode in which the head is shaken, the eyes and brows are moved; the cheeks, nose, lips, chin and neck can all be used to convey subtle themes. All this will be clear from the directions of Rāghavabhaṭṭa in his commentary on the *Abhijñānaśākuntala* for depicting the *bhramarabādhā* (attack by the bee), *śṛṅgāralajjā* (amorous bashfulness), *kusumāvacaya* (gathering of flowers) and *prasādhanā* or *alaṅkāra* (wearing ornaments).[2] Thus there are many themes which are indicated by means of tokens and gestures in Sanskrit plays. In reality the art of *āṅgikābhinaya* was fully developed and an object, which was not procurable, must have been represented by means of bodily gestures.

DANCING

Dancing in India flourished under royal patronage and every king and chieftain had his band of musicians, court-dancers and painters. People of good family used to be well versed in these arts, and music and dancing formed an important part of their education. But dancing was not confined solely to the educated classes. Folk dances in a multitude of forms has played an important part in the communal life of the people. Indian dancing is a traditional art and as such it has fixed ends and ascertained means of operation. God Śiva in his well known aspect of *Naṭarāja* is pre-eminently the lord of dances. After the destruction of the scarifice of Dakṣa, Śiva danced with various gesticulations to the tune of music. He imitated all the principal gods and assumed different postures. These dances were known as *piṇḍībandhas*.[3]

The position of hands, feet, waist, thighs, abdomen, back and chest are vital in dance. Sometimes motion is slow and sometimes quick. These movements are called *mātṛkā*[4] or mothers of dance. A combination of three or four of these is a *karaṇa* or action. One hundred and eight such actions (*karaṇas*)[5] are enumerated in the *Nāṭyaśāstra*. Different combinations of these actions are called *aṅgahāras*[6] or gesticulations. The *Nāṭyaśāstra* enumerates 32 such gesticulations. There are four different ways

[1] *NS-KM*, XXV; *KSS*, XXVI.
[2] Rāghavabhaṭṭa in his commentary on *Śāk*, pp. 24, 29, 86, 99.
[3] *NS-KM*, IV. 233–242a; *KSS*, IV. 246b–56; *GOS*, IV. 257–66.
[4] *NS-KM*, IV. 54b–58; *KSS*, IV. 55b–60; *GOS*, IV. 56–60.
[5] *NS-KM*, IV. 32b–54a; *KSS*, IV. 34–55a; *GOS*, IV. 34–55.
[6] *NS-KM*, IV. 16b–26a; *KSS*, IV. 18–27; *GOS*, IV. 18–27.

to end the dance gracefully and they are called *recakas*.[1] All these *recakas*, *aṅgahāras* and *piṇḍībandhas* were designed by Śiva after the destruction of the sacrifice of Dakṣa. He taught Taṇḍu the art of dancing and hence dancing has been known as *tāṇḍava*.

The temple at Chidambaram where the *tāṇḍava* is believed to have been performed is one of the most beautiful temples in India, dedicated to Śiva in his aspect of Naṭarāja. In the most inner enclosure is the *nṛtta-sabhā* or hall of dance. It consists of a stone platform with 56 stone pillars with dance poses exquisitely carved on them. This hall is at least 1,400 years old and is one of the earliest of Indian temple monuments. Towards the gateways there are 108 bas-relief panels, depicting a dance of Śiva and his consort Pārvatī. There are many fine examples of classical dance poses in the temples at Ellora in Aurangabad, Elephanta near Bombay, Bhuvaneshvara near Puri on the Bay of Bengal, and in numerous temples scattered all over south India.

Delighted with the performance of the drama, the *Tripuradāha*, Śiva ordered Taṇḍu to teach Bharata the art of dancing. Sages asked Bharata why the dance was included in a dramatic performance. It did not help the story nor did it produce an emotion. Acting was quite sufficient for those purposes. Bharata's explanation was this: "Dances do not help dramatic action but beautify it. They are very popular, especially on auspicious occasions."[2]

The *Nāṭyaśāstra* recognises two types of dance, *tāṇḍva*, the violent dance of men, invented by Śiva himself, and *lāsya*, the tender amorous dance of Pārvatī. Because of its special importance *lāsya* is carefully analysed into ten parts by the *Nāṭyaśāstra*.[3] It shows the essential union of song and dance. The divisions of *lāsya*, of course, appear to ignore their nature as parts of a dance, but it must be remembered that the motions of performers are essential in the performance.

We obtain a clear idea of dancing from a critical study of the first two acts of the *Mālavikāgnimitra* and first act of the *Ratnāvalī*.

The science and art of dancing are known as *abhinayavidyā* in *Nāṭya-śāstra*. This is divided into two parts, *śāstra* (science) and *prayoga* (performance). The latter is further distinguished into *kriyā* (self-acting) and *saṅkrānti* (imparting lessons in dancing).

The actual performance consists of two parts, *aṅgasauṣṭhava* (graceful

[1]*NS-KM*, IV. 231b–232; *KSS*, IV: 240–246a; *GOS*, IV. 250b–256.

[2]*NS-KM*, IV. 244–48; *KSS*, IV. 258b–263a; *GOS*, IV. 268b–273a.

[3]*NS-KM*, XVIII. 170–81; *KSS*, XX. 138–51; *DR*, III. 52–53, p. 73; *SD*, VI, *sūtras*, 241–51, pp. 393–94.

contours) and *abhinaya* (gesticulation, expressing sentiment). Graceful contours can be exhibited in a twofold manner, through *viralanepathyā* (thin costume) and body control.

Then, begins the real work of the dancer, Mālavikā, in the present case. She takes up a stanza of four lines, first hums the tune and afterwards sings it aloud. Thereafter she gesticulates with a view to bringing out the sentiment which permeates the piece.

Bhāvas form the most important feature of *abhinayavidyā*. The two dance masters (*abhinayācāryas*) Haradatta and Gaṇadāsa have been described as two *bhavas* incarnate. Similarly the lesson in *abhinaya* which is imparted to Mālavikā by Gaṇadāsa has been described as *bhāvika*. Any movement or emotion difficult of representation was called *duṣprayojya* as an instance of which is given *calita*, a dance in which the dancer, while representing the sentiments, gives expression to his own feelings. The success of an actor lies in his bringing in bodily form a particular emotion. The *bhāva* becomes *śarītī* when the *calita* is performed by Mālavikā Parivrājikā describes it as faultless art and is full of appreciation for it.[1]

The maids in the *Ratnāvalī*, dance before the kings, who shows deep appreciation of their art.[2]

In the *Mṛcchakaṭika* also there are references to dancing. *Viṭa*: "stop there, Vasantasenā, your steps show skill in a dance." Saṁsthānaka calls Vasantasenā a dancing girl (*lāsikā*).[3]

In the *Bālacarita* there is reference to a Hallīṣaka dance. Girls of cowherds, though naturally charming, look extremely beautiful when dressed up in garments of varied hues. Their male young ones have drums and are singing. "Dāmodara: come now, belle of the station, wood garland, crescent and gazelle, we must do this dance made for herdsmen. Girls: As you tell us, master. Saṅkarṣaṇa: Dāmaka and Meghanāda, beat the drums. Both: Right, Master (All dance). Old Herdsmen: Bravo, that's good. Well sung. Well danced. I will dance a bit myself. No I am tired."[4]

Thus it can be seen from dramas that dancing was very popular with spectators.

DIALOGUE

Ancient dramatists gave great importance to dialogues and proper

[1]*Māl*, II. 8, p. 29.
[2]*Rat*, I. 16, p. 15.
[3]*Mṛch*, I. 17, p. 15; 23, p. 17.
[4]*Bālacarita*, III, pp. 539–40.

dramatic delivery. The *Nāṭyaśāstra* emphasizes on the choice of words in a play and calls them the body of the dramatic art (*nāṭya*). *Vācikābhinaya* (verbal representation) mainly consists in the use of proper pronunciation, modulation, accent and rhythm.[1] Use of different dialects and proper forms of address to persons according to their ranks or social status are also included. These rules are very elaborate and are well adapted to bring out the lyrical qualities of a play and will be discussed in chapter 8.

The value of an instructive or entertaining dialogue was well understood in India and religious scriptures, the *Vedas*, the *Upaniṣads*, the *Saṁhitās*, the *Mahābhārata*, the *Tantras*, the *Purāṇas* and even the *Jātakas* or the *Baudha-ākhyānas* are in the form of conversations. In fact another name of the Veda is *śruti*—what was heard in conversation. The *Nāṭyaśāstra* insists on weighty dialogue and says the words employed in dramas should be suggestive, deep in meaning, approved of by Vedas and acceptable to all persons.[2]

The dialogues between Ātreyī and Vāsanti in the *Uttararāmacarita*, between Sāgarikā and Susaṅgatā in the *Ratnāvalī*, between *Kaśyapa* and *Śakuntalā* in the *Abhijñānaśākuntala*, between Bhīmasena and Draupadī in the *Veṇīsaṁhāra*, between Urvaśī and Pururavas in the *Vikramorvaśīya*, between Cāṇakya and Candanadāsa in the *Mudrārākṣasa* are lively and deep in meaning. The language of Bhāsa is very simple, natural and touching, alternating with simple figures of speech. The language of Kālidāsa is remarkably easy. Bhavabhūti in the *Uttararāmacarita* uses somewhat more difficult language. In his other two plays, and especially in the *Mālatīmādhava*, it is more elaborate and difficult. The *Mṛcchakaṭika* presents fewer difficulties than any of these dramas.

Ordinary dialogues in Sanskrit plays are for the greater part in prose, but reflections or descriptions and poetical fancy take the form of verse. Many kinds of metre from *anuṣṭubh* to *daṇḍaka* are used by them.[3]

Intonation (*kāku*) is change of voice under different emotions such as fear, grief and anger. *Dhvanervikāraḥ*, connoting variations or modulation of sound in the intonation, can be considered to be the generic definition of *kāku*. By the definition given by *Amarakośa*[4] it becomes clear that *kāku* is of feminine gender and stands for the emotions as pointed out above. Though the definition given by Amara Sinha is histrionic in

[1] *NS-KSS*, XV. 1–4; *GOS*, XIV. 1–4; *Agnipurāṇa*, CCCXXXIX, 49b–53.
[2] *NS-KM*, XXVII. 42–46a; *KSS*, XXVII. 45–49a.
[3] *NS-KSS*, XV. 37–47; *GOS*, XIV. 42–52.
[4] *Amarakośa*, 1 canto, p. 30, "*Kāku striyāṁ vikāro yaḥ Sokabhityādibhirdvaneh*".

its essence yet it relates also to music as mostly these feelings are the innermost base of a musical experience.

The word *kāku* is applicable to both dramaturgical and musical literature. Dramatic aspect of *kāku* is exhibited in detail by the *Nāṭyaśāstra* of Bharata while its musical aspect is given by the *Saṅgītaratnākara*. But here as we are mainly concerned with dramatic practice, we take up only the injunctions of *Nāṭyaśāstra* in this respect.

Kāku is a word of negation which is used in a manner implying the affirmative, as in question of appeal. In such cases the intended meaning is suggested by a change of the voice. Slow (*vilaṁbitā*) intonation is desired in the comic, the erotic and the pathetic sentiments. In the heroic, the furious and the marvellous sentiments the excited (*diptā*) and high (*uccā*) intonations are praised. Fast (*drutā*) and low (*nīcā*) intonations have been prescribed in the terrible and the odious sentiments.[1] Thus the intonation should be made to follow the states (*bhāva*) and the sentiments (*rasa*).

Vithyaṅgas, the constituent parts of *Vīthī*, are purely of the rhetorical kind. They are often mentioned in the rules of theorists and serve the purpose of enhancing the beauty of presentation of plays.[2]

[1]*NS-KM*, XVII. 108–118a; *KSS*, XIX. 46–58; *GOS*, XVII. 115–29.
[2]*NS-KM*, XVIII. 156–68; *KSS*, XX. 118–33; *GOS*, XVIII. 113b–126a.

Fig. 10: Dancing party from Fort Wall, Sri Sailam

Fig. 11: Music and dancing party of Harsaleshwar Temple, Halebid
(Courtesy: Archaeological Survey of India, New Delhi)

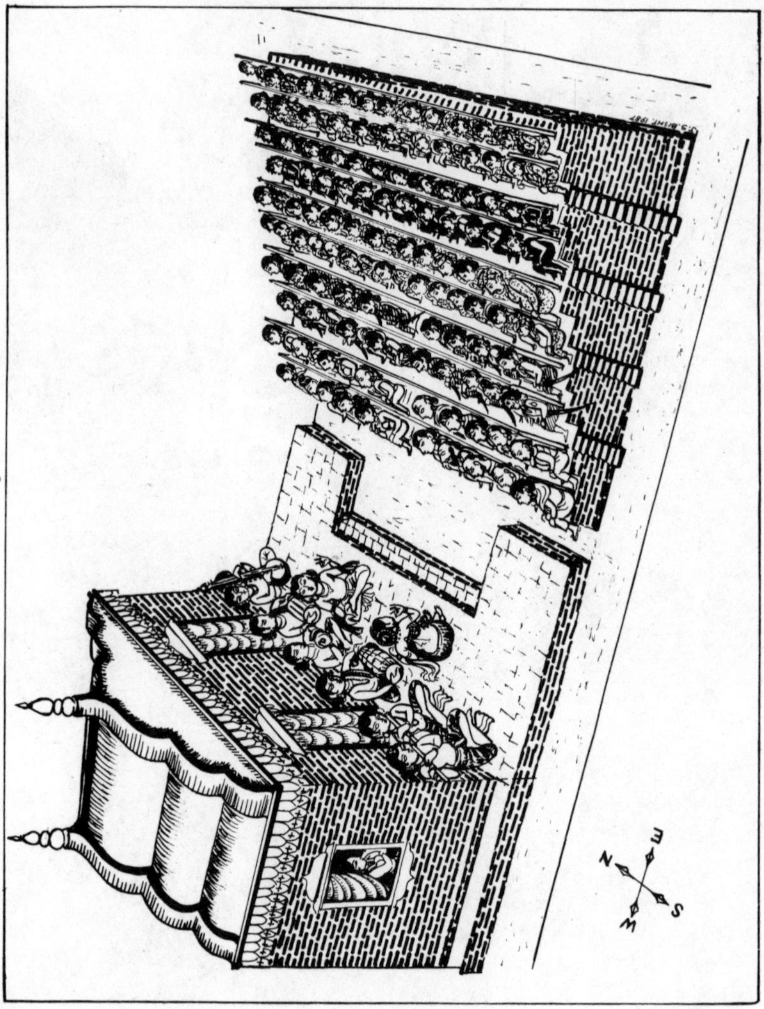

Fig. 12: Diagram of seating arrangement of musicians in an orchestra on the Raṅgaśīrṣa as

CHAPTER SEVEN

The Troupe

ROLES OF CHARACTERS (*BHŪMIKĀ*)

We shall now deal with the types of people allowed to play roles in Sanskrit dramas. Actors were selected for their gait, speech, gestures and disposition. Divine personages were represented by persons whose physiques were well built and who spoke delightfully. Those, who were fat and tall, whose voice was deep like thunder and who had terrifying eyes, eyebrows and faces, were selected for the roles of *rākṣasas*, *dānavas* and *daityas*. The roles of princes were assumed by wise actors, of good appearance and voice and of virtuous disposition; of generals and ministers by persons who were brave, clever in conversation and possessed of clear vision; and of chamberlains and learned *śrotriyas* by persons who had pale eyes and long noses. Persons, who were slow, dwarfish, hunch backed, of deformed noses or cheekbones, of ugly faces, badly dressed and ill-tempered, played the parts of servants. Wearied persons were represented by those who were lean and thin, while persons in normal health were represented by fat persons. The manager would, however, use his discretion to select actors keeping in view the feeling, actions and nature of the characters. The characters were represented according to their country, dress and appropriate appearance.[1]

In Sanskrit plays the roles were of three different qualities: *anurūpā*, similar to the nature of the person represented, *virūpā*, contrary to the nature, and *rūpānusāriṇī* imitative by nature. *Anurūpā* is that which is represented by an actor of the same age and sex. In *virūpā* a child plays the role of an old man or an old man takes the role of a child. In *rūpānusāriṇī* a man plays the part of woman. A man's role may be played by a woman and vice versa according to the desire of the manager, but an old man or a boy should not be made to play the role of each other. When a man's role is given to a woman it should be done with great care. Thus the *Nāṭyaśāstra* expressly admits of three modes of representation: roles may be taken by persons of appropriate sex and age; roles of the old may be taken by the young and vice versa.[2] The assumption of women's roles by men has, curiously enough, very early evidence; for the *Mahābhāṣya*

[1]*NS-KM*, XXXV. 1–20a; *KSS*, XXXV. 1–8.
[2]*NS-KM*, XXVI. 1–5; *KSS*, XXXV. 15–20.

mentions the word *bhrūkuṁsā* which was used to denote a man who was personating a woman.[1] The *sūtradhāra* in the *Ratnāvalī* and the *Priyadarśikā* plays the part of Vatsa, his younger brother that of Yaugandharāyaṇa in the former play[2] and that of Dṛḍhavarman in the latter[3]; in the *Mālatīmādhava*, the *sūtradhāra* and *Pāripārśvika* assume the roles of Kāmandakī and her pupil Avalokita, respectively.[4] The enactment of women's roles by men was not by any means the normal practice. The *naṭī* normally plays an important female role as in the *Karpūramañjarī*.[5] In the *Kuṭṭanīmata*, where an actual representation of the first act of the *Ratnāvalī* is described, a woman is found in the role of the princess.[6]

Bharata states that women are delicate (*sukumāra*) and hence they should be represented by women alone. *Nāṭya* should be performed by women well versed in the dramaturgic *śastra*.[7] Learned teachers should instruct women in terms of the *Nāṭyaśāstra* for theatrical representation was a delicate (*sukumāra*) subject. Roles in *śṛṅgāra* sentiment should be left to women, for they have delicate gestures and well-formed limbs.

In *nāṭya*, two kinds of performances, *sukumāra* and *āviddha* are followed to present emotions and sentiments. *Nāṭaka, prakaraṇa, bhāṇa, vīthī* and *aṅka* are varieties of the delicate (*sukumāra*) type. *Āviddha* is full of war, motions and agitation. It involves too much of cutting, tearing and fighting; there is also the use of indecent language. Hence women should not take any part in it. The styles known as *sātvatī* and *ārabhaṭī* are employed in it. *Ḍima, samavakāra*, *vyāyoga* and *ihāmṛga* are its species. Their *āviddha* performances were to be done by *devas, dānavas* and *rākṣasas* who were violent by nature and full of vigour.[8]

NĀṬYĀCĀRYAS

Poets, directors, stage managers, musicians, scene-designers and painters come under the category of *nāṭyācāryas*, according to the *Nāṭyaśāstra*. Among *nāṭyācāryas*, the *sūtradhāra* is the foremost as he guides actors, arranges the paraphernalia, directs the performance and above all is responsible for the successful presentation of the play. According to the *Nāṭyaśāstra*, the *sūtradhāra* should be a master of sciences and arts,

[1] *Mahābhāṣya*, II, p. 196.
[2] *Rat*, I, prelude prose, p. 7.
[3] *PD*, prelude prose, pp. 3–4.
[4] *MM*, *prastāvanā*, p. 12.
[5] *Kar. M, prastāvanā*, p. ii.
[6] *Kuṭṭanīmata—KM*, 852–927, pp. 104–10.
[7] *NS-KM*, XXVI. 6–13a; *KSS*, XXXV. 21–23a, 24b–29.
[8] *NS-KM*, XXVI. 20–25; *KSS*, XXXV. 23b–24a, 30–36.

know countries, and costumes and customs prevalent in them. He should be well versed in languages, the science of dramaturgy and versification. He should have good knowledge of music, musical instruments, political science, geography, astrology, anatomy, history, law and emotions and sentiments. He should be able to foresee the purport of his own exposition. These are the minimum qualifications of a *sūtradhāra*. In addition, he is a poet, has excellent memory and intellect, is grave and generous. He should be in good health, sweet-tempered, self-controlled, of a forgiving nature, righteous, not avaricious, truthful and impartial.[1]

The *sūtradhāra*, the chief actor, whose name denotes that he was thought of as an architect conversant with histrionics, is occasionally styled head of the troupe. He is essentially the instructor of the actors and his designation can be taken to mean a professor. In the *Uttararāmacarita*, Bharata is called *tauryatṛka sūtradhāra*, professor of the three kinds of *saṅgīta* (instrumental music, song and dance).[2] Thus the *sūtradhāra* was an important dramatic personage, controlling the whole company, assuming different roles, sometimes arranging the scenes, sometimes directing the actors and sometimes himself taking an important role in the plays.

According to the dramatic treatises, the *sūtradhāra* had two associates, the *sthāpaka* and the *pāripārśvika*. In his attributes the *sthāpaka* resembles the *sūtradhāra*. Immediately after the preliminaries, another person, similar to the *sūtradhāra* in appearance and qualities is to enter and introduce the play, a function which gives him the designation of the introducer (*sthāpaka*).[3] He does not, however, figure in any of the extant dramas and so the duties assigned by the treatises to the *sthāpaka* must have all been performed by the *sūtradhāra* himself.

According to the *Nāṭyaśāstra*, the *pāripārśvika*'s qualities and qualifications are second only to those of the *sūtradhāra*. He is of middle type, of good form, intelligent and an expert in the performance of his duties. He has full knowledge of instruments. He is an attendant of the *sūtradhāra*. He appears in the prologues of many plays and acts the parts of persons of rank. He receives the *sūtradhāra*'s orders, passes them on to other actors and directs the chorus.[4]

The *Nāṭyaśāstra* also refers to some *ācāryas* expert in preparing materials required for the stage and proficient in directing actors and actresses.

[1]*NS-KM*, XXIV. 93–100; *KSS*, XXXV. 45–52.
[2]*URC*, IV, p. 119.
[3]*NS-KM*, V. 149–54; *KSS*, V. 163–68; *GOS*, V. 168b–69a, 172b–177a.
[4]*NS-KM*, XXIV. 101b–102a; *KSS*, XXXV. 53.

Many types of artisans seem to have been necessary in the presentation of plays.[1]

There is the *mukuṭakāra* who makes crowns (*mukuṭas*) for the characters with the help of different materials as stated in chapter 5 of this book. He prepares various kinds of head-dresses also. The *ābharaṇakṛt* prepares ornaments. The *mālyakṛt* makes garlands. The *veśakāra* prepares dresses. The *citrakāra* paints pictures. The *rajaka* dyes the dresses. The *kāruka* prepares things out of lac, stone, iron and wood. He is an artisan who prepares different items of stage paraphernalia. The *kuśīlava* is an expert in the arrangement of musical instruments and also in playing them. The *nāṭyakāra* leads the characters in a play by directing them in the representation of feelings. The *naṭa* is the performer of *nāṭya* and an expert in using the four kinds of musical instruments. He is called *naṭa* because he represents and imitates the actions of men. He is an expert in the representation of sentiments, feelings and courage. The *nāṭakīyā* is a beautiful woman who can sing and has the capacity to rouse sentiments. She is familiar with the different kinds of musical instruments and has knowledge of rhythm and tune. The *taurika* is the head of warriors and trumpeters, an expert in blowing all musical instruments. Thus artisans are named according to the duties they are called upon to perform.

ACTORS AND ACTRESSES

There is great variety of characters, male and female, introduced in Sanskrit plays. Kings, ministers, high officials and attendants often figured very prominently. Actors and actresses were, however, classified according to their qualifications into superior (*uttama*), medium (*madhyama*) and third rate actors (*adhama*).[2] The principal parts in any drama were, however, a few; the king, the *vidūṣaka*, the parasite, the heroine and her companion were stock types. Theorists give detailed instructions about persons appearing on the stage.

Heroes were (*nāyaka, netṛ*) of different kinds according to their qualities. They were light-hearted (*lalita*), calm (*śānta*), exalted (*udātta*) or vehement (*uddhata*).[3] The self-controlled and light-hearted hero, *dhīralalita*, was free from anxiety, fond of the arts, happy and gentle. The hero in the *Ratnāvalī* is an instance of the *dhīralalita* hero. The self-

[1]*NS-KM*, XXXV. 26–27, 31–37; *KSS*, XXXV. 72–73, 77–84.

[2]*NS-KM*, XXIV. 85–92; *KSS*, XXIV. 1–8.

[3]*NS-KM*, XXIV. 3–5; *KSS*, XXXIV. 17–19; *DR*, II. 1–6a, pp. 35–38; *SD*, III. 35–38, pp. 90–91.

controlled and calm hero, *dhīraśānta*, is a Brāhmaṇa or possessed of the generic qualities of a hero. The heroes in the *Mālatīmādhava* and the *Mṛcchakaṭika* are instances in point. The self-controlled and exalted hero, *dhīrodātta*, is of great excellence, exceedingly serious, forbearing, not boastful, resolute, assertive and purposeful. The heroes in the *Mahānāṭaka* and the *Abhijñānaśākuntala* are instances of this type. The self-controlled and vehement hero, *dhīrodhata*, is dominated by pride and jealousy, devoted to witchcraft and deceit, self-assertive, fickle, irascible and boastful. Examples of this type are rarely found. Various other types of heroes are described, but as they serve no purpose in the actual presentation of Sanskrit plays we do not go into a detailed study of their characteristics.

Sometimes the hero has an antagonist, and he is the *pratināyaka*. He is avaricious, stubborn, criminal and vicious like the *dhīroddhata* hero. He is always painted as passionate and evil-minded.[1] Rāvaṇa, the opponent of Rāma, and Duryodhana, the opponent of Yudhiṣṭhira, are *pratināyakas*.

Among the pleasure companions (*narmasaciva, narmasuhṛd*) of the hero is the *pīṭhamarda* (he who rubs his sides). He is devoted to the hero and is the hero of an episode (*patākā, prāsaṅgika-itivṛtta*).[2] Sugrīva in the Rama dramas and Makaranda in the *Mālatīmādhava* belong to this class.

According to the *Nāṭyaśāstra*, *viṭa* (parasite) is familiar with the ways of courtesans, sweet-tempered, impartial, poetic, able to argue, eloquent and clever. He is amiable in society and versed in arts.[3] Vātsyāyana says that the *viṭa* is a character who squanders away his resources. He is married.[4] In dramas, especially in the *Mṛcchakaṭika*, *viṭa* plays a great part. In the *bhāṇas*, however, the actor appears as a *viṭa* and the role can be taken to have been borrowed directly from the popular stage.

Vidūṣaka (joker) is the most important stock character in Sanskrit plays. He is a Brāhmaṇa and is described bald-headed, hunch-backed, dwarfish, has protruding teetch, a distorted mouth and yellow eyes. He is dressed in rags and skin. He is fond of quarrels and takes pleasure in eating and drinking.[5] His external appearance, dress and gait are meant to evoke laughter. Moreover, he is the faithful companion and friend of

[1] *DR*, II. 9b.

[2] *SD*, III, *sūtras*, 39–42; *DR*, II. 8.

[3] *NS-KM*, XXIV. 102b–104; *KSS*, XXXV. 54–55; *DR*, II, prose, p. 40; *SD*, III, *sūtras* 41.

[4] *Kāmasūtra*, 45, p. 56.

[5] *NS-KM*, XII. 121–22, XXIV. 106; *KSS*, XIII. 136–37, XXXV. 57; *GOS*, XII. 137b–139a; *DR*, II. 9; *SD*, III, *sūtra* 42.

the hero, who calls him a comrade (*vayasya*) and seeks his help in all difficulties, on account of which he often appears very dexterous.

The *śakāra* is an old, popular character and is the brother-in-law of the king. He is irritated without any reason and again appeased, wears gorgeous clothes and jewels, gladly brags of his high connections, but throughout shows himself as ignorant and contemptible. He pronounces *śa* for *sa* and speaks Māgadhī.[1]

To the next circle of the hero's acquaintances belongs the slave *ceṭa*. According to the *Nāṭyaśāstra*, the *ceṭa* is quarrelsome, talkative, physically deformed and knows well whom to respect and whom not.[2]

To the more distant or outer circle (*bāhya*) of acquaintances belong the commander-in-chief (*senāpati*), the successor to the throne (*kumāra*), the different ministers (*mantrin, saciva, amātya*), the judges (*prāḍvivāka*), messengers to distant places (*dūta*) and the court priest (*purohita*).[3]

Detailed instructions on the different types of heroines (*nāyikā*), their qualities, situations and relation to the hero are available. They may be divine women (*divyā*), queens (*nṛpapatnī*), women of good family (*kulastrī*), or courtesans (*gaṇikā*). In their relation to the hero, they may belong to him (*svīyā*), to another (*anyā*) or to all (*sādhāraṇī*).[4] The *svīyā* type of heroine is found in the *Uttararāmacarita*—Sītā, the wife of the hero, Rāma. An *anyā* heroine is either a maiden or a married woman. A married woman should never figure in the principal sentiment, but love for a maiden could be represented in connection with the principal or the subordinate sentiments. An example of the *anyā* type is found in the *Ratnāvalī* and the *Mālatīmādhava* in the love of Vatsarāja for Sāgarikā and Mādhava for Mālatī. In the *sādhāraṇastrī* type falls the courtesan. The *Mṛcchakaṭika* refers to a distinct class of very highly accomplished *gaṇikās* or courtesans, and Vasantasenā, a dancing girl, is introduced as an accomplished heroine with admirable traits of character.

Next to the heroines come their friends, step-sisters, maids and members of the harem. The *Nāṭyaśāstra* describes them as constituting the inner circle (*ābhyantaragaṇa*).[5] To this class belongs the principal queen (*mahādevī*), the second queen (*devī*) and old woman (*vṛddhā*). In addition to these, are woman body-guards (*sañcārikā*) sometimes called

[1] *NS-KM*, XXIV. 105; *KSS*, XXXV. 56; *DR*, II. 44b–45a, p. 56; *SD*, III. 52–53, pp. 99–100.

[2] *NS-KM*, XXIV. 107; *KSS*, XXXV. 58.

[3] *NS-KM*, XXIV. 59b–61a; *KSS*, XXXIV, 67–68.

[4] *NS-KM*, XXIV. 6b–9; *KSS*, XXXIV. 24–25; *DR*, II. 15–23a; *SD*, III, *sūtras* 56–73.

[5] *NS-KM*, XXIV. 15–17; *KSS*, XXXIV. 29–31.

yavanī or greek maidens), women waiting on the king (*anucārikā*) the heroine's personal maids (*paricārikā*) and the door-keeper (*pratihārī*).

There is a third category of roles called *napuṁsaka* (neuter). Bharata includes in this class learned and skilled Brāhmaṇas (*snātaka*) chamberlains (*kañcukīya, kañcukin*) and eunuchs (*varṣadhara, nirmuṇḍa, aupasthāyika*).[1]

SPECTATORS AND JUDGES

Sanskrit dramas demanded the full attention of a cultured audience. It is expressly asserted, as in the dramas of Kālidāsa, Śrī Harṣa, Bhavabhūti and Visākhadatta, that spectators are critical and experienced. In the *Mālavikāgnimitra* the stage manager says: "I am asked by the learned audience to represent on the occasion of the spring festival the play named *Mālavikāgnimitra*." Then on the question whether the *Mālavikāgnimitra* should be played the manager says: "The wise accept one or the other after examination, while the judgment of a fool is led by the experience of others." Thus the *Mālavikāgnimitra* requires the audience to be learned and critical.[2]

In the *Ratnāvalī* the stage manager says: "Ah, I am quite sure, the minds of all the spectators have been won over or are favourably disposed towards us. For, Śrīharṣa is an eminent poet and this audience here is ever disposed to appreciate merit; the story of Vatsarāja is an attractive one in the world, and we are masters of the histrionic art. Each of these circumstances leads to the attainment of the desired object. What to say then when there is a combination of all advantages through my accumulated luck."[3] Here also the audience is supposed to be critical as with that quality alone the merits of a play can be judged.

There is no need to quote any example from Bhavabhūti's dramas. He was a great stylist and had a wonderful command over language. The poetry of his dramas could only be appreciated by a learned and critical audience.[4]

In the *Mudrārākṣasa*, the manager says: "Really I have very great pleasure in acting before an assembly capable of appreciating the merits of poems. Do you ask why? Grain sown by even a fool will thrive if it falls on good soil. The growth of paddy in clusters does not depend on

[1] *NS-KM*, XXIV. 50–52; *KSS*, XXXIV. 61–62.
[2] *Māl*, I. 2 and prose, pp. 2–3.
[3] *Rat*, I. 5, p. 5.
[4] *MM*, IX. 17, p. 184; *URC*, I. 27, p. 27.

the skill of the sower."[1] So in this drama, too, the audience has a high standard and is critical and able to appreciate merits. Thus dramas themselves show that the spectators (*sabhāsad*), were appreciative of the dramatic art.

The *Nāṭyaśāstra* requires that the ideal spectator has keen susceptibility and excellent judgement with ability to feel the emotions of characters as depicted by actors. He should be attentive, an expert in handling the four kinds of instruments, have a knowledge of dresses, dialects, gestures and metres. He should be well versed in the *śastras* and arts and should be religious by temperament. Thus he should have keen intelligence, capacity to examine and weigh the merits of the performance and participate in the pleasures and sorrows depicted on the stage.

In an assembly (*pariṣad* or *saṁsad*) there may be very few who fulfil all these conditions. The spectators can be good, medium and indifferent. They appreciate only that art, dress, action, speech or movement which is intelligible to them. Youths enjoy passionate scenes; religious-minded persons take pleasure in scenes dealing with salvation. The brave delight in the representation of the *bībhatsa* and *raudra* sentiments and of battles. The old are interested in religious stories and *purāṇas*. Boys, fools and women take pleasure in comic scenes.[2] Thus different spectators derive pleasure from different scenes according to their age, country and circumstances.

The *Abhinayadarpaṇa* characterises the audience as a *kalpavṛkṣa*—the tree that answers all wishes. The *Vedas* are its branches, *Śāstras* its flowers and scholars the bees adorning it.[3]

There was a very elaborate arrangement for judging in every detail the success of a performance. According to the *Abhinayadarpaṇa*, the *sabhāpati* or chief of the audience should be wealthy, intelligent, discriminating, an expert in giving awards, versed in music, versatile, celebrated, having pleasing qualities, well acquainted with gestures expressive of desires and moods, without envy or malice, well disposed to people; possessed of righteous conduct, kind, patient, disciplined, versed in arts and proficient in *abhinaya*. His functions are to make pronouncements on the merit of a performance and to distribute rewards to the *sūtradhāra* or leader of the troupe of dancers, musicians and actors.[4] The definition of a *sabhāpati* is also given in the *Saṅgītaratnākara*.[5]

[1] *Mudrārākṣasa*, I. 3, p. 7.
[2] *NS-KM*, XXVII. 47–60a; *KSS*, XXVII. 50–63a.
[3] *AD*, 19.
[4] *AD*, 17.
[5] *SR*, VII. 1345–50.

The *sabhāpati* has advisers. They speak in a dignified manner, have a desire for fame, understand moods (*bhāvas*) and are able to distinguish between merits and demerits. They are versed in arts and polity and are themselves scholars. They can distinguish a dialect from another and possess poetic faculty.[1]

The success of a drama depends on the judgement of the critic (*prāśnika*) who has necessarily to be qualified for the delicate task of judging the merit of the performance. The *Nāṭyaśāstra* gives ten kinds of critics (*prāśnikas*): an expert in sacrifice (*yajñavit*), an actor (*nartaka*), a prosodist (*chandovit*), a grammarian (*śabdavit*), a king (*rājan*), an expert in archery (*iṣvastravit*), a painter (*citravit*), a courtesan (*veśyā*), a musician (*gandharya*) and an officer of the king (*rājasevaka*). When there is a conflict of opinion among spectators, that of the *prāśnika* is listened to.

A critic (*prāśnika*) is an expert in his own province—an expert in sacrifices, a judge in matters of sacrifice, an actor in acting, a prosodist in complicated metres, a grammarian in lengthy speeches, a king in connection with dignity, in dealing with the female apartments and royal roles, an archer in the excellence of the position of the body or general deportment, a painter in judging the manner of salute and dress, a courtesan in representation of passionate scenes, a musician in musical notes and an officer of the king in matters of servitude or courteous demeanour.[2]

We can have a clear idea of the critic (*prāśnika*) if we closely study the *Mālavikāgnimitra* and the *calita* dance scene performed in the *saṅgītaśālā* of king Agnimitra. There is a discussion as to who, Hardatta or Gaṇadāsa, was the better dance master. Parivrājikā was made the judge. She had a keen insight into gestures and other aspects of representation. She faithfully appreciated the merits of the dance of Mālavikā. She said: "All was faultless and in accordance with the rules of the dramatic science. Her limbs, eloquent with expression properly conveyed the sense, and the movement of her feet was perfect in timing. She exactly represented the sentiment. The movement of her fingers was gentle. In the successive development of acting one feeling gave place to another still the interest remained just the same."[3] Critics like Parivrājikā, who could judge every

[1] *AD*, 18.

[2] *NS-KM*, XXVII. 60b–61; *KSS*, XXVII. 63b–68a. The text of *NS* is corrupt here. *Abh. Bh*, and *KM*, do not speak much about the definition of *prāśnikas*. Only *KSS* gives details. Here in verse 64 of *KSS* there should be *śabdavit* in place of *chedvit* and here *rājan* should also be enumerated in the list of ten *prāśnikas*. In verse 66 there should be *iṣvastravit* in place of *iṣṭavāk*.

[3] *Māl*, II, prose, pp. 8, 24, 29.

detail of the representation critically and minutely, were to be found witnessing Sanskrit plays.

SOCIAL POSITION OF ACTORS AND ACTRESSES

We come now to the social position of actors and actresses. The mythological account given by Bharata says that the actors, in a comic vein, made fun of certain holy sages and were cursed with the loss of their status, which, thereafter, came to that of Śūdras. King Nahuṣa, of epic fame, was the first to establish a theatre on earth, compelling the heavenly nymphs and songsters to come down to the mortal world where they married and mixed with mortals.[1] The story of the curse on actors shows that at the time of Bharata actors as a class had become notorious (*nirbrahmaṇya*) and their unclean habits (*śudrācāra*) were detested and shunned by refined society (*nirāhuta*). When they died, their death was unmourned (*aśoca*).

In the *Rāmāyaṇa* an actor, Śailūsa, is found handing over his wife to another.[2]

The *Arthaśāstra* enjoins that pleasure houses or *nāṭyaśālās* for *naṭas*, *nartakas*, instrumentalists and reciters of stories and actors should not be built in the heart of villages, lest their plays should hinder the work of the residents of the place. The *kuśīlava* is described as a Śūdra to be banished. The *Arthaśāstra* mentions *kuśīlavas* with *rūpajivas* in connection with song and music.[3]

Manu seems to have been aware of the influence which the stage exerted on people and he was vehement in denouncing the profession of actors. In fact, he prohibited Brāhmaṇas from becoming actors. Manu imposes only a minor penalty on illicit connections with the views of actors because they were themselves willing to hand over their wives to others for profit. Manu speaks of the professions of *naṭas*, athletes (*bhalla*) and boxers (*malla*) as the lowest means of livelihood and says *kuśīlavas* should be avoided.[4] According to Manu and Yājñavalkya the testimony of a *kuśīlava* is not valid and no Brāhmaṇa should accept food from stage artists[5] a fact attested by the *sūtradhāra* in the prologue to the *Mṛcchakaṭika*, who says he can find none in Ujjain to accept his hospitality.[6]

[1] *NS-KM*, XXXVI. 28–35, XXXVII. 14–18a; *KSS*, XXXVI. 29–37a, 60b–64.

[2] *Rāmāyaṇa*, II. 30. 8.

[3] *AS*, I. 2. 1; I. 1. 3; I. 2. 27.

[4] *Manusmṛti*, VIII. 362, p. 330; XII. 45, p. 475; X. 22, p. 401.

[5] Ibid., IV. 214–15, p. 170; VIII. 65, p. 280; *Yājñavalkyasmṛti*, II. 5. 70–71, pp. 667–68, I. 6. 160b and 161, p. 237.

[6] *Mṛch*, I, pp. 9–10.

The law book of Viṣṇu treats actors as *āyogava*, a mixed caste, representing the fruit of alliances, improper and undesirable, between Śūdras and daughters of Vaiśyas.[1]

That wives of actors who served as actresses were of low morals is illustrated in the *Mahābhāṣya*. It says, the women of *naṭas* mix with different persons as vowels with consonants.[2]

The reputation of actors and actresses was low and uncomplementary. Actresses were considered to be leading an immoral life and lexicographers characterised actors as living on the price of their wives' honour (*jāyājīva* and *rūpājīva*).

On the other hand, however, actors enjoyed the friendship of great kings and eminent dramtists. Traces of a brighter side of the profession are found and this doubtless can be connected with the gradual elevation of the art from humble origins to the rank of refined poetry.

Bharata ranks as a *muni* or holy sage. As he is the originator of the dramatic art, actors are called *bharataputras* or sons of Bharata. Almost everything connected with drama or the stage is named after him. The oldest and most authoritative treatise on dramaturgy, the *Nāṭyaśāstra*, is ascribed to Bharata. The *apsarā* Urvaśī, a nymph, plays a scenic role in heaven before Bharata.

An actress was often, if not necessarily, one of the courtesans. In the *Mṛcchakaṭika*, Vasantasenā is skilled in acting and has in her house maidens learning the art. Vasantasenā is emancipated from her profession of courtesanship and allowed to marry Cārudatta, a learned Brāhmaṇa, by king Śarvilaka thus: "Noble Vasantasenā, the king is pleased to confer on you the title of wife.[3]

Actors are mentioned as welcome guests of princes and intimate friends of poets of status. Bāṇa enumerates actors and actresses among his friends in the *Harṣacarita*.[4] Bhartṛhari refers to their friendship with kings.[5]

Girls belonging to the higher order of the society, like Mālavikā, were instructed in the art of representation. Mālavikā was made a present to the queen by her brother, Vīrasena, deeming her fit to be initiated in fine arts.[6]

In the *Ratnāvalī*, the manager was treated with great respect by kings and requested to act the drama, in the following words: "Manager, enough of prolixity. Today, on the occasion of the spring festival, called

[1] *Viṣṇusmṛti*, XVI. 3, 8, p. 45.
[2] *Mahābhāṣya*, III, p. 7.
[3] *Mṛch*, X, p. 252.
[4] *Harṣacarita*, I, p. 19.
[5] Bhartṛhari 'Subhāṣitatriśati'. *Vairāgyaśaṭakam*, III. 56.
[6] *Māl*, I, p. 9.

with great respect by the multitude of kings who have come here from various regions and who depend on the lotus-like feet of our king, the illustrious Śrīharṣa, I was told that the *Ratnāvalī* should be enacted on the stage." Here the words 'great respect' signify that actors were held in high respect by kings.[1]

Bhavabhūti in the preludes to two of his dramas asserts his friendship with actors.[2] Men, who could effectively declaim the stanzas of Bhavabhūti, must have had both education and culture of a high degree and must have been very different from acrobats and jugglers, dancers and others, whose humble occupations account for the censures of law books and the *Arthaśāstra*. When we think that Bharata, the first teacher of the art of acting and the theatre-director of the stage of the gods, is subsequently designated a *muni* and that in later days men and women belonging to the higher strata of the society appeared on the stage, the conclusion is warranted that respect for the position of actors and their profession was gradually rising.

[1]*Rat*, I, p. 5.
[2]*MM*, prelude prose, p. 8; *Mahāvīracarita*, prelude prose, p. 8.

CHAPTER EIGHT

Conventions

PŪRVARAṄGA

Bharata devotes one entire chapter of the *Nāṭyaśāstra* to describing preliminaries of a play (*pūrvaraṅga*). According to him *pūrvaraṅga* bears this name because ceremonies connected with it are performed at the beginning of the presentation of play on the stage.[1] According to the *Sāhityadarpaṇa*, the term *pūrvaraṅga* is significant as it includes that which the actor does before the play is presented in order to remove all hindrances.[2] The Avaloka on the Daśarūpa, on the other hand, explains the word as derived from *rañji*, to satisfy, and says the name owes its origin to the fact that it satisfies one beforehand.[3]

According to Bharata the *pūrvaraṅga* has twenty different constituent parts. Out of these the first nine are to be performed behind the curtain and the rest on the stage.[4]

Pratyāhāra, bringing in of the musical instruments (*kutapa*); *avataraṇa*, placing of singers (*gāyaka*); *ārambha*, beginning of the rehearsal song of the chorus; *āśrāvaṇā*, tuning of instruments which are played upon by striking (*ātodya*); *vaktrapāṇi*, tuning of the wind instruments (*vādya*); *parighaṭṭanā*, tuning of the stringed instruments (*tantrī*); *saṅghoṭanā*, meant for rehearsing the use of different hand poses for indicating the time beat; *mārgāsārita*, playing together of different instruments, *āsārita*, entrance and practice of the dancing girls—all these are done behind the curtain.

The parts of the *pūrvaraṅga* to be played on the stage are mentioned below. First comes *gīta* song in praise of gods and then *utthāpana*, song on the setting up of the banner of Indra (*jarjara*). Here the *sūtradhāra* appears, followed by two *pāripārśvikas* who carry a water jug (*bhṛṅgāra*) and the banner of Indra. The *sūtradhāra* strews flowers, brings in Indra's banner and cleanses himself with the water of the jug. After this, is performed *parivartana*, stalking round the stage with praise of the guardians of the world (*dikpālastuti*) and adoration of Indra's banner (*jarjarapūjā*). *Nāndī*, praise or a benediction is next

[1] *NS-KM*, *KSS*, *GOS*, V. 7.

[2] *SD*, VI, *sūtra* 22.

[3] Avaloka on *DR*, III. 2.

[4] *NS-KM*, V. 17–30; *KSS*, V. 17–30a; *GOS*, V. 17–30.

recited by the *sūtradhāra* in a middling tone. It consists of twelve or eight *pādas* and after each *pāda*, both the *pāripārśvikas* say *evamastu* (so be it). There follow *vardhamāna*, an increasing intensity of *tāṇḍava* (manly dance); *śuṣkāvokṛṣta*, an introduction in which the *sūtradhāra* recites some verses in a sonorous voice; the *jarjara ślokas*, in praise of the god whose worship is being celebrated, or in praise of a king or of Brahmā; *raṅgadvāra*, when the play (*abhinaya*) begins, the *sūtradhāra* recites a new verse and bows before Indra's banner (*jarjara*); *cārī*, different paces and gestures with an erotic sense; *mahācārī*, similar paces, but more impetuous in degree; *trigata*, conversation between the *sūtradhāra*, the *vidūṣaka* and a *pāripārśvika* in which the *vidūṣaka* speaks all kinds of nonsense; *prarocanā*, announcement of the contents.

According to Bharata these are the constituent parts of a regular *pūrvaraṅga* or a *caturasra pūrvaraṅga*. The *tryasra pūrvaraṅga* is similar but shortened, while in the *citra* (variegated) *pūrvaraṅga* strewing of flowers and dance of the gods etc. are added.[1]

The *pūrvaraṅga* is not a part of the drama proper. Bharata issues a note of warning that there should be some limit to the dance, song and instrumental music introduced so that the audience may not lose patience.[2]

Bhāsa's dramas, the earliest specimen of Sanskrit play, begin with the direction '*nāndyante tataḥ praviśati sūtradhāraḥ*' (i.e. after the introductory music is over, the stage manager enters). This is certainly an old specimen of introduction, according to which the *nāndī* did not form part of the drama proper. In Bhāsa's dramas there are no *prarocanās* or intimations of the contents.

The well established form of beginning in later dramas shows that the practice had become gradually different, as the *nāndī* and the *prarocanā* were incorporated in the drama proper and were composed by the author of the drama. The *pūrvaraṅga* was greatly shortened by its inclusion as a constituent part of the drama, but its principal parts, including dancing, singing and instrumental music were retained. The usual saying *alaṁ ativistareṇa*—enough of formalities—and similar remarks in the beginning of dramas point to this fact. The *Sāhityadarpaṇa* remarks that in all cases the *nāndī* must be retained.[3]

After Bhāsa almost all Sanskrit plays begin with the *nāndī*. This is followed by the prelude, *prastāvanā*. This formality of the *pūrvaraṅga* is

[1] *NS-KM*, V. 139–44; *KSS*, V. 158b–160a, 152–55; *GOS*, V. 155–61.

[2] *NS-KM*, V. 146–48, I. 23; *KSS*, V. 158a, 160b–162, I. 57; *GOS* V. 164b–167a; I. 56b–57a.

[3] *SD*, VI, *sūtras* 23–24.

observed in every kind of drama. Hence it is dealt with here in some detail.

The *Nāṭyaśāstra* prescribes that the *nāndī* should have words invoking blessings (*āśīrvacana*). It should have eight or twelve feet (*pādas*), should be poetically beautiful and should be holy or approved by gods.

The *nāndī* should be in honour of gods. Brāhmaṇas, the king, or it should please these persons. There must be two *pāripārśvikas* by the side of the *sūtradhāra*. While the *sūtradhāra* recites the *nāndī* in a middle tone, the *pāripārśvikas* say *evamastu* (so be it) at the end of every foot (*pāda*). There is also a note that by the proper execution of the *nāndī*, *candra* (moon) is pleased.[1]

According to the *Abhinayadarpaṇa*, after many kinds of charming tunes have been performed in honour of Gaṇapati, the god of the *muraja* drum and other gods, the dancing girl should have the permission of her preceptor to begin dressing herself suitably. Then to destroy evils, to protect living creatures, to please gods, to bring edification to the spectators, welfare to the leader of the *naṭa* group, protection to the dancing girl and to make the teaching of her preceptor fruitful, she begins offering flowers to gods.[2]

According to the Ādibharata, in addition to Bharata's *āśīrvacana* (words of blessings), the *nāndī* should include salutation (*namaskriyā*); it should suggest the plot of the play (*kāvyarthasūcaka*) and should have eight or ten *pādas*.[3]

In the *Agnipurāṇa*, we find that the *nāndī* is one of the 22 divisions of the *pūrvaraṅga*. It adds to the words *āśīrvacana*, of Bharata, prayers to elders and benedictions of cow, Brāhmaṇa and king etc. (*gobrahmaṇa-nṛpādi*).[4]

Abhinavagupta has discussed the various characteristics of the *nāndī* and has clarified the meanings of certain terms used by Bharata in this connection. He explains the word *nitya* as suggesting the daily recital of the *nāndī* i.e. the *nāndī* should be recited every day the drama is performed, unlike some other items of the *pūrvaraṅga*, which may not be practised daily. According to Bharata, the *nāndī* should be in honour of a god, Brāhmaṇa and king. To this, Abhinavagupta has added that it should also be in honour of a *prekṣāpati* i.e. the guest of honour. He adds a note that this *nāndī* is called *prarocanā* when it occurs as an element of *bhāratīvṛtti*.[5]

[1]*NS-KM*, V. 50b, 98–104a; *KSS*, V. 51a, 106–12; *GOS*, V. 50b, 109–115a.
[2]*AD*, 31–34, pp. 4–5.
[3]Ādibharata as quoted by Rāghavabhaṭṭa in his commentary on *Sāk*, p. 4.
[4]*Agnipurāṇa*, CCCXXXVIII. 8–9.
[5]*Abh. Bh*, I, p. 219.

In the *Daśarūpa*, we find that the *nāndī* should please the audience and that the verses must be sweet.[1] In the *Nāṭakalakṣaṇaratnakośa*, it is stated that the *nāndī* is to be introduced by the stage manager.[2]

In the *Nāṭyaśāstra* there is an illustration of the *nāndī* as given by Bharata. The authors of the *Nāṭyadarpaṇa* tell us that the *nāndī* should have six or eight *pādas* and add the terms Sarasvatī, *kavi* and *guṇotkīrtana* (praises of merit) to Bharata's list. The *nāndī* is supposed to remove obstacles in the way of the performance of a play. The *Nāṭyadarpaṇa* also says that the *nāndī* may be composed by the poet or the troupe manager and that it may be recited by the *sūtradhāra, sthāpaka* or *pāripārśvikas*.[3]

According to the *Bhāvaprakāśana*, the *nāndī* is derived from Nandī, the bull of Śiva. The dance of the bull in a particular form becomes worthy of representation. Its worship in that form is called *nāndī*. It is also known as *nāndī* because it delights the audience. In this context the word *nāndī* is derived from *nand*, 'to please'. There must also be the word *candra* (moon) or its synonym in the *nāndī* verse or the poet, at any rate, should indicate or suggest it. The *sūtradhāra* should recite it in a tone neither high nor low (*madhya svara*) and there should be eight or twelve *pādas* or sentences.[4]

In the definition of the *nāndī*, the *Pratāparudrīya* adds the words direct or indirect suggestion of the plot to the words of Ādibharata and others (*kāvyārthasūcaka*). The *nāndī*, according to it, may have eight, twelve, eighteen or twenty-two *pādas*.[5] The *Rasārṇavasudhākara* gives the same description as the *Pratāparudrīya* with a difference in the number of *pādas*. According to the *Rasārṇavasudhākara*, there may be eight, ten or twelve *pādas*.[6]

The *Sāhityadarpaṇa* quotes the *Nāṭyaśāstra* and adds that the *nāndī* should have signifying auspicious objects like *śaṅkha* (conch), *candra* (moon), *obja*, *koka* and *kairava* (different kinds of lotuses) and should contain eight or twelve *pādas*.[7]

In the commentary on the *Abhijñānaśākuntala*, Rāghavabhaṭṭa has quoted definitions of the *nāndī* as given in most of the works on dramaturgy and has added one more definition according to which the *nāndī*

[1] *DR*, III. 4a.
[2] *NLR*, ll. 1089–1100, pp. 46 and 47.
[3] *ND*, IV, pp. 192–93.
[4] *BP*, VII. ll. 19–22, p. 196, ll. 1–14, p. 197.
[5] *PR*, 34 and following prose, pp. 87–88.
[6] *RS*, III. 137–38 and examples, pp. 265–66.
[7] *SD*, VI, *sūtra* 25.

is composed of poems which please the audience, poets and actors. Here, too, the *nāndī* is derived from *nand*, 'to please'.[1]

Thus the *nāndī* should have the following characteristics. It should include *āśīrvacana*, *namaskriyā*, *kāvyārthasūcana*; should be in beautiful verse; *vedanirmita*; should be in honour of gods, Brāhmaṇas, kings, *sabhāpati*, audience, actors; should be recited every day the drama is performed; should have six, eight, twelve, eighteen or twenty-two *pādas*; the *sūtradhāra* should recite *nāndī* in a tone neither high nor low and two *pāripārśvikas* should stand on his sides and utter the word *evamastu* (so be it) at the end of every *pāda*; the moon is pleased by a proper recital of the *nāndī*; it should contain words like *candra, śaṅkha, abja, koka, kairava* or their synonyms; should contain *guṇotkīrtana*; it is derivable from *nand*; it should be accompanied by offerings of flowers; and be composed by a poet or stage manager.

RELIGIOUS CEREMONIES

The entire edifice of the Sanskrit play has a fundamental religious basis. The *Nāṭyaśāstra* was spoken of as the fifth Veda and Bharata, who wrote it, was regarded as the stage manager of the gods. He is said to have received a revelation of the dramatic art from Brahmā, the creator, who entered into meditation and from the depths of the divine thought brought forth the arts of drama, music and dance for the joy of the universe. According to the *Nāṭyaśāstra*, the *Nāṭyaveda* aimed at the attainment of the four *puruśārthas* or objects of human pursuit, namely *dharma* (ethical and spiritual development of the individual), *artha* (social and civic life and the acquisition of wealth), *kāma* (conjugal love and sensual pleasure of environment) and *mokṣa* (attainment of salvation).[2]

Bharata pays great attention to the forms and ceremonies for worshipping the presiding deities of the theatre. They are: *candra* (moon god), *lokapālas* (guardians of the world), Mārutas, Mitra, Agni (fire god), Varuṇa, *ādityas*, Rudras, *bhūtas*, *apsarasa, yakṣiṇya*, the Ocean god, *kṛtānta, nāgarāja*, the rod of Yama, *niyati, mṛtyu*, Indra, *vidyut* (lightning), *yakṣas, piśācas, guhyakas, vajra*, powerful *jarjara*, Brahmā, Viṣṇu, Śiva, Kārtikeya, Sarasvatī and Oṅkāra. The above-mentioned deities should be worshipped with *bali* (offerings) and sacrifices.[3]

Offerings, sacrifices, *mantras*, herbs, recitation and food (*bhakṣya*)

[1]Rāghavabhaṭṭa's commentary on *Śāk*, I, p. 4.
[2]*NS-KM*, *KSS*, *GOS*, I. 14.
[3]*NS-KM*, I. 49–64a; *KSS*, I. 83b–98; *GOS*, I. 82b–97.

should be offered on the *nāṭyamaṇḍapa*. The show should not begin before the offerings are made. If this rule is disregarded, the knowledge of the performer becomes futile and he goes to the nether world. So the stage manager should make the offerings with all ardour. If no worship is offered, the dancer or financier, whoever he may be, is degraded. According to the dramaturgic treatises, he who makes offerings gets the desired object and goes to heaven.[1]

Most elaborate forms of worship are prescribed in connection with the erection of the theatre. Brāhmaṇas are to be fed at every turn, sometimes with rich and sometimes with ordinary food. In the *puṣya* constellation, a white thread, strong enough to measure the building, should be laid around the theatre. If the thread is broken into two pieces, the death of the proprietor is indicated; if it is broken into three, a political disorder will occur in the land, and if it is broken into four, the master of the dramatic art will perish. To avoid these, measurement of the theatre should be done on an auspicious day and Brāhmaṇas propitiated. Deformed and ugly persons should on no account be employed in any work concerning the building. Monks and mendicants should not be allowed to approach the building.

Bharata gives the correct invocation to be used when laying the foundation of the theatre thus: "Oh pillar: as the Himalayas are immovably fixed on the ground, be thou even like them." In the Rohiṇī or Śravaṇa constellation the pillars should be laid and the director of the theatre should observe fast for three days. Jewels, cows and clothes should be distributed in charity.

While erecting the *mattavāraṇīs*, garlands, clothes and perfumes should be given away in charity. Offerings liked by *bhūtas* should be given to the different castes (*varṇas*). Milk should be offered under the pillars of the *mattavāraṇīs*. Food-rice mixed with pulses should be given to Brāhmaṇas.

When constructing the *rangaśīrṣa* jewels and precious stones were laid underneath this (*raṅgaśīrṣa*) by expert builders. On the eastern side of the *raṅgaśīrṣa* diamond is to be kept; lapis lazuli on the south; emerald on the west, coral in the north and gold in the centre.[2]

Bharata devotes the third chapter of the *Nāṭyaśāstra* to a detailed description of the worship of the gods of the stage. When construction of the theatre is over, cows should live there for a week and Brāhmaṇas

[1]*NS-KM*, I. 87–93; *KSS*, I. 119–25; *GOS*, I. 125–31.

[2]*NS-KM*, II. 30b–35, 38–57a, 62b–63; *KSS*, II. **28b–34a; 36b–56a**, 62–69a, 74b–75; *GOS*, II. 33b–39a, 41b–61a, 67–74a, 79b–80.

recite *mantras*. The director is to be initiated and after a three-day fast should salute with folded hands prominent gods, divine beings, *rājarṣis*, *munis*, and dramatic obstacles and success.

Of the varied aspects of the preliminaries, special importance seems to have been attached to the praise of the world's guardians (*dikpālastuti*) and reverence to Indra's banner. *Jarjara* or the setting up of the flag-staff of Indra is the most important of the sacred rites on the stage. The flag-staff is erected in the stage in the evening after the *mantras* have been chanted the day preceding the festivity. On the day of the festivity, all the deities and the flag-staff are worshipped. Brahmā, Śiva, Viṣṇu, Kārtikeya and the three great serpents Śeṣa, Vāsuki and Takṣaka are supposed to preside in the five knots of the flag-staff. The first part of the staff is wrapped in white linen, the second in blue, the third in yellow, the fourth in red and the fifth in multicoloured cloth. Different deities are invoked with different *mantras* according to the *Nāṭyaśāstra*.[1]

DIALECTS

The atmosphere in Sanskrit plays in characteristically romantic, but a curious element of realism is introduced by the use of many dialects, according to the status of various characters. The gods, most of the Brāhmaṇas and princes spoke pure Sanskrit and female characters Prākṛta. The audience, which could follow the minute variations of dialects, enjoyed this introduction of realism. Dramas like the *Dūtavākya*, where pure Sanskrit is used, or like the *Karpūra-mañjarī*, where pure Prākṛta is used, are indeed very rare.

The use of specific dialects for characters seems to be determined on the strength of a rule of Viśvanātha, who, in the *Sāhityadarpaṇa* says: *Yaddeśam nīcapātraṁ tu taddeśyaṁ tasya bhāṣitam*.[2] But it is not always correct to say that because a character speaks Śaurasenī he or she must be the native of Śūrasena country. The dialect of a character appears to have been fixed by convention, and although in the *Mṛcchakaṭika* this rule is observed with fair rigidity, one cannot say that it is universal.

According to theorists, Sanskrit is the language of members of the higher castes such as kings, Brāhmaṇas, learned men, ministers and generals. Occasionally the senior queen, female ascetics and members

[1]*NS-KM*, III. 1–15; 31b–32a, 65–67a, 74, 81–83, 93; *KSS*, III. 1–16, 33b–34a, 75–77a, 84, 92–94, 104; *GOS*, III. 1–17a, 34, 75b–77, 84b–85a, 92b–95a, 104b–105a.

[2]*SD*, VI. 168.

of the harem also speak Sanskrit.[1] Such is the case with some allegorical female characters in the *Prabodhacandrodaya*[2] and similar other dramas. Sanskrit should also be used when people speak on war and peace, on omens and similar subjects. In the *Pañcarātra*. Bṛhannalā actually turns from Prākṛta to Sanskrit to describe a fight.[3] Women, children and men in low stations speak Prākṛta.[4]

The rules laid down by Bharata for the use of Prākṛta dialects in the Sanskrit plays are simple. According to him—and Sāgaranandin[5] supports him—the main Prākṛta dialect to be used in dramas must be Śaurasenī. However, he allows latitude to writers to use other dialects as the dramatic form of poetic composition draws its characters from different countries. Bharata enumerates seven principal Prākṛta dialects for use in dramas. They are: Māgadhī, Avantijā, Prācyā, Śaurasenī, Ardhamāgadhī, Bālhikā and Dākṣiṇātyā. He gives also a list of sub-dialects (*vibhāṣas*) such as Śākārī Ābhīri, Cāṇḍalī, Śābarī, Drāviḍī, Auḍrī and Vānaukasī.[6] Mahārāṣṭrī has not been mentioned by Bharata nor by Sāgaranandin but by Viśvanātha in the *Sāhityadarpaṇa* which is a late work belonging to about AD1380[7] Mahārāṣṭrī has in fact no place in Sanskrit dramas and in early days its use seems to be restricted to poetic compositions only.

The principal Prākṛta dialect used in the dramas was Śaurasenī, both for prose and verse. It could be used by anybody in the drama. It was famous as the popular dialect of the Doab of the Yamunā and Gaṅgā. According to theorists, it is the language of the heroine, her friends and attendants and generally of women of good families. It is also spoken by ordinary men.

The *vidūṣaka* and others spoke Prācyā, which was hardly different from Śaurasenī, while rogues employed Avantijā.

Ardhamāgadhī was spoken by slaves (*ceṭas*), sons of kings (*rājaputras*) and masters of guilds (*śreṣṭhins*).

Māgadhī was spoken by inmates of the royal harem, by diggers of subterranean entrances, inn-keepers and watchmen. It was occasionally used by the hero while in difficulty for self-protection. According to the *Daśarūpa*, Māgadhī and Paiśācī were the languages of the low people.[8]

[1]*NS-KM*, XVII. 31, 36b–42a; *KSS*, XVIII. 29b–30a, 34b–40a; *GOS*, XVII. 32b–33a, 38–43; *DR*, II. 64, p. 61; *SD*, VI, *sūtra* 168.

[2]*Prabodhacandrodaya*, V, pp. 167–68.

[3]*Pañcarātra*, II. 29–32, p. 400.

[4]*NS-KM*, XVII. 32; *KSS*, XVIII. 33b–34a; *GOS*, XVIII. 30b–31a.

[5]*NLR* ll. 2148–2157, p. 90.

[6]*NS-KM*, XVII. 46–55; *KSS*, XVIII. 44–54a; *GOS*, XVII. 47b–56; *SD*, VI, *sūtra* 168.

[7]*SD*, VI. 168.

[8]*DR*, II. 65–66.

Bharata says Dākṣiṇātyā should be spoken by warriors, police officers and gamesters. Bālhikā, according to the same source, is the native speech of the Khasas who belong to the north.

Coming to the use of sub-dialects or *vibhāṣās*. Śākārī was assigned to the Śakāra and the Śakas and other groups of the same nature, and Cāṇḍālī to the Pulkasas and the like. Ābhīrī or Śābarī was prescribed for those who lived in places where elephants, horses, goats, sheep, camels or cows were kept. Drāviḍī was the speech prescribed for forest-dwellers and the like. It has been observed that Ābhīrī and Drāviḍī dialects are not available in any extant dramas. Generally cowherds. Outcasters and foresters used their own forms of speech. Even mischievous imps had their appropriate jargon and *piśācas* or goblins, when introduced on the stage, spoke a dialect of Prākṛt known as Paiśācī.

The commentary of Pṛthvīdhara on the *Mṛcchakaṭika* has shown vividly the Prākṛta dialects used in dramas[1] and has particularly pointed out that *Mṛcchakaṭika* uses four principal Prākṛta dialects and three sub-dialects— Śaurasenī, Āvantī or Avantijā, Prācyā, Māgadhī, Śākārī, Cāṇḍālī and Ḍhakkī.

INJUNCTIONS AND PROHIBITIONS

We now proceed to examine some of the peculiar but important injunctions and prohibitions laid down by dramaturgic treatises to be observed on the stage.

In order to maintain an idealistic atmosphere not only was a tragic end forbidden but other important and far-reaching restrictions were also imposed. Propriety and decorum were emphasized. Grim realism was not to be presented, for this would not exalt the mind. Painful, disgusting and debasing scenes were to be avoided. Long journeys, murders, fights, revolts in kingdoms, sieges, eating, bathing, kissing, embracing, loosening the *nīvī* and pressing of breasts were not to be represented on the stage.[2]

The older dramatists, however, acted with greater freedom. Thus in the *Ūrubhaṅga* of Bhāsa, Duryodhana dies on the stage[3] and in the *Mṛcchakaṭika*, Vasantasenā is strangled by Śakāra.[4] The injunctions apparently came to be strictly adhered to in later times.

The Sanskrit drama does not entirely exclude tragedy. It excludes the

[1]The commentary of Pṛthvīdhara on *Mṛch*, pp. 1–2.
[2]*NS-KM*, XXII. 279–83; *KSS*, XXIV. 285–89.
[3]*Ūrubhaṅga*, I. 35, p. 498. [4]*Mṛch*, VIII, prose, p. 183.

direct representation of death as an incident and insists on a happy ending. It recognizes some form of tragedy in its pathetic sentiment (*karuṇa rasa*) and love in separation (*vipralaṁbha śṛṅgāra*); the tragic interest is almost central in some plays. In the *Mṛcchakaṭika* and the *Abhijñānaśākuntala*, for instance, the tragedy does not indeed occur at the end but earlier, and in the *Uttararāmacarita*, where the tragic element prevails throughout, it occurs in an intensive form at the beginning of the play. Thus the foremost characteristic feature of Sanskrit plays is the total absence of the distinction between tragedy and comedy. It is a mixed composition in which joy and sorrow, happiness and misery, seriousness and levity are mixed, and in which good and evil, right and wrong, truth and falsehood are blended. But towards the end harmony is always restored and order succeeds disorder, tranquillity, agitation and the mind of the spectator is made peaceful by the happy termination of the story.

Only sweet and exalted sentiments and emotions are to be presented on the stage but minute details of the subject that are deficient in sentiments and unsuitable are to be reported. Things that are not to be represented on the stage and events that extend over a long time are to be related in inter-acts called *arthopakṣepakas*.

Five kinds of inter-acts are distinguished: *viṣkaṁbhaka*, *praveśaka*, *cūlikā*, *aṅkāvatāra* and *aṅkamukha*.[1]

The *viṣkaṁbha* or *viṣkaṁbhaka* relates, at the beginning of an act, events which are happening or which have happened. When a longer interval has elapsed between two acts or important events have happened, the new act is introduced with a *viṣkaṁbhaka*. The *Nāṭyaśāstra* lays down that it should be introduced in the first of the five joints (*sandhi*). This practice is not always followed in dramas. What matters is the kind of persons appearing on the stage. These are either the people of the middle class, in which case the *viṣkaṁbhaka* is called pure (*śuddha*) and is in Sanskrit, or persons appear with people of a lower status in the mixed *viṣkaṁbhaka* (*saṅkīrṇa*) with Prākṛta as the language.

The *praveśaka* in relation to the *nāṭaka* and the *prakaraṇa* is to occupy a place between two acts. It should not consist of the exploits of the superior and the middling characters and there should be no exalted speech in it. Its language should be Prākṛta.

Voices behind the curtain which relate facts constitute *cūlikā*.

The remaining two *arthopakṣepakas* are of a somewhat different kind. The *aṅkāvatāra* comes between two acts or within an act and relates to the purpose of the germ (*bīja*). Bharata explains an *aṅkamukha* as a

[1]*NS-KM*, XIX. 104–11; *KSS*, XXI. 108–16.

preceding allusion to the beginning of an act when this act is separated (*viśliṣṭa*) from it. The *Daśarūpa* calls it *aṅkāsya* and explains it as an announcement of the beginning of an act at the close of the preceding one when the matter of the following act is not an immediate continuation of the earlier one.[1] The *Sāhityadarpaṇa* observes, however, that some authorities take it as an *aṅkāvatāra* and explains *aṅkamukha* as an illusion to the entire following contents of a piece inside an act.[2]

According to the dramatic rules (*nāṭyadharma*) some parts of the matter in hand are to be heard by all persons present on the stage while other parts are not expected to be so heard. The former is known as 'aloud' (*prakāśa*) and the latter 'aside' (*svagata*). An 'aside' is also called *ātmagata*. The adverbial forms *ātmagata* and *svagata* occur frequently in stage directions. Other forms of addresses are personal address (*janānta* or *janāntika*) and that spoken in confidence (*apavārita*). Personal address is mutual conversation in the presence of other persons who are excluded with a gesture by the hand with three fingers raised (*tripatākā*). A confidential speech (*apavārita*) is a secret shared by a person turning round to another and is meant to be heard only by the person addressed. Then there are imaginary conversations (*ākāśabhāṣita*). When an actor says "What do you say" without the presence of any other actor and appears as if he hears the answer, it is called the *ākāṣabhāsita*.[3] This device is frequently employed in a monologue play (*Bhāṇa*).

The *Nāṭyaśāstra* prescribes a set of words for calling the different characters according to their position. The words are given in the following: Gods, great sages, persons well versed in different Vedas and priests were called by men and women alike as '*bhagavan*' (holy one). Kings were called by Brāhmaṇas at their pleasure by their names. A Brāhmaṇa was usually called '*ārya*' (noble one); a king '*mahārāja*' (great king); a teacher, *ācārya* (professor); and an old person, '*tāta*' (father). A minister was called '*amātya*' (councillor) or '*saciva*' (minister) by a Brāhmaṇa and '*ārya*' (sir) by others. Persons of equal status were called by their names. The lord of a chariot was addressed by the charioteer as '*āyuṣman*' (long-lived one) and an ascetic, '*sādho*' (blessed one). A pupil or a son was addressed as '*vatsa*' (child), '*putraka*' (son), '*tāta*' (a term of endearment) or by the name of his *gotra* by father or preceptor. A king was called '*deva*' (lord) by servants and people in general, and as '*bhaṭṭa*' (Prākṛta form of *bhartā*) (sire) by members of his harem and '*rājan*' (king) by *ṛṣis* (sages). The *vidūṣaka* was called *vayasya* (friend) by the king. A husband was

[1]*DR*, I. 58–63a.

[2]*SD*, VI, *sūtras*, 54–65.

[3]*SD*, VI, *sūtras*, 137–40; *DR*, I. 63b–67.

addressed as '*āryaputra*' (noble one's son) by his wife in her youth. Wives of king were called '*bhaṭṭinī*' (mistress), '*svāminī*', (madam) and '*devī*' (lady) by members of the harem according to their status. A slave girl was called '*hañje*' (hey child) and a courtesan '*ajjukā*'; an old woman '*attā*' and the wife '*priye*' (my dear) in an erotic sentiment. These conventions were faithfully followed in Sanskrit plays.[1]

Sanskrit dramas are often very long. There are Sanskrit dramas like the *Bālarāmāyaṇa* of Rājeśkhara which are equal in volume to three dramas of Shakespeare. Dramas are usually divided into acts. The common word for an act is *aṅka*; only in the sub-class, *saṭṭaka*, the act is called *javanikāntara*. According to Bharata, an *aṅka* is *rūḍhiśabda* i.e. he knows no etymology.[2] The *Avaloka* on the *Daśarūpa* says that the *aṅka* signifies the mother's lap, because the act helps the development of the theme.[3]

The number of acts varies according to the kind of drama. In the principal classes there are at least five and at the most ten acts. In each act the hero must appear, and the number of persons present on the stage should not be too many. Three or four was considered to be a convenient number. This number was, however, often exceeded. Further, a subject treated in one act should not spread over more than one day. Different matters may be pressed together in one act. Every one should leave the stage at the end of an act.[4]

The Sanskrit drama lays the greatest importance on the successful portrayal of sentiments and does not insist on quick movement of action. There are very few dramas in Sanskrit which cannot maintain the interest in their action. Ancient rhetoricians held that a dramatist should set before him the creation of sentiment (*rasodbhāvana*) as his chief object.[5] Besides the major plot, Sanskrit critics welcome the development of subsidiary incidents and situations. The fundamental 'unity of action' is to be observed, it is true, but only in the Shakespearian sense.

The 'unity of time' was ignored both in theory and practice, but so far as the drama as a whole was concerned, a sense of dramatic propriety demanded that an act should be arranged with a single purpose exemplified by the doings of a single day. Accordingly an act by itself created its own allusion. But between acts many years may elapse; in the *Abhijñānaśākuntala*,

[1]*NS-KM*, XVII. 64–91; *KSS*, XIX. 1–29a; *GOS*, XVII. 65–94a.

[2]*NS-KM*, XVIII. 14; *KSS*, XX. 14; *GOS*, XVIII. 14.

[3]Avaloka on *DR*, III. 30b–31a.

[4]*DR*, III. 36b–38, *NLR*, ll. 295–304.

[5]*NS-KM*, VI, prose, p. 62; *KSS*, VI, prose, p. 71; *GOS*, VI, prose, pp. 274–89.

Bharata's growth from birth to boyhood is described[1] and in the *Uttara-rāmacarita* no less than twelve years pass between the first and second acts.[2] Time may slide over twelve or sixteen years and the audience may learn of it from the chorus or a short dialogue.

Similarly, the 'unity of place' is not observed. In an act the place is practically the same except for small distances which are suggested by means of some brisk movement on the stage. But change of locality sometimes occurs within the same act, as for example, when a journey through air in a celestial car is performed. Generally in the subsequent act, the scene may open at any other place, even in a celestial region. The concluding stages of a long journey are symbolically represented so that the audience travels and reaches the destination in its imagination and then stays for the act in that locality. The idea of the locality is often picturesquely suggested by means of exquisite poetic descriptions. In plays such as the *Ratnāvalī*, where a royal intrigue is presented, all the acts are confined to the several chambers or gardens of the palace itself. But such a restriction is voluntary on the part of the dramatist and is not imposed on him by the strict rules of dramaturgy.

[1] *Śāk*, VII, p. 185.
[2] *URC*, II, p. 52.

CHAPTER NINE

Nature and Types of Drama

NṚTTA, NṚTYA AND NĀṬYA

Sanskrit dramaturgists have very early distinguished between the art of histrionic (*nāṭya*) and the art of dancing (*nṛtya* or *nṛtta*). As some types of drama are based on *nṛtya* and others on *nāṭya*, it is essential for us to understand clearly these terms before we study the forms of drama and their actual presentation.

Nṛtta and *nṛtya* are derived from *nṛt* and *nāṭya* from *naṭ*.[1] There is reference to *nṛt* in the *Ṛgveda*,[2] while the earliest use of *naṭ* is found in Pāṇinī,[3] proving thereby that *nṛt* was an earlier form. *Naṭ* is found to have been used in the senses of dancing and acting.[4] *Nāṭya,* too, has been assigned both these senses in certain works. That *nāṭya* had both these senses of dancing and acting is also seen in the *Mālavikāgnimitra*. It speaks of a *nāṭya* called *chalika*, *chalita* or *calita* which was acted to the accompaniment of dance by Mālavikā. It was certainly not a drama, nor was it a mere *nṛtya* type. As there is express mention of acting according to the prevalent sentiment (*yathārasamabhinayati*) after the stanza recited by Mālavikā, it is obvious that it was a type which involved *abhinaya*, and this was the technical nature of *nṛtya*. It seems that Kālidasa recognised the principle that *bhāva* (emotion) was at the root of *nṛtya* as he called two *ācāryas*, Gaṇadāsa and Haradatta, *bhāvas* incarnate. Thus also *calita* was a *nṛtya* type. *Nāṭya* here refers to *nṛtya*.[5] The *Mālavikāgnimitra* also recognizes *nāṭya* in the sense of drama. In it *nāṭya* is characterised as a composition in which *lokacarita* (ways of the world) are seen and which necessarily refers to the drama proper, rather than to an ordinary *nṛtya*.[6] The same is the nature of *nāṭya* as used in the *Nāṭakalakṣaṇaratnakośa*.[7] The *Bhāvaprakāśana* alone describes *nṛtta* as *rasāśrayam* (dependent on sentiment), thus equating it with *nāṭya*.[8]

But in order to understand clearly the import of these terms, we shall

[1]*Pāṇini*, IV. 3. 129; V. S. Apte, *Practical Sanskrit-English Dictionary*, pp. 534 and 540: '*naṭ ac iti naṭaḥ*'; '*naṭasyedam kṛtyaṁ syañ iti nāṭyaṁ*'.

[2]*Ṛgveda*, X. 18. 3; 29. 2; VIII. 24. 9.

[3]*Pāṇini*, IV. 3. 110–11.

[4]*Siddhānta Kaumudī Tiṅanta*, p. 444. '*Naṭa nṛttau. Itthameva pūrvamapi paṭhitaṁ. Tatrāyaṁ vivekaḥ. Pūrvaṁ paṭhitasya nāṭyamarthaḥ. Yatkāriṣu naṭavyapadesaḥ*.'.

[5]*Māl*, II, prose, p. 24.

[6]*Māl*, 4, p. 7.

[7]*NLR*, ll. 266–68, p. 12.

[8]*BP*, VII, ll. 7–12, p. 181.

have to keep in mind the subtle distinction between *bhāva* and *rasa*. The *Daśarūpa*, after defining *nṛtya* and *nṛtta*, adds: '*ādyam padārthābhinayo mārgo deśī tathā paraṁ*' i.e. the former, a representation of an object, is called 'high style' (*mārga*), and the latter 'popular style' (*deśī*). Similar meaning is attached to the words *nṛtya* and *nṛtta* in the *Saṅgītaratnākara*, the *Pratāparudrīya* and the *Siddhānta Kaumudī*.[1] This clearly makes *nṛtya* a more evolved form of *nṛtta*. *Nṛtta* is the original form of entertainment on which *nṛtya* was an improvement. Thus *nṛtta* involved *tāla* (rhythm) and *laya* (tune) only and not *bhāva* (emotion) while *nṛtya* was essentially connected with *bhāva* (emotion) and producing *bhāva* (emotion) in the minds of the audience is an art far more advanced than mere *gātravikṣepa* (bodily movement). *Nṛtta*, thus, is dance, while *nṛtya* is mimetic art.

According to the *Nāṭyaśāstra*, *nṛtta* had no purpose other than delighting people.[2] Abhinavagupta gives the following divisions of *nṛtta*: *masṛṇa* (tender), *uddhata* (violent), *masṛṇamiśra* (tender but mixed), *uddhatamiśra* (violent but mixed), that which includes harmonious motions of hands and feet as in *recakas* and *aṅgahāras*, that which includes music leading to *abhinaya* and that which follows music and *vādyatāla* (rhythm of musical instrument) with harmonious motion of the limbs. It will be seen that the first four divisions are based on a principle distinct from the one on which the last three are based. These three can be resolved into two types, one which has pure *gātravikṣepa* (bodily movement) and in which hands and feet are moved in harmony with *bhāṇḍavādya* (play on a musical instrument) and the second which includes *abhinaya*, with harmonious motions of limbs to the tune of music. These two types of *nṛtta* are further taken as distinct from *nāṭya* as is clear from a passage of the *Abhinavabhāratī*[3] which says that the first type, which is *nṛtta*, was quite distinct from *nāṭya* and the second type, which is *nṛtya* was useful in *nāṭya*. Thus both these are distinct from *nāṭya*.

Abhinavagupta says that the *abhinaya* required in *nṛtta-kāvyas* is distinct from the *abhinaya* required in *nāṭya*. In *nṛtta-kāvyas*, *nartakī*, a female dancer, resorts to *aṅgavyāpāra* (movement of limbs) by proper gesticulation, movement of eyes etc.; but all this is to attract the king in whose presence she dances. Thus the *abhinaya* of a *nartakī* excites the king's passion, but the *abhinaya* of a *naṭa* is to personate somebody and

[1] *DR*, I, 7–9; *SR*, VII. 3b, 17b, 28, 29; *PR*, 'Nāṭakaprakaraṇa', 1–2, prose, pp. 72–73; *Siddhāntakaumudī Tiṅanta*, p. 444.

[2] *NS-KM*, IV. 244–48; *KSS*, IV. 258b–263a; *GOS*, IV. 268b–273a.

[3] *Abh. Bh*, I, pp. 182–84. '*Prathama bheda laukike svatantranṛtte devatātoṣaṇādau vā Dvitīyaḥ pūrvaraṅgavidhau pariśiṣṭanṛttalakṣyatayā.*'

thus he has to show feelings, as experienced by another person and make them manifest on the stage by visible representation. A *nartakī* does not play any role and has nothing to represent visibly. All that she has to do is to attract the king's heart by personal appeal, as it were, through her gestures. She does not put on the dress of any other person. Thus *āhāryābhinaya* is almost absent in her case. Abhinavagupta says his second variety of *nṛtta* is a sort of *abhinaya* but it can produce only *bhāva* (emotion), not *rasa* (sentiment) which would be evoked only by *nāṭya*, and is, therefore, distinct from this second variety of *nṛtta*.[1] Abhinavagupta does not use the term *nṛtya* but signifies both *nṛtta* and *nṛtya* of the *Daśarūpa* by the use of *nṛtta*.

From the point of view of evolution, first comes *nṛtta*, then *nṛtya* and last *nāṭya*. *Nṛtta* is mere dance, *nṛtya* has gestures added to it, while *nāṭya* has speech too. *Nāṭya* incorporated all the three items—dance, music and speech—which are so essential for the successful presentation of a play.

MAJOR TYPES OF DRAMA *(RŪPAKAS)*

Bharata was conversant with ten kinds of *rūpakas*, and his divisions and descriptions remained authoritative for later theorists.[2] In course of time, they started all kinds of novelties, leading to further divisions and sub-divisions. They have not, however, attempted to alter anything of the ten *rūpakas* described by Bharata. The novel creations have been classified as sub-classes. The *Daśarūpa* gives details about *naṭikā* for the first time. The *Bhāvaprakāśana* gives an elaborate description of twenty minor kinds of dramas which are styled *uparūpakas*. The *Sāhityadarpaṇa* describes eighteen kinds of dramas which are designated as *uparūpakas*. The *Agnipurāṇa* mentions seventeen minor kinds of dramas in addition to the ten *rūpakas*.[3] But the recognition of *uparūpakas* signifies that later dramas which did not fit in with Bharata's description of *rūpakas* were treated and systematised as new kinds of drama. With the exception of the so-called *nāṭikā* and *troṭaka*, these sub-classes have exercised no apparent influence upon dramatic literature.

The chief point of distinction between *rūpaka* and *uparūpaka* is that an *uparūpaka* mainly deals with bodily gestures and music, which occupy a

[1] *Abh. Bh*, I, pp. 177–78.

[2] *NS-KM*, XVIII. 1–3a; *KSS*, XX. 1–3a; *GOS*, XVIII. 1–3a.

[3] *DR*, III, 42b–48; *BP*, IX, pp. 255–68; *SD*, VI, *sutras* 4–6; *Agnipurāṇa*, CCCXXXVIII. 1–7.

secondary position in *rūpaka*. Thus *uparūpaka* places greater emphasis on *kāyābhinaya* (bodily gestures) while *rūpaka* requires *sātvika* temperament and other *abhinayas*. The *Bhāvaprakāśana* very clearly says that *rūpakas* were *rasātmaka* (dependent on sentiment) and *uparūpakas* were *bhāvātmaka* (dependent on emotion). It calls *uparūpakas* as *nṛtyabhedaḥ* (species of *nṛtya*) and *rūpakas* as *nāṭyabhedaḥ* (species of *nāṭya*). The distinction that *nāṭya* is *vākyārthābhinayātmaka* and *nṛtya* is *padāthābhinayātmaka* also points to the same principle.[1]

Now we shall first describe the major types of drama (*rūpakas*) and then the minor types (*uaparūpakas*) as given in the dramaturgic treatises.

Nāṭaka: According to Bharata, when the peculiarities of society were sought to be connected with certain gestures or when the actions of gods, *ṛṣis*, kings or of the members of a society were copied, they came to be called a *nāṭaka*. All *vṛttis* should be in their proper place in a *nāṭaka*, consisting of from five to ten acts. An act should contain various appropriate actions and events of not more than one day. According to the *Daśarūpa*, in a *nāṭaka* the hero should be endowed with attractive qualities of the type known as the self-controlled and exalted (*dhīrodātta*) and should be glorious, desirous of winning fame, very energetic, a preserver of the three Vedas (*trayī*), a ruler of the world, of renowned lineage, a royal seer or a god. The subject matter should contain the five elements of action corresponding to the five dramatic stages and should be divided into five junctures (*sandhis*), and these junctures should again be divided into 64 sub-divisions. The *patākā*, *prakarī* and *viṣkambhaka* should be employed. One sentiment, either the heroic or the erotic, is to be made the principal sentiment, all others being made subordinate. The marvellous sentiment should be employed only towards the end.[2]

Prakaraṇa: In the *prakaraṇa* class all the *vṛttis* can be employed. According to the *Daśarūpa*, the action should be invented and should take place on the earth. A minister, a Brāhmaṇa, or a merchant, of the type known as self-controlled and calm (*dhīrapraśānta*), under going misfortunes and having virtues, the search for pleasure and wealth being his chief objects in life, should be the hero. The remaining features such as junctures, introductory scenes and sentiments are as in the *nāṭaka*. In a *prakaraṇa,* the heroine may be of two kinds: the high-born wife of the hero or a courtesan. In some plays, there is only the high-born woman; in some plays only the courtesan; and in some, both. High-born women

[1] *BP*, VII. ll. 7–8, p. 180; ll. 7–8, p. 181; VIII. ll. 11–12, p. 221.

[2] *NS-KM*, XIX. 118, 123; XVIII. 10–12; *KSS*, XXI. 123–28; XX. 10–12; *GOS*, XVIII 10–12; *DR*, III. 22b–27, 33b–34a; *SD*, VI, *sūtra*, 10; *PR*, 'Nāṭakaprakaraṇa' 32–33, p. 87; *NLR*, 12–53, pp. 1–3.

remain indoors, the courtesan outside, and the two should never meet. Because of these varieties of heroine the *prakaraṇa* is of three kinds: *śuddha*, with the wife as heroine; *vikṛta*, with the courtesan; and *saṅkīrṇa*, with both. This mixed variety (*saṅkīrṇa*) abounds in rogues.[1]

Samavakāra: In the *samavakāra* class also the contents are borrowed from well known (*prakhyāta*) legends of gods and demons. It is to consist of three acts presenting the three kinds of deception, the three kinds of excitements or the three kinds of love. The first act should last for twelve *nāḍikās*; the second, for four; and the third, for two; a *nāḍikā* being equivalent to 24 minutes. This kind of drama is called *samavakāra* because various themes are scattered about (*samavakīryante*) in it. It may have as many as twelve characters.[2]

Īhāmṛga: In the *īhāmṛga* dramas the story is of a mixed type-party legendary and partly invented. It is divided into four acts with three junctures. The hero and the opponent of the hero may either be human or divine, without restriction; they should be renowned persons and of the type known as self-controlled and vehement, the latter committing improper acts by mistake. There are scenes of wrath but the characters are prevented from dashing into battle by some artifice.[3] The *īhāmṛga*, according to the commentary on the *Daśarūpa*, owes its name to the fact that in it a maiden, who is as difficult to be obtained as a gazelle, is demanded.[4]

Ḍima: In the *ḍima* the subject must be well known and all the styles may be employed in it except the gay style. Its heroes, sixteen in number, should be gods and *gandharvas*, all of them vehement. It contains all the sentiments except the comic and erotic.[5] According to the commentary on the *Daśarūpa*, the name *ḍima* is equivalent to *saṅghāta* (injuring), inasmuch as the heroes always come to blows among themselves.[6] It is also to include incidents such as an earthquake, fall of meteors, an eclipse of the sun or the moon, battle, personal combat, challenge and angry conflict.

Vyāyoga: To the old-popular stage also belongs the *vyāyoga* which

[1]*NS-KM*, XVIII. 93–47; *KSS*, XX. 49–53; *GOS*, XVIII. 45–49; *DR*, III. 39–42; *SD*, VI, *sūtras*, 224–26; *PR*, 'Nāṭakaprakaraṇa', 35, p. 88.

[2]*NS-KM*, XVIII. 109–123a; *KSS*, XX, 65b–81a; *GOS*, XVIII. 62b–77a; *DR*, III. 62b–68a; *SD*, VI, *sūtras* 234–40; *PR*, 'Nāṭakaprakaraṇa' 46–49, pp. 90–91.

[3]C.O. Haas, *The Daśarūpa: A Treatise on Hindu Dramaturgy* by Dhanañjaya, p. 105.

[4]*NS-KM*, XVIII, 123b–28; *KSS*, XX. 81b–86; *GOS*, XVIII. 77b–82; *DR*, III. 72b–75, *PR*, 'Nāṭakaprakaraṇa', 52–53, p. 92.

[5]C.O. Haas, op. cit., pp. 100–1.

[6]*NS-KM*, XVIII. 130–34; *KSS*, XX. 88–92; *GOS*, XVIII. 84–88; *DR*, III. 57–60a, *SD*, VI, *sūtras* 241–44; *PR*, 'Nāṭakaprakaraṇa', 42–44, p. 90.

derives its name from the fact that in it many men disagree with one another (*vyāyujyante*). The plot does not last for more than one day, and there is a lot of fighting and dissension, in which, however, women play no part. It is one-act play.[1]

Aṅka: An *aṅka* or *utsṛṣṭikāṅka* is a one-act drama. The plot in it is usually to be well known, but it may sometimes be otherwise. It relates to one's fall and is to be furnished with male characters other than those who are divine. It abounds in the pathetic sentiment and treats of women's lamentations and despondent utterances at a time after battles and violent fighting have ceased to rage. Small plays inserted into dramas are often designated *aṅkas*.[2]

Prahasana: The *prahasana* (farcical comedy) has been borrowed from the popular stage. The poet takes the plot from everyday life and surrounds it with all kinds of illusions, wordy disputes and dissensions between rogues and worthless persons. There are two kinds of *prahasana*, the pure (*śuddha*) and the mixed (*saṅkīrṇa*). In the *śuddha* type, Śaiva *gurus* (*bhagavat*), Brāhmaṇas and persons belonging to various strata of society appear, each one speaking his special dialect or devoting himself to his special calling. In the *saṅkīrṇa prahasana*, courtesans, slaves, eunuchs, parasites (*viṭa*) and rogues (*dhūrtas*) appear. According to the *Daśarūpa* and the *Sāhityadarpaṇa*, there is yet a third kind of *prahasana*, the distorted type (*vikṛta*), where eunuchs and chamberlains appear as gallants.[3]

Bhāṇa: The *bhāṇa* has also a popular origin. The piece is acted by a single actor who appears as a man of the world and indeed as the principal *viṭa*. For this purpose he describes partly his own adventures and partly those of others. He uses the monologue (*ākāśabhāṣita*) and pretends to see and hear others. He acts, speaks, asks questions and answers on behalf of the imaginary persons. He makes suitable gestures. It is clear that the *bhāṇa* has developed from the pantomime or the musical dance and this explains why *lāsya* is employed in it. It is also a one-act play.[4]

Vīthī: Similar to the *bhāṇa* was the one-act *vīthī*. The *vīthī* was acted by two players. The *Sāhityadarpaṇa* remarks that according to the opinion of any anonymous authority, three actors may also appear, one playing

[1]*NS-KM*, XVIII. 135–138a; *KSS*, XX. 94–97a; *GOS*, XVIII. 90–93a; *DR*, III. 60b–62a; *SD*, VI, *sūtras* 231–33; *PR*, 'Nāṭakaprakaraṇa', 45, p. 90.

[2]*NS-KM*, XVIII. 138b–145; *KSS*, XX. 97b–104; *GOS*, XVIII. 93b–100; *DR*, III. 70b–72a; *SD*, VI, *sūtras* 251–52; *PR*, 'Nāṭakaprakaraṇa', 51, p. 92.

[3]*NS-KM*, XVIII. 146–151a; *KSS*, XX. 106–111a; *GOS*, XVIII. 101–107a; *DR*, III. 54–56; *SD*, VI, *sūtra* 264; *PR*, 'Nāṭakaprakaraṇa', 38–41, p. 89.

[4]*NS-KM*, XVIII. 151b–154; *KSS*, XX. 111b–115a; *GOS*, XVIII. 107b–111a; *DR*, III. 49–51, *SD*, VI, *sūtras* 227–30; *PR*, 'Nāṭakaprakaraṇa', 36–37, p. 89.

the role of a person placed high in life (*uttama*), another of the middle rank (*madhyama*) and a third one of the lowly (*adhama*). In all cases the conversations are with imaginary persons (*ākāśabhāṣita*).[1]

MINOR TYPE (*UPARŪPAKAS*)

While the *rūpakas* are considered to be major forms of drama (*nāṭya*), the *uparūpakas* (dance compositions) as minor forms of drama. In the latter, music and dance predominate and most of them are forms of dance-drama or regular dances (*nṛtyaprabandhas*). Though *vīthī* and *bhāṇa* are said to be major types of drama, yet seeing their nature we can even classify them among the *uparūpakas*. The *rūpakas* delineate a full *rasa vākyārthābhinaya* a full story and all the four *abhinayas* while *uparūpakas* present a *bhāva* or *bhāvas*, *padārthābhinaya*, only a fragment of a story and are lacking in one or more of *abhinayas*, e.g. Kathakali lacks in *vācikābhinaya*. Thus the scope of naturalistic features, *lokadharmī*, is reduced in the *uparūpakas*.

Nāṭikā: Bharata refers at one place in the *Nāṭyaśāstra* to a kind of play called the *nāṭī* or *nāṭikā*. In *nāṭikā* according to the *Daśarūpa*, the plot contains an invented story as in the *prakaraṇa*, but the hero is a renowned king and of the self-controlled and light-hearted type and the principal sentiment is the erotic, with its various characteristics. The heroine is near the hero because of her connection with the harem. Through her hearing and seeing him, a newly awakened passion arises in the hero in regular stages. The hero is apprehensive of the queen. The *nāṭikā* contains all junctures except *vimarśa* and the four sub-divisions of the gay style (*kaiśikī*) which is represented by the four acts.[2]

Troṭaka: The *troṭaka* has five, seven or nine acts. It deals with gods and men and in each act the *vidūṣaka* appears. The tenth *aṅga* of the *garbhasandhi* is called *toṭaka* or *troṭaka* and this word signifies 'confused, excited speech'. We also hear of a dance called *troṭaka*.[3]

Goṣṭhī: The *goṣṭhī* is a one-act drama in which nine or ten ordinary men and five or six women appear.[4] It does not contain lofty discourse but represents love and enjoyments (*kaiśikīvṛtti*) and *mukha, pratimukha*

[1]*NS-KM*, XVIII. 155; *KSS*, XX. 115b–117; *GOS*, XVIII. 111b–113a; *DR*, III. 68b–70a; *SD*, VI, *sūtras*, 253–59; *PR*, 'Nāṭakaprakaraṇa', 50, p. 91.

[2]*NS-KM*, XVIII. 106; *KSS*, XX. 62–63; *GOS*, XVIII. 57; *DR*, III. 43–48; *SD*, VI, *sūtras* 269–72.

[3]*NS-KM*, XIX. 82; *KSS*, XXI. 89; *DR*, I. 40–41; *SD*, VI, *sūtra* 273.

[4]*SD*, VI, *sūtras* 274–75.

and *nirvahaṇa* junctures are employed. It mainly depicts Kṛṣṇa's exploits in killing demons.

Saṭṭaka: The *saṭṭaka* is nothing but a *nāṭikā* entirely written in Prākṛta without *viṣkambhaka* or *praveśaka*. The acts are not called *aṅkas* but *javanikāntaras*. The marvellous sentiment prevails in it. Like the *troṭaka*, the *saṭṭaka* also employs a specified kind of dance.[1]

Nāṭyarāsaka: The *nāṭyarāsaka* is likewise a one-act piece with changing time and rhythm (*bahutālalayasthiti*).[2] The comic and the erotic sentiments are chiefly employed in it. It contains *mukha* and *nirvahaṇa* junctures but some say that *mukha, garbha, vimarśa* and *nirvahaṇa* junctures are found in it. As far as we can judge, it is a kind of ballet and pantomime.

Prasthāna: The *praṣthāna* or *prasthānaka* has two acts. In it the hero and the heroine are slaves or servants and *bhāratīvṛtti* is employed. The Avaloka on the *Daśarūpa* says that the *prasthāna* is a kind of imitative dance (*nṛtyabheda*).[3] Abhinavagupta states that in this piece, imitation of the gait and movement of animals like elephants is found.

Ullāpya: The *ullāpya* is a one-act piece. It is full of fighting and *asragīta*, i.e. background music played from behind the stage with reference to the plot.[4] According to some, it should be in three acts, have four heroines and abound in combats.

Kāvya: The *kāvya* contains one-act and is a comedy (*hāsya*). Different kinds of songs such as *khaṇḍamātrā*, *dvipadikā* and *bhagnatāla* are prescribed for it. There are amorous speeches and is full of the comic and devoid of *ārabhaṭīvṛtti*. According to the Avaloka on the *Daśarūpa*, the *kāvya* is a kind of imitative dance and is an interplay of song and dance.[5] If the whole song-poem is one *rāga*, it is called *kāvya* but if it is found in a variety of *rāgas*, it is *citra-kāvya*. *Gīta-Govinda* belongs to *citra-kāvya* type.

Preṅkhaṇa: In the one-act *preṅkhaṇa*, there is no *sūtradhāra*. The *nāndī* and *prarocavīa* are sung behind the curtain (*nepathe*). It contains *mukha, pratimukha* and *nirvahaṇa* junctures. Angry interlocution and simple combats form its subject.[6]

Rāsaka: The *rāsaka* is a one-act piece in which five persons appear. The *Bhāratī* and *Kaiśikī vṛttis* and a variety of languages and dialects are employed in it. It contains *mukha* and *nirvahaṇa* junctures but some admit *pratimukha* juncture also. The Avaloka on the *Daśarūpa* says that

[1]Ibid., *sūtras* 276–277a.
[2]Ibid., *sūtras* 277b–279.
[3]Ibid., *sūtras* 280–81, on *DR*, I. 8.
[4]Ibid., *sūtras* 282–83.
[5]Ibid., *sūtras* 284–85, Avaloka on *DR*, I. 8.
[6]Ibid., *sūtras* 286–87.

it is a kind of *nṛtya*, with a piece consisting of singing and dancing.[1] It was a show (any kind of irregular stage-performance by a number of persons) performed in the open on streets amidst a gathering of people in quadrangles and temple courtyards.

Nāṭya Rāsaka otherwise called *carcarī* dance is performed in spring and in honour of the king e.g. the one in the beginning of the *Ratnāvalī*.

Saṁlāpaka: The *saṁlāpaka* has three or four acts. In it the hero is heretic and sentiments other than the erotic and the pathetic are employed. Representation of beseiging a city, treachery, combat and confusion are depicted.[2]

Srīgadita: It has one-act. The name *Śrīgadita* is assigned to it because the word *śrī* often comes up and because the goddess *śrī* appears singing and reciting. It chiefly employs Bhāratīvṛtti and contains *mukha, pratimukha* and *nirvahaṇa* junctures. According to the Avaloka and *Daśarūpa*, *śrīgadita* is a kind of mimic dance.[3]

This type of composition depicts love in separation, featuring a lady of the family and her lady friend (*sakhi*). The heroine narrates the qualities of her lover who is attached to her friend and complains against her. The similarity of this theme with that of the *varṇas* occurring in Bharatanāṭya songs is quite visible.

Śilpaka: The *śilpaka* has four acts in which all the *vṛttis* are allowed and the comic and quietistic sentiments are excluded. Descriptions of burning grounds (*śmaśāna*) and similar things are found in it. The hero is a Brāhmaṇa and the secondary hero a low character. Probably it was a kind of pantomime.[4]

Vilāsikā: The species of one-act drama is also called *vināyikā* by some writers. In it erotic sentiment is predominant and *mukha*, *pratimukha* and *nirvahaṇa* junctures are used. It has an inferrior hero. Others include it in *durmallikā*.[5]

Durmallī or *durmallikā*: *Dombi* or *dombālikā* is a type like the nautch, performed by a single *nartakī*. Songs are sung by accompanying singers while the dancer dances. The *durmallī* has four acts. The first act lasts for three *nāḍikās* and the *viṭa* appears in it. The second, in which the *vidūṣaka* appears, lasts for five *nāḍikās*, and the third, with the *pīṭhamarda*, lasts for six *nāḍikās*. The fourth is that in which citizens appear

[1]*SD*, VI, *sūtras* 288–90; Avaloka on *DR*, I. 8.

[2]Ibid., *sūtras* 291–92.

[3]Ibid., *sūtras* 293–95; Avaloka on *DR*, I. 8.

[4]Ibid., *sūtras*, 296–300.

[5]Ibid., *sūtras*, 301–2.

for ten *nāḍikās*. In this form of dramatic piece hero is of an inferior character. *Bhāratī* and *Kaiśikī vṛttis* and junctures except *garbha* are employed.[1]

Prakaraṇikā: The *prakaraṇikā* is a *nāṭikā* with the hero and heroine drawn from the rank of *sārthavāhas*.[2]

Hallīśa: The *hallīśa* has one act, with the *kaiśikīvṛtti* predominating in it. It contains junctures, *mukha* and *nirvahaṇa* only. There is plenty of music and dancing in it.[3] *Hallīśaka* is a circular dance.

Bhāṇikā: The *bhāṇikā* is a one-act piece containing the *mukha* and *nirvahaṇa* junctures only and the *vṛttis bhāratī* and *kaiśikī*, with a heroine of high family and a vulgar hero. According to the Avaloka on the *Daśarūpa*, *bhāṇī* is a kind of musical dance.[4]

The *Abhijñānaśākuntala* and the *Veṇīsaṁhāra* are specimens of *nāṭakas*; the *Mṛcchakaṭika* and the *Mālatīmādhava* of *prakaraṇa*; the *Pāñcarātra* of Bhāsa and the *samudramanthana* in the *rūpakaṣaṭka*, of Samavakara; and *Rukmiṇī-haraṇa* of *Īhāmṛga*. The *Tripuradāha* is a *ḍima*, the Kirātārjunīya, a *vyāyoga* and the *Hāsyacūḍāmaṇī* a *prahasana*. *Bhāṇas* are preserved in the collection known as the *caturbhāṇi*. The *Ratnāvalī* and the *Priyadarśikā* are *nāṭikās* and the *Vikramorvaśīya* is a *torṭaka*. There are not many examples of *uparūpakas* except *nāṭikas* and *troṭakas*.

It is needless to trace the gradual development of *uparūpakas* and *rūpakas*, because the earliest dramas of Bhāsa and Kālidāsa are in a developed form and we can only suppose that there must have been a large number of dramas, major or minor, in earlier times. These dramas do create an impression that they had already reached the highest stage of dramatic perfection.

A *saṭṭaka* was exemplified by Rājaśkhara's *Karpūramañjarī*, a complete Prākṛta counterpart of the *nāṭikā*.

ART OF WRITING A SANSKRIT DRAMA

Drama (*nāṭya*)[5] is the imitating of situations. It is seen and is called *rūpaka* because of the assumption of parts by actors. It is tenfold and is based on the sentiments. The ten chief varieties of drama (*nāṭya*) are: the *nāṭaka*, *prakaraṇa*, *bhāṇa*, *prahasana*, *ḍima*, *vyāyoga*, *samavakara*, *vīthī*, *aṅka*

[1]Ibid., *sūtras*, 303–5.
[2]Ibid., *sūtras*, 306.
[3]Ibid., *sūtras*, 307–8.
[4]Ibid., *sūtras*, 309–12; Avaloka on *DR*, 8, p. 2.
[5]*DR*, I, 7, 8, 11.

(*utsṛṣṭikāṅka*) and the *īhāmṛga*. Moreover there are eighteen minor types of dramas called *uparūpakas*. Classification is done according to subject-matter, hero and sentiment: All the major and minor types of drama are held to resemble the *nāṭaka* in their general character. So *nāṭaka* is only taken into consideration while suggesting the pattern for writing a Sanskrit drama.

The *nāṭaka* should have a celebrated story for its plot such as the famous story of the *Rāmāyaṇa* for instance, that forms the plot of the drama *Rāmacarita* etc. It should be possessed of the five junctures: the *mukha*, *pratimukha*, *garbha*, *vimarśa* and the *upasaṁhṛti*. It should have the qualities of vivacity (i.e. a steady glance, a striking gait and laughing voice), prosperity etc. described. It should contain or represent personages (or characters) contributing, to the various prosperities of the hero i.e. it should have mighty assistants for the hero. It should be abounding with the sentiments of pleasure and pain as also with variety of flavours as are clearly exhibited in the stories of Rāma, Yudhiṣṭhira. It is declared that the *nāṭaka* should consist of from five to ten acts.

The hero should be of the sort characterised high spirited but temperate and firm, powerful and virtuous, being either a royal sage of renowned family such as Duṣyanta, or a god such as the holy Kṛṣṇa or a demigod i.e., one who, though a god, thinks himself a man, such as the divine, Rāmacandra.

The principal flavour must be one only, being either the erotic or the heroic, all other flavours should be subordinate, and the marvellous exhibited in the fulfilment of the end or in the last juncture, viz., the conclusion. There must be four or five important personages engaged in the business of the hero, and the *nāṭaka* must be so composed as to end like a cow's tail. According to one view, each of the acts is to be gradually made shorter than the one preceding while others say that as in a cow's tail some hairs are short and some long, so in the *nāṭaka* some important incidents are to be completed in the first or opening juncture (*mukha-sandhi*), some in the juncture *pratimukha*, and similarly the other incidents are to be distributed among the other junctures, without trying to make them equal, in number, in every juncture.[1]

When the stage-manager (*sūtradhāra*) has gone out after disposing of the preliminaries (*pūrvaraṅga*) at the beginning of the play, another actor entering in like manner i.e. with Viṣṇu-like stride, shall introduce the drama indicating what is to come (*sthāpaka*).

A play dealing with god or one dealing with mortals or commingled,

[1] *SD*, VI. 277.

as either of these, he shall allude to the subject-matter (*vastu*), or the germ (*bīja*) or the opening (*mukha*), or to one of the characters (*pātra*) e.g. '*rāmo mūrdhni nidhāya*' stanza from the *Udāttarā-ghava* of Māyurāja (allusion to subject-matter), *Ratnāvalī*[1] (allusion to the germ), *Abhijñā-naśākuntala*[2] (allusion to a character).

After propitiating the audience with pleasing verses that hint at the subject of the composition, he shall use the eloquent style (*bhāratī*—manner of speaking chiefly in Sanskrit, employed by actors) sometimes arousing expectancy by means of praise of the matter in hand e.g. *Priya-darśikā*.[3] The introduction (*āmukha*) or induction (*prastāvanā*) is that variety of eloquent style in which the stage manager (*sūtradhāra*) addresses an actress (*naṭī*) or an assistant (*mārṣa*) or the jester (*vidūṣaka*) on a matter of his own, in bright conversation, hinting at the matter in progress. Of this there are three forms, the opening of the story: (1) *kathodghāta* in which a character enters taking up a remark of the stage-manager or the meaning of such a remark, which corresponds with some incident connected with himself; (2) the entrance of a character (*pravṛttaka*)—the entering of a person hinted at by the similarity of the nature of the season described; and (3) and particular presentation (*prayogā-tiśaya*)—excess of representation. The stage manager, after hinting at the theme and a character with any one of these elements shall go out at the end of Induction (*prastāvanā*) and then begins the detailed Presentation of the subject-matter.

Hero: Self-controlled and exalted (*dhīrodātta*) endowed with superb characteristics—the incident for which he is renowned should be made the principal subject of a play.

Story: Whatever, in the original story, is at all unsuited to the hero or inconsistent with the sentiment, is to be omitted or arranged in some other way. e.g. treacherous killing of Bālī was omitted by Māyurāja in the *Udāttarāghava*. Same incident was altered by Bhavabhūti in the *Mahāvīracarita*, where Bālī is represented as coming because of his friendship with Rāvaṇa, in order to kill Rāma (who thereupon slays him in self-defence, not treacherously).

Arrangement of Dramatic Structure: After determining upon the beginning and end of the play and after dividing it into five parts, the author should further more break up into small sections the divisions called junctures (*sandhis*). The subject-matter which consists of the five

[1]*Ratnāvalī*, 1–6.

[2]*Śāk*, 1. 5.

[3]1. 3.

elements of the Action[1] corresponding to the five stages[2] is first divided into five junctures[3] and these again into their various sub-divisions numbering 64.[4] Incidents of the episode (*patākā*) employing less junctures and episodical incident (*prakarī*) without any junctures should be done.

At the beginning of the play, one should put an explanatory scene or an Act, according to the appropriateness of the action. (Explanatory scene—*viṣkambhaka*—subject matter required but without sentiment should be represented by such a device). But when the subject-matter proceeds with sentiment right from the start, then there should be at the beginning an act, following up the hints (given) in the introduction.

The five *arthaprakṛtis* "five elements of the plot" which are defined by the ancient theorists as "means of accomplishing the fruit or the ultimate end"[5] occupy a very vital place in the technique of Sanskrit drama. They form an inevitable link in the plot-development. They are *bīja* (seed or germ), *bindu* (recollection of the motive force), *patākā* (episode), *prakarī* (incident) and *kārya* (fruit or denouement).

According to Abhinavagupta the *arthaprakṛtis*[6] are primarily of two types: inanimate and animate. He further subdivides the inanimate into two types: principal (*mukhya*) and subordinate (*gūḍhatra*). The former is *bīja* and the latter *kārya*. The animate also is likewise subdivided into two: principal and subordinate. The former is *bindu*, while the latter is further subdivided into two: (i) *svārthasiddhiyuta* i.e. concerned with the attainment of one's own object. (ii) *parārthasiddhiyuta* i.e. concerned with the accomplishment of the other's object only. Thus the first one is *bindu*, the second one is *patākā* and the third one is *prakarī*.

This division is highly significant. Accordingly *bīja* and *kārya* are inanimate causes of plot-development while *bindu*, *patākā* and *prakarī* are animate causes.

If we look at the nature of *bīja* it is not a concrete thing as it is in the form of an idea or a desire. For instance, in a drama of love the *bīja* will be in the form of springing of desire for each other in the hearts of the hero and the heroine. A drama dominated by the heroic sentiment may have stimulation or provocation to fight as its *bīja*. This clearly indicates that *bīja* naturally constitutes an idea or force which is abstract and not any concrete entity. This is what Abhinavagupta must have in mind when he calls *bīja* as inanimate (*jaḍa* or *acetana*).

[1] *DR*, I, 18. [2] Ibid., 19.
[3] Ibid., 22–23. [4] Ibid., 24–54.
[5] *Sanskrit Drama*, p. 298.
[6] *Abh. Bh*, in *NS*, *GOS*, XIX "*jaḍacetanatayā dīrghakaraṇam*", etc., p. 12.

Kārya is also essentially not different from *bīja* as in fact, it is the *bīja* which ultimately transforms itself into *kārya* or fruit. *Bīja* is the cause and *kārya* is the effect. The effect should obviously be of the same nature as the cause. So *kārya* also ought to be inanimate.

Now turning to the animate group which includes *patākā, prakarī* and *bindu* we find that *paṭākā* and *prakarī* from the episodes and incidents which are often introduced in a drama. These episodes and incidents are directly related to human beings and hence may rightly be regarded as animate causes.

Bindu consists in *a* very important element in a drama in as much as it provides a link or a sort of a rallying point especially in places where very often the main purpose is likely to be lost sight of on account of various disgressions which are essential for sustaining and diversifying the interest in a drama. The purpose in placing *bindu* in the animate group may be explained thus: The essential nature of *bindu* is to afford link, the task being accomplished by the words or the doings of a character, *bindu* is thus inseparably connected with some animate person and hence metaphorically (by *lakṣaṇā*) may be considered as animate. Out of these five *arthaprakṛtis* it is quite evident that *bīja* and *bindu* are principal. *Bīja* is the motive force that goes to develop the action in the play and pervades the entire story. Similarly *bindu* is also highly important inasmuch as it contributes to the effective plot-development. Like *bīja*, *bindu* also pervades the entire story and serves as a link to the digressions in the form of episodes and incidents with the main story. Thus *bīja* and *bindu* are principal (*mukhya*), and *kārya, patākā* and *prakarī* are comparatively less important.

Thus the classification of *arthaprakṛtis* as given by Abhinavagupta and followed by Rāmacandra and Guṇacandra is highly significant enabling as it does to comprehend the place and importance of each of the *arthaprakṛtis* in a drama.

Let us analyse the *Mudrārākṣasa*, a *nāṭaka* from the point of elements (*arthaprakṛtis*) of the drama. It is in seven acts. The hero is Candragupta, possessed of the qualities of the *dhīrodātta nāyaka*. The prevailing sentiment is *vīra* or heroism. The *bīja* (seed) is cast where Cāṇakya gives expression to his design and his firm resolve to make efforts to force Rākṣasa to accept ministerial office under Candragupta and thereby to give stability to his rule. The *bindu* (drop) is the gaining of Rākṣasa's seal-ring by Cāṇakya which enables him to forge a letter to entrap Rākṣasa. The *patākā* in this play is the long dialogue between Rākṣasa and Virādhagupta indicative of the utter failure of the counter-efforts of Rākṣasa and the success of his adversary. The *prakarī* or the fourth element of the plot is, in this play, the report brought by Karabhaka about the sham quarrel between Cāṇakya and his pupil. The *kārya* (final object of the plot) is the final surrender of Rākṣasa with the words '*kā gatiḥ eṣa prahvosmi*'.[1] (i.e., what course is there? I am willing.)

As regards its development a dramatic plot has five stages or conditions called *avasthās*: (1) *ārambha* (setting the enterprise), (2) *yatna* (effort), (3) *prāptyāśā* (prospect of success), (4) *niyatāpti* (some attainment through removal of obstacles not completely), and (5) *phalāgama* (attainment of desired object). A playwright should provide some links (*sandhis*) to connect these *avasthās* with the principal and subordinate parts of the main action (the episodes and incidents). They are five in number, answering to the five *arthaprakṛtis*, each of which they join with its corresponding stage, viz., *mukha, pratimukha, garbha, avamarśa* and *nirvahaṇa* also called *upasaṁhāra*.

The *mukha sandhi* is the combination of the *bīja* and *āraṁbha* wherein the seed is sown, with all its *rasas*. In the *pratimukha* there is the means (*yatna*) to the chief and, which herein sprouts up. In the *garbha* there is attainment and non-attainment of the desired end, implying a further sprouting up of the original *bīja*. There are impediments, but the main plot gains ground under resistance. The *avamarśa sandhi* is that in which the seed attains a more luxuriant growth than in the *garbha*, being accompanied by *niyatāpti* of the end, but whose final result is postponed further off by fresh impediments of various sorts as in the *Abhijñānaśākuntala* (the king's forgetting Śakuntalā after marriage owing to Durvāsā's curse). The *nirvahaṇa* or consummation is the harmonious combination of all the aforesaid parts in the final catastrophe.

The *Mudrārākṣasa* is purely a political drama (*nāṭaka* specie. It has for its theme the winning over of Rākṣasa, the hostile minister of the Nanda dynasty in Magadha, to the side of Candragupta, the new king, set on the throne of the Nandas by Cāṇakya. The unity of action is admirably maintained, all the events being made to converge to one end, viz., the conciliation of Rākṣasa. Well designed at the beginning, vigorously pushed on now under cover, now on open tract, though resisted yet ever advancing straight towards the goal and turning to profit the incidental events on the way, and rapidly developing into complete success, the plot possesses the chief requisites of a piece of art—unity in variety, entire subordination of the individual factors to one idea and plan and the harmonious co-operation of the parts to one crowning effect.

[1]*Mudrārākṣasa*, act VII (Prakāśaṁ) after *śloka* 16.

CHAPTER TEN

Presentation of Plays

ACTUAL PERFORMANCE

The *Nāṭyaśāstra* presupposes the existence of a large number of dramas enacted in very early time such as *The Fall of the Asuras, Churning of Nectar from the Sea* and *Burning of the Three Cities*.[1]

Aśvaghoṣa wrote the *Śāriputraprakaraṇa*, portions of which are available in manuscript. The drama was, it is doubtless, intended for religious edification. Its style is simple. It is probable that it was enacted before the public so as to propagate the Buddhist faith. But it cannot definitely be proved.

The discovery of thirteen dramas written by Bhāsa went a great way to prove the high pitch of perfection the Indian stage had reached in ancient days. One cannot but agree with Winternitz when he says that "Kālidāsa and Bhavabhūti may be greater poets, greater masters of language than the author of these plays, but I know in the whole of Sanskrit literature no drama that could compare as a stage play with any of the thirteen plays ascribed to Bhāsa".[2] Indeed those dramas are the works of a genius who was thoroughly conversant with the technique of the stage and who, it is apparent, knew what actual stage representation is.

The scenes, in which Santuṣṭa, Maitreya, Vasantaka, Śakāra, Sudhākara Madhyama are presented, show that these plays contain sufficient humour essential for a play meant for the stage.

Svapnavāsavadattā (vision of Vāsavadattā) was presented on the stage by the University of Hawaii under the direction of Shanta Gandhi in 1974.[3]

Now coming to the dramas of Kālidāsa, we find that the *Mālavikāgnimitra* was performed at a spring festival in Vidiṣā. The *Vikramorvaśīya* is found in two recensions. The difference between the two versions comes into bold relief in act IV. While the north Indian version contains a series of Apabhraṁśa verses and directions on the method in which they should be sung and represented, all this is

[1]*NS-KM*, I. 22; IV. 1–10; *KSS*, I. 56; IV. 1–11; *GOS*, I. 55b–56a; IV. 1–11.
[2]Winternitz, *Some Problems of Indian Literature*, p. 129.
[3]*Sanskrit Drama in Performance* edited by Baumer and Brandon, 1981.

wanting in the south Indian recension. This *nāṭaka* was also meant for the stage. The *Abhijñānaśākuntala* is the last and the best work of Kālidāsa. It has been translated into almost all the European languages and has been staged in various parts of Europe and India. Even today the *Abhijñānaśākuntala* staged in all parts of India.[1] *Abhijñānaśākuntala* was staged by the University of California at Los Angeles in 1979 as a part of its Asian Performing Arts Summer Institute and Festival.[2]

Further the *Avadānaśataka* says that a *nāṭaka* was performed at the bidding of Krakucchanda in the city of Śobhāvatī by a troupe of actors. The director undertook the role of the Buddha and members of the troupe, the roles of monks.[3]

I-tsing, who visited India in the last quarter of the seventh century, relates that "king Śilāditya versified the story of the Bodhisattva Jīmūtavāhana, who surrendered himself for a *Nāga*. This version was set to music. He had it performed by a band accompanied by dancing and acting, and thus popularised it in his time."[4] This might refer to the *Nāgānanda*.

In the *Kuṭṭanimata* of Dāmodaragupta, actual performance of the first act of the *Ratnāvalī* has been described in detail.[5]

There are plays within plays as in the *Priyadarśikā*. Queen Vāsavadattā desires to have a play represented in which her own meeting with Udayana in Ujjain is represented.[6]

Bhavabhūti is known today for his three plays, the *Mahāvīracarita* (or usually called *Vīracarita*), the *Mālatīmādhava* and the *Uttararāmacarita*. The *Mahāvīracarita* opens with the sentence: "The audience orders that a drama with certain specified qualities be staged. Later it is stated that the poet is a friend of the actors." Similarly in the *Mālatīmādhava*, it is said that the audience order the *sūtradhāra* to stage a drama, possessing certain characteristic qualities and the poet entrusts his work to actors out of his spontaneous friendship with them. In the *Uttararāmacarita*, no reference is made to the poet's friendship with actors and the *sūtradhāra* starts requesting the audience to listen to what he has to say.[7]

[1] *Māl*, prelude I, prose, p. 2; *Vik*, prelude, I, 2, p. 3; *Śāk*, prologue, I, p. 8.

[2] *Sangeet Natak*, Journal of the Sangeet Natak Akademi, 1980 by Philip B. Zarrille.

[3] *Avadānaśataka*, II. 75, pp. 29–30; Keith, *Sanskrit Drama*, p. 43.

[4] I-tsing, *A Record of the Buddhist Religion as Practised in India and the Malay Archipelago (A.D. 671–695)*, trans. by J. Takakusu, pp. 163–64.

[5] *Kuṭṭanīmata*—KM, III. 852–927, pp. 104–10; Bombay edition, 875–928, pp. 336–68.

[6] *PD*, III, pp. 30–43.

[7] *Mahāvīracarita*, I, prologue 2–3 and prose, pp. 6–8; *MM*, prologue prose, pp. 8 and 10; *URC*, prelude, prose, p. 3.

Rājaśekhara's dramas were meant to be acted. He won fame in the court of the Pratihāras of Kānyakubja. In the *Karpūramañjarī*, which is apparently his first drama, produced at the request of his wife, Avantisundarī, and not at the bidding of the king, his patron, he relates that he bore the title of '*Bālakavi*', '*Kavirāja*'. He calls himself the teacher of Nirbhayarāja. Nirbhayarāja was Mahendrapāla of Kanauj whose inscriptions dated from AD 893–907, are available. The *Bālarāmāyaṇa* was produced at his behest, and the unfinished *Bālabhārata* was intended for representation at the court of Mahendrapāla's successor, king Mahipāla, whose inscriptions date from AD 914–17. References are also available for the staging of the *Viddhaśālabhañjikā*, the fourth drama of Rājaśekhara.[1]

In the *Anargharāghava*, the actor declares that he has come to exhibit a drama superior to that played by a rival and asserts that the dearest desire of a player is to satisfy the public and win back the favour he has lost. This also shows that *nāṭkas* were sometimes enacted in a spirit of competition.[2]

There are more popular dramas, the plots of which are loosely constructed out of well-known stories from the *Mahābhārata* or the *purāṇas*. A dramatist has composed speeches in beautiful verses, the rest being left to the actors on the stage to extemporise. The *Mahānāṭaka* is an instance in point.

The *Dūtāṅgada* of Subhaṭa appears to be the oldest among the later shadow plays. It was represented in honour of Kumārapāladeva on 7 March 1243, and certainly on the orders of the Cālukya lord Tribhuvanapāla in Gujarat.[3] It contains only one act and treats the same subject as is contained in the seventh act of the *Mahānāṭaka*. This shows that portions of plays like the *Mahānāṭaka* were represented on the stage in one form or the other.

Kṛṣṇamiśra, author of the *Prabodhacandrodaya*, says in the introduction to his *nāṭaka* that it was produced at the request of Gopāla in the court of king Kīrtivarman whom Gopāla had reinstated in his kingdom, after the Cedi king Karṇa, who had driven him out, had been conquered.[4]

In south India even now Sanskrit plays are acted. Bhāsa's dramas, the *Abhijñānaśākuntala*, the *Nāgānanda*, the *Subhadrā Dhanañjaya*, the *Tapti-svayaṁvara*, the *Mahānāṭaka*, the *Bhagavadajju* and the *Mattavilāsa* are very popular there.

[1]*Kar. M*, I, *prastāvanā*, II. 12, p. 10; *Bālarāmāyaṇa*, prologue, pp. 2, 5; *Bālabhārata*, prologue, p. 2; *Viddhaśālabhañjikā*, prologue, pp. 4–5.

[2]*AR*, prologue prose and 3–4, pp. 6–10.

[3]*Dūtāṅgada* of Subhaṭa, I, p. 2.

[4]*Prabodhacandrodaya*, prologue 3 and prose, pp. 10–14.

Kakṣyā Division: Zones of the stage should be fixed taking into consideration of the type of the theatre-hall. When one is in a particular zone of the stage, it will only change when one walks out of it.[1]

It is from the convention of the zonal division that one is to know whether the place in which the scene has been laid is a house, a city, a garden etc.[2] As modern device of the change of scenes was not available in ancient theatre, the convention of the zonal division on the stage indicated the locality in which different sets of characters performed their different actions.

Zonal division should relate to location: (a) inside, (b) outside, (c) in the middle, (d) to a place far, and (e) to a place near.[3] According to convention of the zonal division, those, who entered the stage earlier, should be considered as being inside a house or a room while those, entering it later, are to be taken as remaining outside it. He who enters the stage with the intention of seeing those entering earlier, should report himself turning to the right.[4]

If a person goes out from inside the house on any business, he is to make his exit with the very same door by which he entered. If after going out he is to re-enter that house, he will make his exit, if necessary, by the door through which the men, who entered later, came. If, per chance, he goes along with latter, re-enters the house with the latter, or by himself alone, another zone should be prescribed for the two. This other zone should be indicated by their order in walking.[5]

Going about on the stage in observing local usages, will be in two ways, viz., by entering from the right and by entering from the left. In the Āvantī and the Dākṣiṇātyā local usage, the going about on the stage will be from the right, and in the Pañcālī and the Ọḍhra-Māgadhī it will be from the left. In case of the Āvantī and the Dakṣiṇātyā local usages the door to be used in entering should be the northern one, while in case of the Pañcālī and Oḍhra Māgadhī local usages the southern door should be used. But in view of the special assembly, place, occasion and expression of meaning, these rules may be combined. In musical plays (*gānakādi*) these rules should be simplified. One should produce them in disregard of the multiplicity of local usages.[6]

The arrangement of the instruments (drums etc.) should be done between the two doors of the tiring room. The direction, which the

[1]*NS*, *KSS*, XIV, 1, 3. [2]Ibid., 4.
[3]Ibid., 8. [4]Ibid., 9, 10.
[5]Ibid., 11–15.
[6]Ibid., 36 and prose and 51, 52, 55.

instruments and the two doors of the tiring room face, should always be considered as the east in course of the dramatic performance.[1]

How a particular character should walk with others, is to be understood by the rank one holds in society. With equals, one should walk side by side, with one's inferiors, one is to walk surrounded by the latter and hand-maids walk in front of their master. The same place if much walked over will be taken as distant land. Nearby lands or lands of medium distance are to be indicated on the same principle. If a person departs on business to a distant place, this is to be indicated by closing the act with his departing and mentioning again this fact in an Introductory scene (*praveśaka*). To indicate the attainment of an object one is to traverse a measure of distance. Incidents in a play occurring for a *kṣaṇa*, a *muhūrta*, a *yāma* and a day are to be accommodated in an act in pursuance of the germ of the play. But a month or a year is to be understood as finished with the end of an act; and events occurring more than one year after, should not be put in an act.[2]

The zones of the stage and allied conventions concerning the movements of men are to be observed in a play in connection with Bhāratavarṣa (India). The *yakṣas*, *guhyakas* and followers of Kuvera, *rākṣasas*, *bhūtas*, *piśācas*, *gandharvas*, *apsarās*, *gaṇas*, *nāgas*, *siddhas* and *brahmarṣis*, *daityas* and *dānavas*, *pitṛs* should be placed in Jambudvīpa where the different mountains of their dwellings exist. According to the various needs of the play, gods and demigods are to move to cities, forests, seas or mountains through the sky, by an aerial car, by their occult power or by different other acts. But while in disguise in a play, gods and demigods are to move on the ground, so that they may be visible like human beings. Their exploits should be represented according to their habits and powers, but their costumes and make-up should be like that of human beings. All the conditions of gods are to be made human. Hence they should not be represented as winkless which they traditionally are. Their states should be first indicated by glances and then represented by bodily gestures and postures.[3]

Experts in dramatic production should put the zonal division on the stage after having knowledge of the four local usages and the two practices (*dharmī*, *lokadharmī* and *Nāṭyadharmī*).[4]

PORTRAYAL OF SENTIMENT (*RASA*)

Sanskrit plays insist on the portrayal of specific sentiments on the stage,

[1] *NS*, *KSS*, XIV. 2.
[2] Ibid., 24, 25.
[3] Ibid., 26–35.
[4] Ibid., 77–79.

and we should, therefore, clearly understand how each of the sentiments was represented. The eight sentiments found in the Sanskrit dramas are the erotic, the comic, the pathetic, the furious, the heroic, the terrific, the repulsive and the marvellous.

The erotic sentiment (*śṛṅgāra rasa*) has two aspects: it may be in union or in separation. In union it should be represented with joy in the eyes and face, smiles and sweet words, equanimity and rejoicing and pleasant movements of the limbs. In separation it should be accompanied by self-disparagement, debility, apprehension, envy, weariness, painful reflection, longing, drowsiness, sleep, dreaming, wakening, sickness, derangement, swoons, stupefaction and death.

The comic sentiment (*hāsya rasa*) is produced by strange dresses, ornaments, impudence, fickleness, roguery, senseless drivels, ridicule, description of people's defects etc., and is represented by the movement of the lips, teeth, nose and cheeks, by fully expanded or contracted glances, perspiration, grimaces and by keeping the hands on the hips.

The pathetic sentiment (*karuṇa rasa*) is represented through tears, lamentation, drying up of the mouth, change of colour, trembling, sighs and loss of memory.

The furious sentiment (*raudra rasa*) is shown in bloodshot eyes, prespiration, frowning, gnashing of teeth and biting of lips, blowing of cheeks, wringing of hands, hurling various weapons, cutting asunder the head, the trunk and the arms.

The heroic sentiment (*vīra rasa*) is represented by calmness, patience, prowess, pride, enthusiasm, influence, masterfulness and by words expressive of challenge.

The terrific sentiment (*bhayānaka rasa*) is represented by the trembling of hands and feet, restless eyes, change of colour and voice, stupefaction, contraction of limbs, palpitation of the heart and by parched lips, palate and throat.

The repulsive sentiment (*bībhatsa rasa*) is represented by contortions of the face and eyes, the covering up of the nose and lowering of the head followed by uncertain steps.

The marvellous sentiment (*adbhuta rasa*) is represented by eyes opened wide, restless glances, horripilation, perspiration, joy, repeated appreciative exclamations, cries of '*ha, ha*' and agitation of fingers or toes.[1]

[1]*NS-KM*, VI. 15; prose, pp. 63–64; 48, prose, pp. 64–67; 68, 72, 74, prose, p. 68; 76; *KSS*, VI. 15, prose, p. 73; 48, prose, pp. 74–77; 68, 72, 74, prose, p. 78; 76, *GOS*, VI. 16, prose, pp. 301–10; 55, prose, pp. 313–14, 318, 320–21, 325, 327; 84, 89, 93, prose, p. 330; 96. See 'English translation of *NS* chapter VI' in the *NS* of Bharata chapter 6 by Subodhacandra Mukerjee.

The *Abhijñānaśākuntala*, the *Uttararāmacarita* and the *Veṇīsaṁhāra* mainly depict the erotic, pathetic and heroic sentiments, respectively. If a *nāṭakamaṇḍalī* wants to have the desired effect upon the public, it should employ actors and actresses wearing appropriate dresses, make-up and acting according to these directions.

SUCCESS

There are certain factors indicative of the success of the presentation of Sanskrit plays. *Siddhi* (success) was of two kinds: *mānuṣī* (human) and *daivikī* (divine) depending on speech, temperament and gestures, and relating to various emotions and sentiments. *Mānuṣī siddhi* (human success) has ten features, and the *daivikī siddhi* (divine success) two; and such features consist mostly of various temperaments expressed vocally (*vāṅmayī*) and physically (*śārīrī*). *Vāṅmayī siddhi* (vocal success) is of eight kinds: *smita* (smile), *ardhahāsya* (ordinary laughter) *atihāsya* (excessive laughter), *sādhukāra* (well done), *ahokāra* (how wonderful), *kaṣṭa* (how pathetic), *pravṛdhanāda* (tumultuous applause) and *avakruṣṭa* (swelling uproar).

A remark or acting through words of double meaning which produces a smile from spectators comes under *smita*. *Ardhahāsya* is a situation in which one laughs ordinarily. If a joker with his intelligence makes a king weep when he is happy or makes him laugh when he is sad, the spectators laugh heartily. This *siddhi* is called *atihāsya siddhi*. When the dialogue is fine, the spectators say '*sādhu*', '*sādhu*' (well done). This is *sādhukāra siddhi*. A wonderful scene or event that evokes from the spectators the spontaneous exclamation, '*aho*' (how wonderful) comes under *ahokāra siddhi*. When a pathetic scene is exquisitely presented the hearts of the spectators melt and they say: *hā kaṣṭam, hā kaṣṭam* (how pathetic). This is *kaṣṭa siddhi*. When a very wonderful scene is presented, spectators not only exclaim '*aho*' (how wonderful) but shout 'bravo, bravo'. This is *pravṛddhanāda siddhi*. When a character rebukes or blames another, spectators also sometimes hate the despised and they give expression to their hatred by swelling uproar. This is *avakruṣṭa* or *sādhikṣepa siddhi*.

Śārīrī siddhi (physical success) is said to occur when the hair of spectators stand on ends and they rise on account of excessive delight or begin to crack their fingers. This *siddhi* is of two kinds. The first kind follows dialogues exciting wonder or enthusiasm and the second, scenes of quarrels and excitement when spectators become one with the *naṭa* (actor). If the conduct of the spectators becomes one with the conduct of the actors representing different emotions and sentiments the play may be pronounced to be a really good play.

The *daivikī siddhi* (divine success) is obtained when an actor identifies himself with a character whom he is impersonating and when there are no obstacles, no noise, no unusual occurrence in the course of the presentation of a play and the auditorium is full. Obstacles may arise from four sources:from the fault of actors, from any enemy, from gods and lastly from portentous calamity. When an actor assumes a role contrary to his nature or acts contrary to the way in which he should play a certain role or recites a speech of another character by mistake, or does not know the use of artificial objects prepared according to the method described in the *āhāryābhinaya*, or other things being good speaks in a peculiar tone, obstacles are said to arise from the fault of the *naṭa*. Sometimes singers and instrumentalists commit mistakes in singing or tuning the instruments, sometimes the dramatist makes mistakes in the production of the *nāṭya*. These obstacles may also be included in the first category. When a play is on, some enemies of the actor raise voices of hatred such as 'fie upon thee' or shout very loudly so that the actor's voice cannot be heard, or clap sharply, or throw cowdung or stones at him and thus create obstacles, it is an attack from the enemies. Obstacles arising from the gods are: strong wind, fire, rains, fear from an elephant or a serpent, stroke of lightning, appearance of ants, insects and ferocious animals. Obstacles resulting from portents (*autpātika*) are those due to earthquake, storm, falling of meteors and the like. The two kinds of obstacles, which cannot be remedied in the representation of a play, are faults due to a natural calamity and the running out of water from the *nāḍikā*.

It is understood that in ancient India time was measured by a water vessel of a particular size with a well-defined tube (*nāḍika*) at its bottom.

The *siddhis* (successes) and *ghātas* (obstacles) are carefully noted before a troupe is declared successful and the proficiency of a *nāṭakamaṇḍalī* conceded. The merits and defects of *nāṭakamaṇḍalīs* were recorded by *siddhilekhakas* (recorders of successes and obstacles). *Siddhilekhakas* were experts in discriminating the *siddhis* (successes) and obstacles and they were not all of the same age. Their experience was wide and varied. It was on the recommendation of *siddhilekhakas*, who observed the performance of every actor of every company and the *siddhis* and obstacles, that the question of offering the *patākā* (banner), a kind of trophy, to a *nāṭakamaṇḍalī* was decided. If there was no agreement among *siddhilekhakas* as to which troupe should receive the *patākā* (banner) the opinion of *prāśmikas* (critics) was taken. *Prāśnikas* were considered arbitrators (*pañca*). If after taking the opinion of *prāśnikas* two *nāṭakamaṇḍalīs* were considered to be equal in merit, the king, whose judgement was final, was asked to award the *patākā* (banner). If, however, the king also could not come to a decision, the *nāṭakamaṇḍalīs* were both awarded *patākās* (banners).[1]

Thus we find that the dramatic art was highly developed in ancient India and that the Sanskrit dramas were actually played on the stage and there was a competition between the *nāṭakamaṇḍalīs* in the successful portrayal of their dramatic art which mainly constituted the depiction of a particular *rasa* (sentiment) in the minds of spectators and there was a sufficiently large number of *siddhilekhakas* and *prāśnikas* who would judge their merits and give the *patākā* (banner) to the victorious *nāṭakamaṇḍalī*.

[1]*NS-KM*, XXVII. 1–41, 62–67; *KSS*, XXVII. 1–44, 73–79.

Fig. 13 : Scene from *Abhijñānaśākuntalam* directed by Mrs Vijaya Mehta (Courtesy: Sangeet Natak Akademi, New Delhi)

Fig. 14: The Sūtradhāra in Bhāsa's *Madhyamavyāyoga*
(Courtesy: National School of Drama and Asian Theatre Institute, New Delhi)

Fig. 15: Scene from *Mudrārākṣasa* directed by B.V. Karanth
(Courtesy: National School of Drama and Asian Theatre Institute, New Delhi)

CHAPTER ELEVEN

National Theatre

IDEA OF A NATIONAL THEATRE

A national theatre is a crying need in free India. With the attainment of independence, attempts are being made to Indianize the administration and education. The feeling is growing that fine arts such as music, dancing, painting and above all dramatic art as presented in the theatre should have state patronage and should be developed on national lines based on the technique observed on the ancient Indian stage but modified according to the needs of the present times. Even if we cannot fail to observe that the modern Indian theatre is profoundly influenced by the west, we must not forget that India had a great national theatre of her own in the past. The modern Indian stage can certainly be remodelled on the lines of the stage in ancient India to suit the native genius of the country.

The development of the stage during the last century incorporating features from the provincial theatres, from the primitive Tamil theatre to the most artistic one of Bengal—reveals a great variety of culture. But a fundamental unity is found in the midst of this great diversity. Mythological heroes have commanded reverence throughout the country. Love of the emotional, the imaginative and the idealistic rather than of the intellectual and the purely realistic is a national trend. Sanskrit plays are performed now mostly in universities, colleges and in the temples of the South.

Sanskrit plays are also staged today but not regularly. In recent years, notable attempts have been made to revive an interest in Sanskrit dramas to meet educational objectives. The Brāhmaṇa Sabhā of Bombay, The Music Academy of Madras, Rabindra Bharati University of Calcutta, Banaras Hindu University of Vārāṇasī, Delhi University, Delhi through organizing the Inter-college Sanskrit drama competitions and other distinguished centres of Sanskrit learning are striving hard to stage Sanskrit plays for maintaining interest in students and entertaining the educated public. In theatre structures (*kuṭṭampalam*) in South, portions of Sanskrit plays are still performed. In Ujjain, Conference on Sanskrit dramatic literature, is held annually and the invited groups stage Kālidāsa's dramas particularly. Sanskrit plays *Mṛcchakaṭika, Madhyamavyāyoga,*

Mattavilāsa, Mālavikāgnimitra, Ūrubhaṅga have been staged by eminent dramatists recently. These productions which contain elements, conventions, techniques and devices relating to more than one traditional theatre, are bound to serve as landmarks on our contemporary theatre scene.

The vision of *Vāsavadattā* i.e. *Svapnavāsavadattā* of Bhāsa was excellently staged at the University of Hawaii, USA in March 1974.

It is clear from the evidences put forward in chapter 10 that Sanskrit plays were actually performed in ancient India and that they can be staged exquisitely even today in the same fashion.

Before giving the suggestions for establishment of a National Theatre in India, we should understand the trends of folk theatre and modern theatres.

The folk theatre of India has flourished along with the classical theatre. Folk art forms are stage performances, which are equally important as classical ones are spontaneous not following a fixed course or a very rigid conventional mode and were performed for the masses mostly in temples and village squares. Through the folk theatre, the thread of our cultural heritage and the identity of the Indian art have been preserved as they symbolise the habits, traditions and the culture prevalent in the villages. Even in the field of aesthetics a special stress is laid on the study of folk art as an important element of society.

Folk art covers a vast field. Not being strict and conventional in its forms it is expressed in variegated facets. There is a specific mode of folk art which takes its origin from the native soil and the specific genius of a group of people. Every state in India possesses its own characteristic folk drama.

The degraded forms of fold amusements including sexual jokes and vulgarity of the medieval period, which consisted in haphazard incidents, loose spectacular representations of the life and deeds of Rāma Kṛṣṇa etc. were the lineal descendants of the most ancient types, *bhāṇa* and *prahasana*. The *bhāṇa* and *prahasana* came into greater prominence after the eleventh century AD when the classical drama declined in importance. In this connection the role of *uparūpakas*, minor forms of drama, which are replete with music and dance, is of great importance as they serve the link or common ground where the classic met the popular.

The details of staging of Indian folk theatre, a popular form of entertainment and employment of costumes, make-up, rituals, brilliant spectacle, its performances are interesting. The cycles of plays such as *Rāmalīlā* based on the *Rāmāyaṇa* in Rāma Nagar, Vārāṇasī and elsewhere;

Rāsalīlā performances in temples throughout India, mainly in Mathura; *Navaṭaṅkī* in different styles in Uttar Pradesh, Punjab and Rajasthan; *Svāṅga* in Haryana and western Uttar Pradesh, *Kaviyālā* in Himachal Pradesh and mostly broadcast from Simla Radio; the provocative gestures and erotic clowning of the famous *tamāśā* women in Maharashtra; the highly stylized *Chhau* mask drama of Seraikella, Bihar; the bewitching heroines portrayed by *Jātrā* male actresses in Bengal, Orissa and eastern part of Bihar; *Aṅkiyā Naṭa* propagating Vaiṣṇava tenets of Assam; *Prahlāda Nāṭaka* and *Pala* singers in Orissa; *Naqāla* of Punjab; *Bhāṇḍa Pathera* or *Jaśna* of Kashmir; *Khyāla, Bhīla Gaurī* and puppet plays of Rajasthan; *Bhavāi* of Gujarat; the stirring tales of heroes, gods and demons of the spirited *Yakṣagāna* dance opera, consisting of music and its ritualistic conventions in Karnataka; *Bhāgavata Melā, Kuchipuḍī* art, *Therukoothu* art, *Kuravanjī* of Tamil Nadu; *Burrakathā* and four varieties of *Vīdhi Nāṭakam* of Andhra; all are facets of this immensely varied art. Certain characteristics are common to the folk drama; the use of outdoor settings and arena stages, the telescoping of time and space by a commentator singer, the integration of music and dance with dramatic action, the emphasis on stylization and significance of colour; the role of the clown who reveals life through mockery and humour; the direct involvement of the audience with the performance.

The folk play is performed in a variety of arena settings: round, parabolical, horizontal, square and multiple set stages with different types of gangways and 'flower paths'. The folk actor uses very few props. He creates palaces, rivers, forests, battle scenes and royal courts by the sorcery of his art.

The modern Indian stage in its process of evolution has absorbed the cultural richness of the classical drama, the folk traditions of the medieval times and above all the influence of the West.[1]

The Madras theatre in fact includes the Tamil, Telugu and Kanarese theatres. The Tamil theatre still indulges in medieval practices—plaintive songs and acrobatic feats—to arouse enthusiasm. The professional companies in Tamil Nadu still take up mostly mythological themes like *Daśāvatāra* and enact them in spectacular settings, dazzling scenery and costumes borrowed from the Parsi stage. Though the actors are not educated and cultured yet they are superb in depicting indigenous arts of Dravidian dances and songs. Rukmini Devi Arundale has established the Kalākṣetra for revival and propagation of Bharata Nāṭyam in Adyar,

[1]R.K. Yajnik, *The Indian Theatre*, for the influence of European Theatres on the Modern Indian stage.

Madras. The Telugu stage is, on the other hand, developing more rapidly, while going through the mythological, bookish, historical and social types of productions. The Kanarese theatre is making remarkable progress in Bangalore and some noteworthy companies are coming into existence in Mysore.

Bengal has a regional theatre which has gone far ahead in realizing the ideal of a true synthesis of old and new forms, without of course, actually reviving the old folk theatre. The Bengali stage is highly artistic. The repertory system is followed. Its distinguishing feature is that all feminine roles are played by women. Not only this, but young girls are also employed to play the roles of boys. The novel use of song and dance is another special feature of the Calcutta stage.

Like the Bengali theatre, the Marathi theatre began mainly under British influence, but soon emancipated itself from it and established a considerable repertoire which is good as literature as well as for purposes of the theatre.

Scenes and costumes in Marathi theatre lack splendour. It concentrates its effort on natural acting and scientific music. It follows the system of alternating serious scenes with light ones. We cannot but remark that gradually religious inspiration is being lost and growth of a secular element based on realistic farce and contemporary satire is noticed in Marathi productions. Further, there we come across an excessive use of songs on the Marathi stage.

The Professional Parsi theatre came into existence in 1890. The Parsis took up both Gujarati drama and stage. They put commercial success based on this formula "give the public what it wants" above artistic achievement. The Parsi theatrical companies did not attach much importance to the realization of sentiment and it was observed that the aggrieved actress sang songs in the midst of tragic scenes. So Parsi theatres, whose sole purpose was to give public what it wanted, however crude it might be, became purposeless as the film and talkies were introduced in India. Now efforts are being made to improve the theatrical activities in Gujarat. The Naṭa Maṇḍala now presents *Menā Gurjarī* and other Gujarati folk plays in a marvellous manner.

Fundamental distinction exists between the Parsi and Gujarati companies on the one hand and the Marathi and Bengali troupes on the other. The Marathi and Bengali companies do not thrust extra comical stuff or farcical songs like the Parsi companies. The Marathi and Bengali plays are artistic wholes.

The Hindi theatre, comparatively a later development, has been influenced by touring Parsi companies and it has been developing in Uttar Pradesh after the appearance of the dramatist, Bharatendu Harish Chandra. During the Muslim rule in India the main places of dramatic shows were temples and monasteries, where on the occasion of festivals people used to entertain themselves mostly by the performance of *Rāmalīlā* and *Kṛṣṇalīlā*. With the disappearance of the Parsi theatre, there was no stage properly speaking in north India. By far the greatest contribution to the Hindi stage has surely been made in recent years by the actor producer, Prithviraj Kapoor, who started his Prithvi Theatre in 1945 in Bombay. Prithviraj did a real service to the country by bringing life and vigour to the Hindi stage. The theatrical performance of Prithviraj were very simple, natural and timely, and had a great appeal to the minds of the cultured.

In spite of the fact that modern Indian theatres have made considerable progress, none of the theatres in India is perfect nor has any of them the capacity of answering the demands for a national theatre. Some of the lines on which the foundation of a national theatre can be based are suggested here below.

There is no lack of inspiration in the remnants of the broken tradition of our theatre. Though India cannot gain much by reviving the formalism of the ancient theatre, it is likely that it will gain enormously by inquiring into its old craft of comedy, tragedy, farce and the morality plays. A constant return to folk feeling, which is rooted in the real life of our people, can bring a genuine sense of reality to the Indian stage today. The *Rāsa*, the *Navaṭaṅkī*, the *Rāmalīlā,* the *Kṛṣṇalīlā*, the enactment of the victory of the Pāṇḍavas over the Kauravas, the Muharram, the Holi as well as the several harvest dance dramas are the apotheosis of the old drama survivals which are an important reservoir of energy, from which a new living art of the theatre can be enriched.

It may be suggested in the present content that alongside with the creation of new plays, effort should be made to stage the plays of Bhāsa, Kālidāsa, Bhavabhūti, Tagore, Prasāda etc., in the different provincial languages and Hindi. The arrangement should be made for translation, abridgment and the modification of their language. Really talented and cultured people, who can understand and appreciate dramatic art and who have genuine love for self-sacrifice, should be asked to make arrangements for the establishment of a national theatre in India.

A fundamental unity must be maintained in the direction of the stagecraft followed in different theatres. This can be done by relying on the ideals and culture of the country as a whole. On the ancient stage, feminine roles were generally played by women, but this tradition was discontinued after the Muslim conquest on account of the insecurity of the times and the purdah system. The practice must again be revived in order to bring realism in character representation. The orthodox Indian notions of propriety and decorum must be maintained. In the *Abhijñānaśākuntala*, Duṣyanta brings his lips close to his beloved but does not kiss on the stage. Western life as reflected in European productions in India was perfectly natural in its place, but when it was foolishly aped on the Indian stage, it was bound to result in demoralizing our theatre. The conventional intrigues between lovers and married women common in many French plays, which are being freely followed on the Indian stage, should altogether be stopped.

Preparation of a correct colour scheme is essential. If colours are prepared according to the *Nāṭyaśāstra* and the *Viṣṇudharmottara* as described in chapter five, a high degree of success in the presentation of plays may be attained. The hair, beards, ornaments and dresses described in books on Sanskrit dramaturgy are fully suitable for plays in any Indian language. Though modern means of representing objects can be used, the ancient Indian methods should not be entirely overlooked.

Construction of the stage cannot be so crude now as in ancient times, but the ancient technique may be revived to suit modern conditions. The use of curtains and wings should be elaborately developed. Music, dancing and histrionics for the modern stage should be employed on the models of ancient India. A great number of songs are generally introduced in all possible contexts—fighting heroes and dying heroines sang on the Parsi stage—and the beauty of native music is marred by the introduction of European tunes to the accompaniment of the Indian musical instruments. This combination of Indian and European music should be discarded once for all. The practice of introducing everywhere European patterns of music, dialogue and dancing should also be abandoned.

Truly Indian National Theatre must be a place, where purely Indian dramas whose object is to produce *rasa* in the minds of the spectators are performed, where a highly developed colour scheme is employed, where the hair, dress and other equipment follow the pattern of Indian life, where classical music, dance and histrionics are encouraged, in short, where the ideals of Indian society are maintained. To achieve the above ideal the Government of India should encourage dramatists, dancers and musicians of worth and reputation. They should also help in the establishment of a truly Indian theatre where all kinds of plays, whether in Sanskrit or any modern Indian language, may be performed according to the requirements of the day. A happy combination of ancient techniques and modern requirements will surely provide a very strong foundation to the National Theatre.

Such efforts have been started by the Government of India by establishing Sangeet Natak Akademi and the National School of Drama and Asian Theatre. An annual all-India festival or experimental plays is presented by Sangeet Natak Akademi. A scheme to support the efforts of young directors in quest of an indigenous theatre idiom, inspired by the traditional/folk theatre of the country, is launched by the Sangeet Natak Akademi in 1984 and from that time onwards several zonal festivals have been organised in South, East, North and West zones in collaboration with the state Sangeet Natak Akademis and departments of culture annually.

The National School of Drama and Asian Theatre Institute was established with the object of promoting a vibrant theatre movement of contemporary relevance and taking root in the traditions and the cultural diversities of the country. Today, the School is linked to comparative theatre development in the world. It teaches talented and enthusiastic young theatre lovers in a scientific method the theory and practice of drama by guiding them to specialize in the art of acting, stage management efficiently and direct the actors and actresses in performing all kinds of roles (*abhinayas*) in the play to its all-round successful finish.

CHAPTER TWELVE

Epilogue

The origin and development of Sanskrit plays have been detailed in this work only as an introduction to the elaborate description of the subjects connected with the actual presentation of plays on the stage. The Sanskrit drama is religious in character and Indian in origin. The Sanskrit drama or *nāṭya* is evolved from *nṛtta* and *nṛtya* and means a representation of situations. Conventions, which were observed on the ancient Indian stage, were peculiar and, as such, had no connection with the practices of the stage prevalent in other countries. The Sanskrit dramas were written partly in Sanskrit and partly in the different Prākṛta dialects. An idealistic atmosphere was maintained on the stage. Not only was a tragic end forbidden, but other important restrictions were also imposed. Propriety and decorum were emphasized and the dramatist had to observe the 'decencies' of the stage. Things as should not be represented and events as extended over a long time, were related in interacts, the so-called *arthopakṣepakas*. A certain set of words was used on the stage for calling the different characters. The unities of time and place were not observed in most of the plays and the unity of action was observed in the sense that everything, which was shown on the stage, gave expression to that sentiment for the depiction of which the drama was written. The entire edifice of the Sanskrit play has got a fundamental religious basis. The play begins and ends with benedictions in the form of *nāndī* and *bharatavākya*. The actual performance of the play was preceded by preliminaries, the essential aim of which was to secure the favour of the gods for its successful representation. Thus Sanskrit drama with its novel peculiarities and having religious tinge in the course of its beginning, development and conclusion, is purely of Indian origin and is national in character.

Various theories have been advanced by European scholars to explain the origin of Sanskrit drama, but they all fall to the ground as they deal with only individual aspects of Indian drama and do not treat it as a whole. The object of Sanskrit plays is to bring satisfaction to the audience by evoking *rasa*, the transcendental pleasure in its mind. It is a novel aspect which is not found in the dramas of any other country. Plays were enacted during fairs, in temples, at general festivals in different seasons, at the pleasure of the poet's patron or before the learned assembly and at village festivals and ceremonies.

The possible correct measurements and the construction of different parts of the theatre are given in this work after interpreting and harmonizing the conflicting texts of the *Nāṭyaśāstra* with the help of the commentary written by Abhinavagupta. It has been shown very carefully that in ancient India plays were enacted in the *saṅgītaśālā* of the palace, in the courtyard of the temple and in open spaces in villages. Spectators in the palace theatre consisted of kings, courtiers, learned Brāhmaṇas and high state officials, in the temple theatre, of devotees, learned Brāhmaṇas and the general public; while public theatres were meant for village people and the public. Bharata's description of theatres, their construction, size and shape, position of the stage, orchestra, auditorium and of elaborate practices to be performed in the form of preliminaries and religious ceremonies continuing for many days in connection with presentation of Sanskrit plays, all support the view that theatres were of a permanent nature, but as we do not find an archaeological evidence of a permanent theatre we cannot be definite about this. It is certain that there were theatres for the general public built on a temporary basis, as the main spectators were the populace in such play-houses. Though nine types, or even eighteen types of theatres can possibly be determined according to space and time, yet, broadly speaking, for practical purposes the theatre was of three types i.e. *vikṛṣṭa* (rectangular), *caturasra* (square) and *tryasra* (triangular). In it the stage was double-storeyed and it was divided into *kakṣyās*. Most probably it did not jut out into the auditorium in any case. The decorations on it were to be in harmony with oriental splendour, colour and brilliance. Regarding the four main pillars in the auditorium it is noteworthy that no pillar was to be in the centre and that the four were dedicated to the four castes, the lowest included. This reveals, curiously enough, a partially democratic basis of Indian theatrical art, four colours being associated with the four castes, white, red, yellow and blue respectively. There were other columns, too, perhaps for those not included in caste system. Galleries were to be formed one behind the other. The seats in the auditorium were to be arranged in the manner of a ladder to ensure visibility. They were to be made of wood and bricks, one and a half feet higher above the ground. There were at least three doors in a theatre, but there could be as many as six doors: two from *nepathyagṛha* leading into *raṅgaśīrṣa*, one in the auditorium, one by which the *naṭa* enters with his wife, two others existing on the southern and northern sides of *raṅgapīṭha*. As to the roof of the theatre it is quite possible that there were theatres of both kinds—open-air theatre where there was no roof and theatre where there was possibly a roof.

Special attention has been given in outlining the methods of arrangement of scenes and preparation of various kinds of stage paraphernalia. It is clearly proved that the curtain was not imported from Greece or elsewhere outside India and was definitely of Indian origin and was called by the name of *yavanikā*, *javanikā* or probably *yamanikā*. There was only one curtain and it was drawn aside and not removed or rolled up. However, there might possibly be minor curtains also which could be used for making divisions i.e. *kakṣyās* on the stage. Something has also been said about Indian painting in order to show that the curtain must have been coloured according to the *rasa* of the drama to be enacted. Four different timings of representation of Sanskrit plays are mentioned which exclude meal timings and midnight hours. However, the plays could be performed at any time by the order of the patron or the king.

Animals and other objects which were exhibited on the stage were either made up of bamboos covered with cloth or made up of cloth alone, and in some cases their motion was shown through mechanical means. Weapons and other hard substances were prepared from shellac, mica, cloth, clay etc., and thus were handy. *Alaṅkāra*, comprising dresses, garlands and ornaments, and *aṅgaracanā*, including colouring of the body, hair and beards, were peculiarly prepared and employed on the stage having due regard to country, age and above all to the main sentiment of the play.

Those objects which could not be represented on the stage by means of materials suggested above due to the absence of the materials or otherwise, were shown through mimicry. The science of histrionics was so much developed and so highly valued as to be taught to high born ladies as an accomplishment. Gestures and movements were not realistic and were often made with reference to imaginary objects. For instance, a gesture might show that a bee was worrying a maiden, though no actual bee would be visible. A particular movement of the body might show a person ascending to or descending from a palace which might not actually be represented on the stage. The code of gestures and movements prescribed for the different limbs was binding on the *naṭa* (actor). The *naṭa* had no room for being original by inventing gestures etc., for that was the business of masters (*ācāryas*) of the art who knew its theory and practice.

In ancient theatre musicians used to sit in *raṅgaśīrṣa* between the two doors leading to *nepathyagṛha*. Music was prevalent on the stage in order to add charm to the special dramatic actions presented on the stage. It may be remarked here with emphasis that the orchestra could be organized on the ancient Indian stage with the help of four kinds of instruments i.e., *tata* (stringed musical instruments), *suṣira* (wind instruments), *avanaddha* (instruments of percussion i.e. drums) and *ghana* which were struck against each other (cymbals, bells and gongs). The reason is obvious because various kinds of instruments, which are required for the performance of a play on the stage, are Indian in origin and because they can serve to strike a particular *rasa* as desired in a particular Sanskrit play and because they have a rich variety and are used even today in orchestral form in south India and at the dances of prominent dancing masters like Uday Shankar and Ram Gopal.

As to who should play a particular role is a very important subject which is treated in this work. In Sanskrit plays, the roles are of three different nature: *anurūpā*, similar to the nature for the person he is acting; *virūpā*, contrary to the nature for the person he is acting; *rūpānusāriṇī* imitative by nature. In *anurūpā* women take the roles of women, and men, those of men. In *virūpā,* the child plays the role of an old man or an old man takes the role of a child. In *rupānusāriṇī*, if a man plays the part of a female character it is called imitative acting. A man's role may be played by a woman according to the desire of the manager, but an old man and a boy should not be made to play the role of the opposite sex. This item of work is very significant and valuable as drama is the true representation of life.

The qualities and usefulness of different *nāṭyācāryas*, who were proficient in one or more branches of art connected with drama, are also described in this work. This shows the height of development of dramatic art in ancient India. Elaborate education in the science of dramatic art was imparted by *naṭyacāryas* to actors and actresses who appeared on the stage. Well-trained *ācāryas* used to prepare different materials required for the stage.

Actors and actresses were despised as low and were denied some of the privileges of the highest caste but, on the other hand, they enjoyed the friendship and love of great kings and eminent dramatists like Bhavabhūti.

The specialities of spectators and judges are described in detail as they are peculiar to Sanskrit plays which were enacted on the stage. This feature of the Sanskrit play significantly proves that dramatic art was critically observed and judged.

Sanskrit plays mostly were intended to be actually presented on the stage. There might be some literary dramas also which were meant for reading only but the number of such dramas was very small. As the aim of every Sanskrit play was to portray one main sentiment, it is carefully shown how different *rasas* were presented on the stage. The system of advertisement, though crude, was in existence. Arrangement was made for the judgment of the dramatic art which was shown on the stage by two or more theatrical companies. *Siddhilekhakas*, whose duty was to write the qualities i.e. different kinds of successes (*siddhis*) and obstacles (*ghatas*), existed in a sufficiently large number. They used to count them, pronounce judgment and offer *patākās* (banners) to the winning party. In case there was a conflict of opinion among the *siddhilekhakas*, reference was made to *prāśnikas*, who were considered to be the best arbitrators in different kinds of dramatic art. If they also failed to give correct opinion about the respective merits of the different companies, the matter was referred to the king whose judgment was final. In case the king also would not able to pronounce his judgment owing to their equal merits, both the parties were offered *patākās*.

Thus we can assert that the art of presenting Sanskrit plays on the stage was developed to high excellence in ancient India and that the standard of the taste of cultured and *sahṛdaya* people was so high that they could appreciate and realize the portrayal of sentiment, the transcendental joy, for the realization of which the drama was specially enacted on the stage.

Even now the Sanskrit dramas like *Mṛcchakaṭika, Svapnavāsavadattā, Mudrārākṣasa, Ratnāvalī* and other popular dramas are staged in Indian and foreign universities and are appreciated by the learned, cultured and critical audiences.

The *bhāṇa* and *prahasana* came into greater prominence after the eleventh century AD when the classical drama declined in importance. The forms of folk amusements, were the lineal descendants of the *bhāṇa* and *prahasana*. Every state in India possesses its own characteristic folk drama. The folk play is performed in a variety of arena settings: round, parabolical, horizontal, square and multiple set stages with different types of gangways and flower paths. The epics and the *purāṇas* formed the main source of inspiration for classical as well as medieval representations, but in one case there was concentration on a special episode and in the other a clumsy reproduction of all the principal incidents of the *Rāmāyaṇa*.

Bhāgavatam in south India, *yātrās* in Bengal, *Liḷita* in Maharashtra, *Bhavaī* in Gujarat, *Rāmalīlā, Rāsalīlā* and *Navaṭaṅkī* of Upper India and devotional romances of Gopichand, Puran and Hakikat in Punjab are the most ancient folk plays prevalent from medieval times.

The modern Indian stage, in its process of evolution, has absorbed the cultural richness of the classical drama, the folk traditions of the medieval times and above all the influence of the West. While understanding the trends prevalent in Madras theatre, the Bengal theatre, the Marathi theatre, the Parsi and Gujarati theatre and the Hindi Theatre, it can be ascertained that the development of the stage in the last century from the primitive Tamil theatre to the most artistic one in Bengal reveals a great variety of culture. The theatrical development in India has got a great setback owing to the popularity of the 'talkies' in Hindi, Marathi, Gujarati and other vernaculars produced by the Indian film companies, which can afford to pay fabulous royalities to actors and actresses and attract them to screen.

Though there is some activity in the field of theatre in different parts of the country, it is highly inadequate. We are making an effort to achieve all round progress, and we should not neglect the theatrical art. The Government of India has shown keen interest in developing and helping the musical, dancing, dramatic and theatrical arts by establishing Sangeet Natak Akademi and the National School of Drama and Asian Theatre. The Government have been encouraging dramatists, dancers, musicians and instrumentalists and have given national awards to Prithviraj Kapoor, Sombhu Mitra and Ebrahim Alkazi, eminent directors and producers; Uday Shankar, Rukmini Devi Arundale, Vyjayantimala Bali, prominent dancers; Omkar Nath Thakur, Mushtaq Hussain Khan, M.S. Subbulakshmi, high class musicians; Bismillah Khan, Ravi Shankar, Rājeswari Padmanabhan, well-known instrumentalists and honoured them in a befitting manner. This is not enough. The Government should invite well known artists to co-ordinate the salient features of the different theatres of the country and evolve a unified national theatre for India.

Bibliography

SANSKRIT DRAMAS AND WORKS ON DRAMATURGY AND OTHER ALLIED TOPICS

Agnipurāṇa by Vedavyāsa, Vangavasi edn., Calcutta, Śaka 1812.

Anargharāghava by Murārī, with commentary of Rucipati, *NSP*, Bombay, 1929.

Abhijñānaśākuntala by Kālidāsa, with notes by M.R. Kale, Bombay, 1934.

Abhidhānaratnamālā (a Sanskrit Vocabulary), ed. with a Sanskrit-English Glossary by Th. Aufrecht, London, 1861.

Abhinayadarpaṇa by Nandikeśvara, ed. by Manomohan Ghosh, *CSS*, no. 5, Calcutta, 1934, rep., Calcutta, 1957.

Abhinavabhāratī by Abhinavagupta, in manuscript form copied from MSS. Government Oriental Manuscript Library, Madras contained in Sarasvati Bhawan Library, Sanskrit Government College, Varanasi. Also available in *Nāṭyaśāstra* published in *GOS*, vol. I, 1926; vol. II, 1934; vol. III, 1954; vol. IV, 1964 and also exist in *Hindi Abhinavabhāratī,* ed. by Nagendra, Delhi, 1960.

Amarakośa, by Amara Siṁha, edited with Hindi notes by Manna Lal, Varanasi, 1937.

Arthaśāstra by Kauṭilya with Śrīmūla commentary of T. Gaṇapati Śāstrī, 1–1, II; II–III–VII. *TSS*, nos. LXXIX and LXXX, Trivandrum, 1924.

Avadānaśataka, ed. by J.S. Speyer II, 8–10, St. Petersburg, 1909.

Āryamañjuśrīmūla-kalpa, ed. by T. Gaṇapati Śāstrī, *TSS*, no. LXX, Trivandrum, 1920.

Uttararāmacarita by Bhavabhūti, ed. by M.R. Kale, Bombay, 1934.

Ṛgveda Saṁhitā, ed. by Max Müller, Oxford, 1973.

Karṇasundarī by Bilhaṇa, ed. by Durgā Prasāda and Kāśīnātha Paṇḍuraṅga Parab, *KM*, no. 7, *NSP*, Bombay, 1895.

Karpūramañjarī by Rājaśekhara, with commentary of Vāsudeva, *KM*, no. 4, *NSP*, Bombay, 1927.

Kāmasūtra by Vātsyāyana with Jaimaṅgala commentary, Varanasi.

Kāvyaprakāśa by Mammaṭa with commentary by Vāmanācārya, Poona, 1933.

Kāvyamīmāṁsā by Rājaśekhara, ed. by C.D. Dulal and R.A. Sastry, *GOS*, Baroda, 1934.

Kuṭṭanimata by Dāmodargupta in *KM* series, pt. III, *NSP*, Bombay, 1887 and also ed. by T.M. Tripathi, Bombay, 1924.

Kundamālā by Diṅnāga, with notes by Vedavyāsa, Lahore, 1932.

Kauṣītaki Brāhmaṇa, Von. B. Lindner, I, Text, Jena, 1987.

Caturbhāni, Śivapurī, Patna, 1922. (It contains the following four dramas: *Padmaprābṛtak* by Śudraka, *Dhūrtaviṭasaṁvādą* by Īśvaradatta, *Ubhayābhisārikā* by Vararuci and *Pādatāḍitaka* by Śyamilaka.)

Daśarūpa by Dhanañjaya, with commentary of Dhanika, *NSP*, Bombay, 1928.

Digghanikāya, ed. by T.W. Rhys Davids and J. Estlin Carpenter, vol. I, *PTS*, London, 1890.

Dūtāṅgada by Subhaṭa, *KM*, no. 40, *NSP*, Bombay, 1922.

Dhvanyāloka by Ānandavardhanācārya, *KSS*, Alaṅkāra Section, no. 5, Varanasi, 1940.

Nāṭakalakṣaṇaratnakośa by Sāgaranandin, ed. by Mykes Dillon, vol. I, Text, London, 1937.

Nāṭyadarpaṇa by Rāmacandra and Guṇacandra, with their own commentary, *GOS*, Baroda, 1929.

Nāṭyaśāstra by Bharata (editions of *Nāṭyaśāstra*: *KM*, no. 42, rep., Delhi, 1983; *KSS*, no. 60, Varanasi, 1929; *GOS*, vol. I, no. 36, Baroda, 1926 vol. II, no. 68, Baroda, 1934; vol. III, no. 124, Baroda, 1954; vol. IV, no. 145, Baroda, 1964. Chs. I–XIV edition by J. Grosset, XVI–XVII by P. Ragnaud in his *Rhetorique Sanskrit*, XIV, XVIII–XX by F. Hall in his edition of *Daśarūpa*); *Bhāratīya Nāṭyaśāstra* written by G.V Ketakar in Marathi, Poona, 1928.

Nirukta of Yāska, with commentary by Durgācārya, Bombay, vs 1982.

Pañcadaśī by Vidyāraṇyasvāmī, with English translation, Bombay, 1912.

Pāravatīpariṇaya by Śrī Bāṇabhaṭṭa, *NSP*, Bombay, 1923.

Pratāparudrīya by Vidyānātha, with Ratnapana of Kumārasvāmin, ed. by Chandra Shekhar Shastri, Madras, 1914.

Pratijñāyaugandharāyaṇa by Bhāsa, commentary by Ramachandra Shukla, Allahabad, 1957.

Prabodhacandrodaya by Kṛṣṇamiśra, with Candrikā and Prakāśa commentaries, *NSP*, Bombay, 1904.

Priyadarśikā by Śrī Harṣa ed. by Jīvānanda Vidyāsāgara, Calcutta, 1874.

Bālabhārata by Rājaśekhara, ed. by Durgā Prasāda and K.P. Parab, *KM*, no. 4, *NSP*, Bombay, 1887.

Bālarāmāyaṇa by Rājaśekhara, with Jīvānanda commentary, Calcutta, 1884.

Bṛhaddeśī of Mataṅgamuni, ed. by K. Sambaśiva Śāstrī, *TSS*, no. XCIX, Trivandrum, 1928.

Bhagvadbhaktirasāyana of Madhusūdana Sarasvatī, with Sanskrit ṭīkā by Goswami Damodara Shastri, Kāśī, 1984.

Bhāvaprakāśana of Śāradātanaya, *GOS*, no. 45, Baroda, 1930.

Bhāsanāṭakacakra, ed. by C.R. Devadhar, *POS*, no. 54, Poona, 1937. (It contains the following 13 dramas of Bhāsa: *Svapnavāsavadattā, Pratijñāyaugandharāyana, Avimāraka, Cārudattā, Pratimā, Abhiṣeka, Pañcarātra, Madhyamavyāyoga, Dūtavākya, Dūtaghaṭotakaca, Karṇabhāra, Urubhaṅga* and *Bālacarita*.)

Manusmṛti by Manu, with commentary by Kullūkabhaṭṭa, and ed. by Vāsudeva, *NSP*, Bombay, 1902.

Mahābhārata, I, with commentary of Nīlakaṇṭha, Poona, 1929, rep., New Delhi, 1979; III and V, ed. by V.S. Sukthankar, Poona, 1937, 1941.

Mahābhāṣya of Patañjali, ed. by F. Kielhorn, Bombay, 1883.

Mahāvīracarita of Bhavabhūti, with commentary of Vīrarāghava, ed. by T.R. Ratnam Aiyar, *NSP*, Bombay, 1901.

Mānasāra Śilpaśāstra, ed. by P.K. Acharya, London, 1933, rep., New Delhi, 1979.

Mārkaṇḍeyapurāṇa of Vedavyāsa, Calcutta, Śaka 1812.

Mālatīmādhava of Bhavabhūti, ed. by M.R. Kale, Bombay, 1928.

Mālvikāgnimitra of Kālidāsa, with commentary of Kaṭayavema, *NSP*, Bombay, 1930.

Mudrārākṣasa of Viśākhadatta, ed. by Śaradaranjan Ray, Calcutta, 1929.

Mṛcchakaṭika of Śūdraka, with commentary of Pṛthvīdhara and notes by M.R. Kale, Bombay, 1924.

Meghadūta of Kālidāsa, with commentary by Mallinātha, ed. by Kāśīnātha, sec. edn., Poona, 1916.

Yājñavalkyasmṛti, Poona, vol. I, 1903; vol. II, 1904.

Raghuvaṁśa of Kālidāsa, VI–X sargas, *KSS*, no. 84, Banaras, 1987.

Ratnāvalī of Śrī Harṣadeva, with notes by M.R. Kale, Bombay, 1925.

Rasārṇavasudhākara of Siṅghabhūpāla, ed. by T. Gaṇapati Śāstrī, *TSS*, no. 1, Trivandrum, 1916.

Rāgavibodha of Somanātha, with Sanskrit commentary, Lahore, Śaka 1817.

Rāmāyaṇa of Vālmīki, with commentary, *NSP*, Bombay, 1824.

Rūpakaṣaṭakam, a collection of six dramas of Vatsarāja, ed. by D. Dalal, *GOS*, no. VIII, Baroda, 1918. (It contains the following six dramas: *Kirātārjunīyavyāyoga* (pp. 1–22), *Karpūracaritabhāṇa* (pp. 23–36), *Rukmiṇīharaṇa Ihāmṛga* (pp. 37–44), *Tripuradāhaḍima* (pp. 75–119), *Hāsyacūḍāmaṇi Prahasana* (pp. 118–48), *Samudramanthana Samavakāra* (pp. 148–92).)

Vikramorvaśīya of Kālidāsa, with Kaṭayavema's commentary and ed. by Cārudeva Śāstrī, Lahore, 1929.

Viddhaśālabhañjikā of Rājaśekhara, with commentary of Jīvānanda, Calcutta, 1873 and with Sanskrit ṭīkā and preface by B.R. Arte and K.R. Godbole, Poona, 1886.

Viṣṇudharmottarapurāṇa, ed. by Madhusūdana Mādhava Prasāda, Bombay.

Viṣṇusmṛti of Viṣṇu, ed. by Julius Jolly, Calcutta, 1881.

Śilparatna of Śrīkumāra, ed. by T. Gaṇapati Śāstrī, *TSS*, no. LXXV, 1922.

Śuklayajurveda Saṁhitā (Vājasaneyī Saṁhitā), with Mantrabhāṣya of Uvaṭācārya and Vedadīpabhāṣya of Mahidhare, ed. by Wasudeo Lakṣmaṇa Śāstrī Pansikar, *NSP*, Bombay, 1929.

Śrīmadbhāgavata Purāṇa, in two khaṇḍas, with Bālabodhinī bhāṣaṭīkā by Govindadāsa Vyāsa 'Vinīta', Saṁvat 1991.

Saṅgītadāmodara of Śrīśubhaṅkara, Calcutta, 1960.

Saṅgītapārijāta of Ahobala Paṇḍita, ed. by Kalindaji, Hatharas, 1941.

Saṅgīta-Makaranda of Nārada, ed. by Maṅgeśa Rāma Kṛṣṇa Telaṅg, *GOS*, no. XVI, Baroda, 1920.

Saṅgītaratnākara of Śārṅgadeva, with Kallinātha commentary I and II by Maṅgeśa Rāma Kṛṣṇa Telaṅg, Poona, 1896, 1897.

Saṅgītasamayasāra of Saṅgītakāra Śrī Pārśvadeva, ed. by T. Gaṇapati Śāstrī, *TSS*, no. LXXXVII, Trivandrum, 1925.

Sāhityadarpaṇa of Viśvanātha, with commentary by Haridāsa Siddhāntavāgīśabhaṭṭa, Nakipur, Vaṅgābda, 1335; *Sāhityadarpaṇa* of Viśvanātha with Vimlaviyakhyaya, Varanasi, 1956.

Siddhānta Kaumudī of Bhaṭṭoji Dīkṣita, with Tattvabodhinī, Subodhinī, Candrāloka commentaries, *SVP*, Bombay, 1926.

Subhāṣitatriśati by Bhartṛhri, ed. by Vāsudeva, Bombay, 1914.

Hanumannāṭaka or *Mahānāṭaka*, with bhāṣaṭīkā, Bombay, 1924.

Harivaṁśa, with commentary, Bombay, 1895 & 1897; *BORI*, Poona, 1969.

Harṣacarita of Bāṇabhaṭṭa, ed. by P.V. Kane, Bombay, 1918.

ARTICLES AND WORKS IN ENGLISH ON INDIAN STAGE AND KINDRED TOPICS CONSULTED AND CITED ONLY WHERE NECESSARY

Acharya, P.K., *A Dictionary of Indian Architecture*, London, 1927, rep., New Delhi, 1979.

———, 'The Play-house of the Hindu Period', *Dr. S.K. Aiyaṇgar Commemoration Volume,* 1936.

Agarwala, V.S., 'Study of Rājaghāṭa Toys', *Nāgarīpracāriṇī Patrikā*, Kārtika Saṁvat, 1977.

Ahuja, R.L., *The Theory of Drama in Ancient India*, Ambala Cantt., 1964.

Ajñāta, *Bhāratīya Raṅgamañca Kā Vivecanātmaka Itihāsa*, Kanpur, 1978.

Ambrose, Kay, *Classical Dances and Costumes of India*, New Delhi, 1980.

Anand, Mulkraj, *The Indian Theatre*, New York, 1951.

Anand, Uma, *The Romance of Theatre*, New Delhi, 1969.

Apte, V.S., *The Practical Sanskrit-English Dictionary*, Bombay, 1925

Banerji, B.N., *Bengali State*, Calcutta, 1943.

Banerji, Projesh, *Naṭarāja—The Dancing God*, New Delhi, 1985.

Basu, B.N., *Kāmasūtra—The Hindu Art of Love*, Calcutta, 1955.

Baumer, Rachel Van M. and Brandon, James R., *Sanskrit Drama in Performance*, Honolulu, 1981.

Bellman, Willard F., *Scene Design, Stage Lighting, Sound, Costume and Make-up: A Scenegraphic Approach*, New York, 1983.

Benegal, Som, *A Panorama of Theatre in India*, Bombay, 1968.

———, General Editor, *Puppet Theatre Around the World*, New Delhi, 1960.

Bhat, G.K., *Theatric Aspects of Sanskrit Drama*, Poona, 1983.

———, *Tragedy and Sanskrit Drama*, Bombay, 1974.

———, *Nāṭyamañjarī Saurabha—Sanskrit Dramatic Theory*, Poona, 1981.

Bhattacharya, Biśwanath, *Sanskrit Drama and Dramaturgy*, Varanasi, 1974.

Bhattacharya, H., *Origin and Development of the Assamese Drama and the Stage*, Gauhati, 1964.

Bloch, T., *Caves and Inscriptions in Ramagarh Hills*, Archaeological Survey of India, Annual Report, 1903–4.

Bose, P.N., *Principles of Indian Śilpaśāstra*, Lahore, 1926.

Bowers, Faubion, *Theatre in the East: A Survey of Asian Dance and Drama*, New York, 1956.

Brandon, James R., *Theatre in Southeast Asia*, Cambridge, Mass., 1974.

———, *Guide to Theatre in Asia*, Honolulu, 1976.

Brooks, Eleanor, *Puppets*, Allahabad, 1956.

Brown, Percy, *Indian Architecture: Buddhist and Hindu*, Bombay, 1956.

———, *Indian Painting*, Calcutta, 1953.

Chakravarti, Cintaharan, articles on 'Saṭṭaka' amd 'Bharata Vākya', *IHQ*, vol. VII, 1931 and vol. VI, 1930.

Chattopadhyaya, Siddheśwar, *Nāṭaka Lakṣaṇa-ratnakośa*, Calcuttta, 1974.

Clements, E., *Indian Music*, London, 1913.

Contractor, Meher R., *Creative Drama and Puppetry on Education*, New Delhi, 1984.

Coomaraswamy, A.K., *The Dance of Śiva*, New Delhi, 1982.

———, 'Hindu Theatre', *IHQ*, vol. IX, Calcutta, 1933.

——— and Kristnayya, D.G., *The Mirror of Gesture*, translation of *Abhinayadarpaṇa*, New Delhi, 1986.

Dalal, Minakshi L., *Conflict in Sanskrit Drama*, Bombay, 1973.

Danielou, Alain, *Northern Indian Music*, London, 1949.

Dasgupta, H.N., *The Indian Stage*, vols. I & II, Calcutta, 1934–38.

De, S.K., *Studies in the History of Sanskrit Poetics*, vol. II, Dacca, 1925.

———, 'The Curtain in Ancient Indian Theatre', *Bhāratīya Vidyā*, vol. IX, 1948.

Dean, Alexander, *Fundamentals of Play Directing*, New York, 1959.

Deva, B.C., *Musical Instruments*, New Delhi, 1977.

Devī, Rāginī, *Dance Dialects of India*, Delhi, 1972.

Dodd, Nigel and Hickson, Winifred, *Drama and Theatre in Education*, London, 1971.

Dayal, Jai, *Prithviraja and His Prithvi Theatres*, Bombay, 1950.

Gangoly, O.C. *Rāgas and Rāginīs*, Bombay, 1948.

Gargi, Balwant, *Theatre in India*, New York, 1962.

Gassner, John, *Masters of the Drama*, New York, 1954.

Ghosh, Manomohan, 'Problems of the Nāṭyaśāstra', *IHQ*, vol. VI, Calcutta, 1930.

———, 'Hindu Theatre', *IHQ*, vol. IX, Calcutta, 1933.

———, *Contribution to the History of the Hindu Drama its Origin, Development and Diffusion*, Calcutta, 1958.

———, *Nāṭyaśāstra Ascribed to Bharata*, vol. I (chaps. I–XXVII), Calcutta, 1951.

———, *Nāṭyaśāstra Ascribed to Bharata*, vol. II (chaps. XXVIII–XXXVI), Calcutta, 1961.

Gode, P.K., Articles on The Bharata-Ādi-Bharata Problem and the MS of Ādi-Bharata in the Government Oriental Library, Mysore, *ABORI*, Poona, vol. XIII, 1931–32.

Gnoli, Raniero, *The Aesthetic Experience According to Abhinavagupta*, Varanasi, 1968.

Gopinath Natanalanidhi, *Abhinaya Prakāśikā*, Madras, 1957.
Gupta, Rākeśa, *Studies in Nāyaka-Nāyikā-Bheda*, Aligarh, 1967.
Gupta, Somanātha, *Parsi Theatre, Origin and Development*, Allahabad, 1981.
Haigh, Arthur E., *The Attic Theatre*, Oxford, 1889 & 1907.
Hartnoll, Phyllis, *A Concise History of the Theatre*, London, 1968.
Hass, C.O., *Daśarūpa*, A Treatise on Hindy Dramaturgy by Dhanañjaya, New York, 1912.
Hatlen, Theodore W., *Orientation to the Theatre*, New York, 1972.
I-Tsing, *A Record of Buddhistic Religion as Practised in India and the Malay Archipelago* (AD 671–95), translated by J. Takakusu, New Delhi, 1982.
Jha, B., 'Treatment of Poetic Defects in Bharata's Nāṭyaśāstra', *JBRS*, vol. ILV, pts. I–IV, March-Dec., 1959.
Jha, Gangānātha, *Kāvyaprakāśa* of Mammaṭa, Allahabad, 1925.
Jones, Clifford Reis, *The Wondrous Crest Jewel in Performance: Āścaryacūḍāmaṇi* of Śaktibhadra, Delhi, 1984.
Joshi, V.P., *The Complete Works of Kālidāsa*, Bombay, 1976.
Kale, K. Narayan, *Theatre in Maharashtra*, New Delhi, 1967.
Kale, Pramod, *The Theatre Universe*, Bombay, 1974.
Kane, P.V., *Introduction to Sāhityadarpaṇa*: *The History of the Alankāra Literature*, Bombay, 1923.
Keith, A.B., *The Sanskrit Drama in its Origin, Development, Theory and Practice*, London, 1964.
Kramrisch, Stella, *Viṣṇudharmottara*, pt. III. Treatise on Indian Painting and Image-making, Calcutta, 1928.
Krishnadas, Rai, *Bhārata Kī Citrakalā*, Prayag, vs 2007.
Krishnaswamy, S., *Musical Instruments of India*, New Delhi, 1971.
Kothari, Sunil, ed., *Bharata Nāṭyam Indian Classical Dance Art*, Bombay, 1982.
Lévi, Sylvain, *Le Theatre Indien*, Paris, 1890; *The Theatre of India*, translated from French into English by Narayan Mukherji, 2 vols., Calcutta, 1978.
Lüders, Heinrich, Sitzungheristic der Konigl Akademic der Wissenchaften Zu Berlin, 1916.
Macdonell, A.A., *A History of Sanskrit Literature*, London, 1905.
Macgowan, Kenneth and Melnitz, William, *The Living Stage*, Englewood Cliffs, N.J., 1955.
Mankad, D.R., *Types of Sanskrit Drama*, Karachi, 1930.
———, 'Hindu Theatre', *IHQ*, Calcutta, vol. VIII, 1932; vol. IX, 1933.

———, *Ancient Indian Theatre*, Vidyanagar, 1950.
Mehta, G.C., *Bibliography of Stageable Plays in Indian Languages*, New Delhi, 1963.
Mielziner, Jo, *The Shapes of Our Theatre*, New York, 1970.
Miśra, Hari Ram, *The Theory of Rasa in Sanskrit Drama*, Chattarpur, 1964.
Monier-Williams, M., *A Sanskrit-English Dictionary*, New Delhi, 1988.
Mukherji, S.C., *The Nāṭyaśāstra* of Bharata, chapter VI edited with an English translation of Rasādhyāya, Paris, 1926.
Mukherji, Sushil Kumar, *The Story of the Calcutta Theatre*, Calcutta, 1753.
Nadkarni, Dhyaneshwar, *New Directions in the Marathi Theatre*, New Delhi, 1967.
Naidu, B.V. Narayanaswami, Naidu, P. Srinivasulu and Pantulu, O.V. Rangayya, *Tāṇḍavalakṣaṇa: The Fundamentals of Ancient Hindu Dancing*, New Delhi, 1971.
Nicoll, Allardyce, *The Development of the Theatre*. A study of theatrical art from the beginnings to the present day, New York, 1966.
Nijenhuis, E. Te, *Dattilam: A Compendium of Ancient Indian Music*, Leiden, 1970.
Panchal, Goverdhan, *Kuṭṭampalam and Kuṭiyaṭṭam*, New Delhi, 1984.
Pandey, K.C., *Comparative Aesthetics*, vol. I, *Indian Aesthetics*, vol. II, *Western Aesthetics*, Varanasi, 1959–72.
Pischel, Richard, *Die Heimat des Pattenspiels*, 1902.
Pischaroti, K.R., 'The Ancient Indian Theatre', *Rajah Sir Annamalai Chettiar Commemoration Volume*, 1941.
Pusalker, A.D., 'Critical Study of the Works of Bhāsa', *JUB*, Bombay, vol. II, pt. VI, May, 1934.
Raghavan, V., *The Number of Rasas*, Madras, 1940.
———, *Some Concepts of Alankāraśāstra*, Madras, 1942.
———, 'Ancient Indian Theatre Architecture', *Journal Triveni*, Madras, 1932–35.
———, 'Nāṭyadharmī and Lokadharmī', *JOR*, Madras, vols. VII & VIII, 1933 & 1934.
———, 'Hindu Theatre', *IHQ*, vol. IX, Calcutta, 1933.
———, Bhoja's *Śṛṅgāra Prakāśa*, Madras, 1978.
———, 'Yantras or Mechanical Contrivances in Ancient India', Transaction no. 10. The Indian Institute of Culture, Bangalore, 1956.
———, *Abhinavagupta and His Works*, Varanasi, 1980.
Rangacharya, Adya, *Drama in Sanskrit Literature*, Bombay, 1867.
———, *The Indian Theatre*, New Delhi, 1980.
Ranganath, H.K., *The Karnatak Theatre*, Dharwar, 1960.

Raha, Kironmoy, *Bengali Theatre*, New Delhi, 1980.

Rao, Subha and Madhas, Achok, *A Note on Ancient Indian Theatre*, New Delhi, 1959–60.

Ridgeway, William, *The Dramas and Dramatic Dances of Non-European Races*, Cambridge, 1915.

———, 'Cult of the Dead' in *JRAS*, 1916.

Sankaran, A., *Some Aspects of Literary Criticism in Sanskrit or the Theories of Rasa and Dhvani*, New Delhi, 1973.

Satyavrat, Usha, *Sanskrit Dramas of the Twentieth Century*, vol. I, Delhi, 1971.

Schuyler, Montgomery, *Bibliography of the Sanskrit Drama*, with an introductory sketch of the Dramatic Literature of India, rep., New Delhi, 1977.

Scott, A.C., *The Theatre in Asia*, London, 1972.

Schechner, Richard, *Environmental Theatre*, New York, 1973.

Sethi, Surjit Singh, *The Theatre of Ibsenites in Punjab*, Patiala, 1976.

Shastri, Harprasad, "The Origin of Indian Drama" in *Journal and Proceedings of the Asiatic Society of Bengal*, NS, vol. V, 1909.

Shastri, K. Vasudeva, *The Science of Music*, Tanjore, 1954.

Shastri, K. Sambasiva, *Balaramabharata*, *TSS*, 1955.

Singhal, R.L., *Aristotle and Bharata*, Hoshiarpur, 1977.

Sircar, Badal, *The Third Theatre*, Calcutta, 1983.

Southern, Richard, *The Seven Ages of the Theatre*, London, 1973.

Sudhākalaśa Vacanācārya, *Sangītopaniṣat-Saroddhara*, A work on Indian music and dancing, Baroda, 1961.

Tagore, S.M., *The Eight Principal Rasas of the Hindus*, with Murthi and Vrindaka, Calcutta, 1880.

Tarlekar, G.H. and Nalini, *Musical Instruments in Indian Sculpture*, Pune, 1972.

Thakurta, Guha P., *The Bengali Drama, its Origin and Development*, London, 1930.

Trivedi, K.M., *The Nāṭyadarpaṇa* by Rāmacandra and Gunacandra. A Critical Study, Ahmedabad, 1966.

Varadpande, M.L., *Ancient Indian and Indo-Greek Theatre*, New Delhi, 1981.

Vātsyāyana, Kapila, *Indian Classical Dance*, New Delhi, 1974.

———, *Traditional Indian Theatre*, New Delhi, 1980.

———, *The Square and the Circle of the Indian Arts*, New Delhi, 1983.

Venkatacharya, T., *The Daśarūpaka* of Dhanañjaya with Avaloka, Madras, 1969.

Warren, C. Lounsbury, *Theatre Backstage from A to Z*, Seattle, 1972.

Watve, G.M., *The Marathi Theatre 1843 to 1960*, Bombay, 1961.
Wilson, H.H., *Select Specimens of the Theatre of the Hindus*, vol. I, London, 1827.
———, *On the Dramatic System of the Hindus*, Calcutta, 1971.
Windisch, E., *Der Griechische Einfluso in Indischen Drama*, 1882.
Winternitz, M., *Some Problems of Indian Literature*, New Delhi, 1978.
Woolner, A.C. and Sarup, Lakshman, *Thirteen Trivandrum Plays* Attributed to Bhāsa, London, vol. I, 1930, and vol. II, 1931.
Yajñik, R.K., *The Indian Theatre*, London, 1933.

Index

SANSKRIT DRAMATIC TERMS, WORKS AND DRAMATISTS

aṁśa 71–72
aṁsopitika 61
akaṁpita 76
Agnipurāṇa 101, 114
aṅka 88, 110, 117, 119, 121; *Aṅkiyā Naṭa* 140
aṅkamukha 108, 109
aṅkāvatāra 108, 109
aṅkāsya 109
aṅga 76, 118
Aṅgārak 65
aṅgada 60, 61
aṅgaracanā 57, 64, 66, 147
aṅgavyāpāra 113
aṅgasauṣṭhava 80
aṅgahāras 80, 113
aṅgula 24, 59, 63
aṅgulīmudrā 60
acetana 124
aṅgulīyaka 60
'ajjukā' 110
aṇu 24
atihāsya 133
'attā' 110
Atharvaveda 1
advibhūmi 27
adbhuta 67, 132
Anargharāghava 9, 16, 129
anucārikā 93
anudātta 71
anumitivāda 12
anuraṇana 41
Anurūpa 87, 148
anuvādī 70, 71
anuṣṭubh 82
anyā 92
apati 49
apaṭikṣepeṇa 44
apanītā 43
Apabhraṁśa 127
apavārita 109
abaraka 67, 68
Abhijñānaśākuntala 15, 48, 49, 52, 53, 58, 67, 79, 82, 91, 102, 108, 110, 121, 123, 126, 128, 129, 133, 143
abhinaya 1, 9, 10, 56, 81, 94, 100, 112–15, 118, 144
Abhinayadarpaṇa 1, 15, 78, 84, 101
abhinayavidyā 80, 81
Abhinavagupta 8, 13, 14, 24, 25, 27, 36, 38, 39, 40, 41, 43, 57, 58, 72, 101, 113, 124, 125, 146
Abhinavabhāratī 27, 41, 46, 48, 63, 72, 113
abhinayācāryas 81
abhivyaktivāda 13
Amarakoṣa 48, 82
Amara Sinha 82
amātya 92, 109
arthaprakṛtis 124–26
Arthhaśāstra 4, 8, 25, 96, 98
arthopakṣepakas 108, 145
Ardhamāgadhī 106
ardhamukuṭa 62
ardhahāsya 133
alaka 66
alaṅkāra 57, 60, 63, 72, 79, 147
alaukika 15
avakruṣṭa 133
avataraṇa 99
Avadānaśataka 4, 128
avanaddha 74, 148
Avanti or Avantijā 106, 107
avarohī 71
Avaloke 58, 99, 110, 119, 121
avamarśa 126
avasthās 126
Avimāraka 44, 46
asoca 96
Aśvaghoṣa 5, 8, 127
asi 59
asita 65
asragīta 119
ahokāra 133

ākāśagāmī 77
ākāśabhāsita 109, 117, 118

ākāśika 78
āgneya 39
ācāryas 78, 109, 112, 147, 148
āṅgika 10, 56
āṅgikābhinaya 76, 78, 79
ātasya 51
ātodya 99
ātmagata 109
Adibhārata 101
ābharaṇakṛt 90
Ābhīrā 63
Ābhīrī 106, 107
ābhyantaragaṇa 92
āmukha 123
āyuṣman 109
āyogava 97
ārabhaṭī 11, 88, 119
ārambha 99, 126
āropya 60
ārohī 71
ārya 109
'*āryaputra*' 110
Āryamañju-śrīmūla-kalpa 50
Āvantī 130
āviddha 88
Āvedhya 60
āśrāvanā 99
āsārita 99
āhārya 10, 56
āhāryābhinaya 56, 60, 64, 67, 68, 114, 134
ākṣepikī 72, 73

Indradhvaja 6, 15
indranīlamaṇi 62
isvastravit 95

īhāmṛga 88, 116, 121, 122

uccā 83
uccitika 60
Uttararāmacarita 7, 16, 19, 52, 53, 56, 82, 89, 92, 107, 111, 128, 133
utsṛṣṭikāṅka 117, 122
utthāpana 99
utpattivāda 12
Udayanacarita 58
udātta 71, 90
Udāttarāghava 99, 123
uddhata 90, 113
uddhatamiśra 113
uparupakas 115, 118, 121, 122, 139
upasaṁhāra 126
upasaṁhṛti 122
upāṅga 76
Upādhyāya 27, 39
Ullāpya 119

Ūrubhaṅga 107, 139
ūha 35

Ṛgveda 1, 2, 112
Ṛṣabha 70

aindrajālikas 4
aiśāna 39

Auḍrī 106
autpātika 134
aupasthayika 93

Odhra-Māgadhī 130

kakṣyā 32, 33, 35, 38, 47, 53, 130, 146, 147
kakṣyāvibhāga 32
kañcukīya, kañcukin 93
kaṭaka 61
kaṇaya 59
Kathakali
kathodghāta 123
kanāta 48
kapota 66
Kapotavarṇa 64
Kapotālī 35
karaṇa 77, 79
karuṇa 14, 66, 108, 132
karṇacūlikā 61
karṇapura 61
karaṇamudrā 61
karṇavalaya 61
Karṇasundarī 54
Karṇikā 61
karṇotkīlaka 61
Karpūramañjarī 88, 105, 121, 129
kalaka 61
kalāpa 61
kaliñja 57, 67
Kallinātha 69

kalpavṛkṣa 94
Kariyālā 140
kasaya 63, 65
kaṣṭa 133
kaṁpana 59
kaṁpita 76
Kaṁsavadha 5
kākapada 66
kāku 82, 83
kāñcī 61
Kāṭhakam 3
Kāmasūtra 8
kāyābhinaya 115
Kalapriyanātha 16, 19
kāruka 90
Kārya 124, 125
Kālidāsa 16, 17, 55, 66, 82, 93, 112, 121, 127, 128, 138, 142
kālīna 58
kāvya 113, 119
Kāvyaprakāśa 14
Kāvyamīmāṁsā 18
kiṅkiṇī 60
kiṅkiṇī-cakravāla 61
Kirātārjunīya-vyāyoga 17, 121
kirīṭ 62
kila 60
Kuchipuḍī 140
Kuṭṭanimata 42, 74, 88
kuṭṭima 35
kuṇḍala 60
kutapa 75, 76, 99
kunta 59
Kundamālā 17
kumbhīpadaka 62
Kuravanji 140
kulastrī 92
kuśīlavas 4, 90, 96
kuhara 35
kṛṣna 66
Kṛṣṇamiśra 129
Kṛṣnalīlā 142
keyūra 60
keśaracanā 66
kaiśikī 11, 118, 119, 121
kokila 70
koṇa 46
Kauśītakī Brāhmaṇa 3
kriyā 80
krīḍanīyaka 1

khaṇḍa 77
khaṇḍapātra 61
khaṇḍamātrā 119
kharjura 61
kheṭaka 59
khyāla 140

gaṇas 1
Gaṇapati 101
Gaṇapati Śāstrī 5
gaṇikas 4, 92
gadā 59
gandharva 62, 70, 95, 116, 131
gati 78
gamaka 70
garbhasandhi 118, 121, 126
gavākṣa (windo) 35, 36
gavākṣa (ornament) 61
gatravikṣepa 113
gāthā 73
Gāndhāra 70, 71
gāyakas 3, 75, 76
gāyikā 75
gīta 1, 69, 99
Gīta-Govinda 119
gūdhatra 124
Guṇacandra 14
Goṣṭhī 118
graha 71
grāma 71
gaura 65, 66

ghaṭṭita 50
ghanam 74, 148
ghātas 134, 149

cakra 59
caturasra 23, 24, 27, 29, 36, 37–40, 100, 146
caturbhāṇi 121
catuṣpada 74
carma 59
carcarī 120
calita 81, 95, 112
cātāka

Candali 106, 107
cāmera 59
cāri 77, 78, 100
citra 100
citrakāra 90
citraturaganyāya 12
citravit 95
citrabhinaya 78
cūḍāmaṇi 60, 61
cūlikā 108
ceṭa 92, 106
ceṣṭita 57

chatra 59
chandovit 95
chalika 112
chalita 112
chāyānāṭaka 7
Chhau 140

jaḍa 124
janānta or *janāntika* 109
jarjara 1, 55, 59, 100, 103, 105
jarjarapūjā 99
jarjara śloka 100
Jaśna 140
javanikā 43, 48, 49, 147
javanikāntara 110, 119
Jātakas 82
jayājīva 97
jāla 35
Jātrā 140
jāti 72
Jṛmbhaka missiles 52

jhallarī 75

ṭhāṭa 72

ḍakkini 75
Ḍima 24, 88, 116, 121

Ḍhakki 107

Taṇḍu 1, 80
tatam 74, 148
Tantras 82
tantrī 99

Tapti-svayaṁvara 129
tamāśā 140
tarala 60
talīya 57
tāṇḍava 1, 80, 100
tāta 109
Tāla 59, 73, 74, 113
tiraskariṇī 43, 48, 49
Tilaka 61
tepita 63
totaka 118
tomara 59
taurika 90
tauryatṛka 69, 89
trigata 100
tripatākā 77, 109
Tripuradāha 2, 80
trisara 60
troṭaka 114, 118, 121
tryasra 23, 27, 30, 36, 37, 40, 100, 146

Therukoothu 140

daṇḍa 24, 59
daṇḍaka 82
dāntapatra 61
dardarika 75
dardura 75
Daśarūpa 9, 58, 99, 102, 106, 109, 110, 113–21
Daśāvatāra 140
dakkinī 75
Dākṣiṇātyā 106, 107, 130
Dāmodaragupta 74, 128
dārukarma 56
dikpālastuti 99, 105
Dighanikāya 3
Diṅnāga 17
diptā 83
divyā 92
dundubhi 75
durmallikā 120
Durmallī 120
duṣprayoja 81
dūta 92
Dūtavākya 105
Dūtāṅgada 16, 129
duḥkhātmaka 14

dṛśyakāvyas 9
deva 109
devī 92, 110
deśī 69, 113
daivikī 133, 134
Drāvidī 106, 107
druta 78, 83
dvāra 35
dvipadikā 119
dvipadīkhaṇḍa 72
dvibhūmi 29

dhanu 59
dharaṇī 35
dharma 103
dharmī 10, 131
dhīralalita 90
dhīrapraśānta 115
dhīraśānta 91
dhīrodātta 91, 115, 123, 125
dhīroddhata 91
Dhūrtavitasaṁvāda 15
dhaivata 70
dhauta 50
dhruvā 43, 72, 73, 74
dhvaja 59
dhvani 10, 69
Dhvanyāloka 10

nakṣatrotpāta 64
naṭa 3, 4, 8, 12, 17, 40, 54, 63, 78, 90, 96, 97, 101, 113, 133, 134, 146, 147
Naṭarāja 75, 79, 80
naṭasūtras 4, 76
naṭī 15, 88, 123
Nandikeśvara 2
Naqāla 140
nartaka 3, 95, 96
nartakī 114, 120
nartana 69
napuṁsaka 93
narmasaciva 91
narmasuhṛd 91
Navaṭankī 140, 142, 149
nāgaraka 4
Nagananda 74, 128, 129
nāgadanta 35
nāṭaka 3, 108, 115, 121, 122, 125, 126, 128, 129
nāṭakamaṇḍalīs 4, 133, 134, 135
Nāṭakalakṣaṇaratnakoṣa 9, 54, 102, 112
nāṭakīyā 90
nāṭamandira 19
nāṭikā 16, 74, 114, 119, 121
Naṭī 74, 118
nāṭya 1, 5, 15, 77, 82, 88, 90, 112–15, 118, 121, 134, 145
nāṭayanti 56
nāṭyagṛha 18, 40
Nāṭyadarpaṇa 14, 73, 102
nāṭyadharma 109
nāṭyadharmī 11, 131
nāṭyamaṇḍapa 18, 23, 29, 41, 104
nāṭyarāsaka 119
Nāṭyaveda 103
nāṭyaveśman 25
nāṭyaśālā 41, 96
Nāṭyaśāstra 3 *passim*
nāṭyakāra 90
nāṭyācārya 78, 88, 148
nāda 69
nāḍikā 116, 121, 134
Nāndī 99, 100, 101–3, 119, 145
nāyaka 90, 125
nāyikā 92
nirgrantha 64, 66
Nirukta 3
nirmuṇḍa 93
nirāhuta 96
nirbrahmaṇya 96
nirvahaṇa 119, 120, 126
niṣāda 70
nīla 64, 66
niyatāpti 126
Nīlakaṇṭha 54
nirvyūha 35, 36
nīca 83
nūpura 60, 61
nṛtta 1, 15, 16, 77, 80, 112, 113, 114, 145
nṛtta-kāvyas 113
nṛtya 1, 112–15, 145
nṛtyaprabandhas 118
nṛtyaśālā 41
nṛtta-sabhā 80
netṛ 90
nṛpapatnī 92

nepathye 44, 119
nepathyagṛha 26, 27, 29, 31, 32, 36, 37, 39, 43, 44, 47, 53, 146, 147
nairṛta 39
naiṣkrāmikī 72–74
nyāsa 71

pañca 135
Pañcadaśī 50
pañcama 70
Pañcarātra 106, 121
Pañcālī 130
paṭa 50
paṭaha 75
paṭi 44, 49, 82
paṭṭisa 59
paṇas 4
paṇava 75
Patañjali 5, 8
patākā 91, 115, 124, 125, 149
patākā (flag) hand 77
pataka (banner) 134, 135
patrapūraka 61
patralekhā 61
pattara 59
padmavarṇa 65
Padmamaṇi 62
parārthasiddhiyuta 124
parighaṭṭanā 99
paricārikā 93
parivartana 99
pariṣad 94
pāthya 1
pāṇavika 75
pāṇḍuvarṇa 64
pāṇi 72
pāṇika 73
Pāṇini 4, 112
pāda 100–3
padapatra 60
Paripārśvika 88, 89, 100–3
Pārvatīpariṇaya 15
pārśvamaulī 62
pārśvagata 62
patra 123
pīṭha 35
piṇḍībandhas 79, 80
pīṭhamarda 4, 91, 120
pīta 64–66
Purāṇas 82, 149
putraka 109
purohita 92
Puṣya 25, 104
puṣṭa 57
pūrvaraṅga 73, 99, 100, 101, 122
pūrvaraṅga caturasra 100
pūrvaraṅga tryasra 100
pūrvaraṅga citra 100
pekkhāghara 41
Paiśācī 106
Prakaraṇa 24, 88, 108, 115, 118, 121
prakaraṇikā 121
prakarī 115, 124, 125
prakāśa 109
prakhyāta 116
prakṣepya 60
Pratapārudrīya 102, 113
Pratijñāyaugandharāyaṇa 44, 58, 59
pratidvāra 35
pratināyaka 91
Pratimānāṭaka 59
pratimukha 118, 119, 122, 126
pratiśīra 49, 62
pratihārī 93
pratyaṅga 76
pratyāhāra 99
pratyūha 35
Prabodhacandrodaya 17, 106, 129
Pramānaṁ 24
prayoga 80
prayogātiśaya 123
prarocanas 100, 101
pralaṁbita 63
pravṛtti 11
pravṛttaka 123
pravṛdhanāda 133
praveśaka 108, 119, 131
praveśikā 72, 73
prasādhana 79
prastāvanā 100, 123
prasthāna 119
prasthānaka 119
Prahasana 24, 117, 121, 139, 149
Prākṛta 6, 48, 49, 73, 105–8, 121, 145
Prācya 106, 107
prāḍvivāka 92

prāptyāśā 126
prāśnika 55, 95, 134, 149
prāsa 59
prāsādikī 72, 73
prāsaṅgika 91
Prahlāda Nāṭaka 140
Priyadarśikā 88, 121, 123, 128
'*priye*' 110
Pṛthvīdhara 107
prekṣāgāra 18
prekṣāgṛha 18
prekṣāpati 101
preṅkhana 119

phalāgama 126

bandhanīya 60
Balibandha 5
Bāṇa 97
bahya 92
bāla 24
Bālacarita 59, 81
Bālabhārata 73, 129
Bālarāmāyaṇa 58, 110, 129
Bālhika 106, 107
bindu 124, 125
bilva 63
bīja 108, 123–26
bībhatsa 14, 66, 132
Burrakathā 140
Bṛhaddeśī 70, 71
Baudha-ākhyānas 82

Bhagavadajju 129
Bhagavadbhaktirasāyana 15
'*bhagavan*' 109
bhagnatāla 119
Bhartṛhari 97
Bhaṭṭa-Lollaṭa 12
Bhaṭṭa-Nāyaka 12
bhaṭṭa 109
'*bhaṭṭinī*' 110
Bhaṭṭoji Dīkṣita 48
bhayānak 14, 66, 132
Bharata 1 *passim*
Bharata Nāṭyam 140
bharataputras 97
bharatavākya 73, 145
bhalla 96
Bhavaī 140, 149
Bhavabhūti 16, 55, 82, 93, 98, 123, 127, 128, 142, 148
bhagavat 117
Bhāgavata Melā 140
Bhāgavatam 149
Bhāṇa 24, 88, 91, 109, 117, 121, 139, 149
bhaṇikā 121
bhāṇī 121
bhāṇḍavādya 113
Bhanda Pathera 140
bhāratī, 11, 101, 119, 121, 123
bhāva 10, 14, 81, 83, 95, 112–14, 118
bhāvika 81
Bhāvaprakāśana 2, 23, 102, 112, 114
bhāvātmaka 115
Bhāsa 5, 8, 82, 100, 107, 121, 127, 129, 139, 142
bhiṇḍi 59
bhūmis 31
Bhīla Gauri 140
Bhūmikā 118
bhṛṅgāra 59, 99
bhendra 57, 67, 68
'*bhojakatva*' 13
bhauma 78
bhramarabadha 79
bhrūkuṁsa 88

makarikā 61
maṇḍapa 27, 35, 39
maṇḍala 77, 78
Mataṅga 69
mattavāraṇa 38
mattavāraṇis 25, 27, 36, 38, 41, 56, 75, 104
Mattavilāsa 129, 139
Madhusūdana Sarasvatī 15
madhya 74, 78, 102
madhyama 70, 71, 90
Madhyama vyāyoga 138
mantrin 92
Manu 96
Manusmṛti 96
Mammaṭa 10
malina 63
malla 96
masṛṇa 113

Masṛṇamiśra 113
mastaki 62
mahācārī 100
mahādevī 92
Mahānāṭaka 17, 20, 91, 129
Mahābhārata 3, 21, 54, 82, 129
Mahābhāṣya 5, 8, 87, 97
'*mahārāja*' 109
Mahārāṣṭrī 106
Mahāvīracarita or *Vīracarita* 123, 128
Mahāvratastoma rite 3
Māgadhī 73, 92, 106, 107
matṛkā 79
Mānasāraśilpaśāstra 19, 24
Mānuṣi 133
Mārkaṇḍeya Purāṇa 3
mārga 69, 113
mārgāsārita 99
mārdaṅgika 75
mārṣa 123
Mālatīmādhava 54, 82, 88, 91, 92, 121, 128
Mālavikāgnimitra 15, 16, 18, 49, 52, 72, 74, 80, 93, 95, 112, 127, 139
mālyakṛt 90
Māyurāja 123
mukuṭa 60, 62, 90
mukuṭakāra 90
mukṭajālā 61
muktāvalī 61
mukha 119–23, 126
mukhya 124, 125
Mudrā 77
Mudrārākṣasa 51, 53, 82, 93, 125, 126, 149
muṇḍāsana 58
muraja 75, 101
mūrcchanā 71
Mṛcchakaṭika 5, 18, 31, 32, 35, 37, 44, 46, 51, 54, 56, 58, 67, 72, 81, 82, 91, 92, 96, 97, 105, 107, 108, 121, 138, 149
mṛdaṅga 4, 75
mekhalā 61
Meghadūta 41, 66
Menā Gurjarī 141
mocaka 60

Yakṣagāna 140
Yajurveda 1, 2
yajñavit 95
yatna 126
yantra 35, 56
yabanikā 46
yamanikā 48, 49, 147
yava 24
yavani 93
yavanikā 43, 48, 49, 147
Yājñavalkya 86
yatra 16, 17, 19, 22, 149
yūkā 24

rakta 64, 66
Raghuvaṁśa 66
raṅgadvāra 100
raṅgapīṭha 27, 29, 36–40, 43–45, 47, 53, 75, 146
raṅgabhūmi 25
raṅgamaṇḍala 25, 38, 39
raṅgamaṇḍapa 38
raṅgaśīrṣa 25, 27, 32, 36, 40, 43–45, 47, 53, 75, 104, 146, 147
raja 24
rajaka 90
rañjita 50
ratnajāla 60
ratnamālikā 61
ratnāvalī (jewel necklace) 61
Ratnāvalī (nāṭikā) 16, 31, 37, 43, 51, 53, 55, 61, 68, 72, 74, 80, 82, 88, 90, 92, 93, 97, 111, 120, 121, 123, 128, 149
raśanā 61
rasa 1, 5, 10–15, 65, 74, 76, 83, 108, 113, 114, 126, 132, 135, 143, 145, 147–49
rasātmaka 115
Rasārṇavasudhākara 9, 102
rasiko naṭaḥ 5
rāga 70–72, 119
Rāgavibodha 69, 70, 71
Rāghavabhaṭṭa 79, 142
rājan 95, 109
Rājaśekhara 73, 110, 121, 129
rājaputras 106
rājamaṇḍalas 4
rājasevaka 95
Rāmacandra 14, 125
Rāmalīlā 139, 142, 149
Rāmāyaṇa 3, 22, 54, 96, 122, 139, 149

Rāsa 142
Rāsalīlā 140, 149
Rāsaka 120
Rukmiṇīharaṇa 54, 121
rucikā 60
rūḍhiśabha 110
rūpa 9
rūpaka 4, 9, 114, 115, 118, 121
rūpakaṣaṭka 121
rūpajīvas 96, 97
rūpānusāriṇī 87, 148
recakas 80, 113
romaśa 66, 67
Rohiṇī 25, 104
raudra 14, 66, 94, 132

lakṣaṇa 125
laya 72, 78, 113
Lāñchita 50
lāsya 2, 80, 117
lāsikā 81
Lalita 149
likṣā 24
lokacarita 112
lokadharmī 11, 118, 131
lokapālas 103
laukika 15

vaktrapāṇi 99
vajra 59
vaṭikā 60
'*vatsa*' 109
vayasya 92, 109
varjura 61
varṇas 104, 120
varṇa (melodious movement) 69, 71, 72
vartalāṭika 62
vardhamāna 100
varṣadhara 93
valaya 61
vaṁśa 75
vaṁśikas 75
vāṅmayī 133
vastu 123
vācika 10, 56
vacikābhinaya 82, 118
Vājasaneyi Saṃhitā 2, 48
vadara 65
vādī 70, 72
vādya 69, 99
vādyatāla 113
vātāyana 35
Vātsyāyana 4
Vānaukasī 106
vāyava 39
vārttikakāra 39
Vikramorvaśīya 17, 45, 82, 121, 127
vikṛta 116, 117
vikṛṣṭa 23, 26, 36–38, 40, 146
vicitra 63, 66
vita 4, 81, 91, 117, 120
vitata 63
vidūṣaka 4, 6, 43, 52, 66, 68, 72, 74, 80, 91, 100, 109, 118, 120, 123
Viddhaśālabhañjikā 50, 129
vināyikā 120
vipralaṁbha 62, 108
vibhāṣas 106, 107
vimarśa 118, 119, 122
viralanepathyā 81
virūpa 87, 148
vilaṁbita 83
Vilāsikā 120
vivādī 70
viṣkambha or *viṣkambhaka* 108, 115, 119, 124
Viśākhadatta 93
viśliṣṭa 109
Viṣṇu 122
Viṣṇusmṛti 97
Viṣṇudharmottara 23, 50, 64, 143
Viśvanātha 105
vīṇā 4, 75, 76
Vīṇāghoṣavatī 59
Vīthī 83, 88, 117, 121
Vithyaṅgas 83
vīra 66, 125, 132
Vīracarita 128
vṛtta 23
vṛtti 11, 115, 119–21
vṛddha 92
vedikā 35, 36
veṇī 66
Veṇisaṁhāra 82, 121, 133
veṇu 4
veśya 95

veśakāra 90
veṣṭita 57, 63
vaidūrya 62
vaiṇika 75
vaitālika vākyas 22
Vaiśyas 97
vyañjanā 13
vyājima 57
vyāyāma 77
vyāyoga 88, 116, 121
vyāla 35
vyālapaṅkti 61

śakāra 92, 107
śakti 59
śākhya 64, 66
Śaṅkuka 12, 27, 39
śaṅkha 75, 102, 103
śataghnī 22
śāntā 90
'*śabala*' 59
sabhāpati 95
śara 59
śaṅkakalāpī 61
Śākārī 106, 107
Śābarī 106, 107
Śariputraprakaraṇa 5, 127
śāritī 81
Śārṅgadeva 70, 72
śikhaṇḍas 61
śikhā 61, 66
śikhājāla 61
śikhāpāśa 61, 66
śikhāpuṭas 61
śilpaka 120
Śilparatna 18, 23
Śilāveśma 41
śīrṣajāla 61
śuddha 63, 66, 108, 116, 117
Śūdra 96, 97
sūdrācāra 96
śūla 59
śuṣkāvokṛṣṭa 100
śṛṅgāra 15, 62, 65, 74, 88, 108, 132
śṛṅgāralajjā 79
śailaguhāhāro 27, 41
Śailūṣa 96
Śauraseni 73, 105, 106
śmaśru 67
śyāma 65, 66
Śravaṇa 25, 104
Śrīgadita 120
Śrī Harṣa 16, 93, 98
Śrīmadbhāgavata Purāṇa 3
śrutis 69, 70, 82
śreṣṭhins 106
śvetā 65

ṣaḍja 70, 71
ṣaḍ-dāruka 75

saṅkrānti 80
saṅkīrṇa 108, 116, 117
saṅgīta 3, 69, 89
saṅghāta 116
saṅghātya 63
Saṅgītapārijāta 69–71
Saṅgītamakaranda 18, 76
Saṅgītaratnākara 18, 83, 94, 113
saṅgītaśālā 42, 95, 146
Saṅgītasamayasāra 70
sanghoṭanā 99
saciva 92, 109
sañcārī 71
sañcārikā 92
sañjīva 57, 67, 68
sañjavana 35
saṭṭaka 110, 119, 121
sattva 13
sandhi 108, 115, 123, 126
sandhima 57
sabhāpati 94, 95, 103
sabhāsad 94
samājas 3
sanavakāra 88, 116, 121
samudramanthana 121
sahṛdaya 13, 149
saṁlāpaka 120
saṁvāda sūktas 2
saṁvādī 70, 71
saṁsad 94
saṁskāras 13
Saṁhitās 82
Sāgaranandin 106
sātvika 10, 56, 115
sātvatī 11, 88

sādhāranīkaraṇa 14
sādhāraṇī 92
sādhikṣepa 133
sādhukāra 133
sādho 109
Sāmaveda 1, 3
sādharaṇastrī 92
sārthavāhas 121
sārvavārṇika 1
Sālabhañjikā 35
Sāhityadarpaṇa 9, 99, 100, 102, 105, 109, 114, 117
siddha 62, 131
siddhi 133, 134, 149
siddhilekhakas 134, 149
Siddhāntakaumudī 48, 112, 113
sita 64, 65
sīmanta 66
sukumāra 88
Subhaṭa 129
Subhadrā Dhanañjaya 129
suṣira 74, 148
sūta 3
sūtra 60
sūtraka 60
sūtradhāra 3, 7, 15–17, 55, 74, 88, 89, 94, 96, 100, 102, 119, 122, 128
senāpati 92
stambha 35
sthāyī 71
sthāpaka 54, 89, 102, 122
sthita 78
snātaka 93
smita 133
stotrīya 64, 66, 87
svagata 109
svara 69, 70, 71
svarita 71
Svapnavāsavadattā 50, 53, 61, 67, 139, 149
Svāṅga 140
svāminī 110
svārthasiddhiyuta 124
svīyā 92
svecchitika 61

'hañje' 110
harita 65
harṣaka 60
Harivaṁśa 3, 54
Harṣacarita 97
hastas 23, 24, 40
hastidanti cuḍiyān 61
Halāyudha 44
hallīśa 121
Hallīsaka 121
hastavī 60
hara 60
hāsya 65, 119, 132
Hāsyacūḍāmaṇi 121
hemasūtra 60

THEATRICAL COMPANIES, ARTISTS AND AUTHORS

Acharya, P.K. 38
Alkazi, Ebrahim 150
Apte, V.S. 48, 112
Arundale, Rukmini Devi 140, 150
ASI, 6, 41
Asiatic Society of Bengal 6
Athenian stage

Bengali stage 141
Bengali theatre 141, 150
Bharatendu Harish Chandra 142
Bismillah Khan 150
Brāhmaṇa Sabhā of Bombay 138
Blöch 6, 46
Böhtlingk 48

Chinese theatre 47
Coomaraswamy, A.K. 36, 47
cult of the dead 7, 8

De, S.K. 44, 48, 49

Folk dances 79
folk theatre 38, 139, 141, 144

Ghosh, Manomohan 36

Gopichand 149
Greek theatre 6, 54
'Greek' theory 8
Grosset, J. 38, 48
Gujarati stage 141
Gujarati theatre 150

Haraprasāda Śāstrī 6
Hakikat 149
Halāyudha 44
Hass, C.O. 116
Hindi stage 142
Hindi theatre 150

I-Tsing 128

Jogimara cave 46

Kalākṣetra 140
Kanarese theatre 140
Keith, A.B. 5, 49
kuṭṭampalam 138
Konow, Sten 48

Lévi, 49
Lüders 7

Madras theatre 140, 150
Mankad 44
Macdonell 42
Maypole theory 6, 8
Monier-Williams 57
Marathi stage 141
Marathi theatre 141
Mitra, Sombhu 150
Modern theatre 139
Mukerjee, S.C. 132
Music Academy of Madras 138
Mushtaq Hussain Khan 150

Naṭa Maṇḍala 141
Natarāja temple 75
National theatre 138, 139, 142, 150
National School of Drama and Asian Theatre 144, 150

Open-air theatre 41

Palace theatre 18, 19, 146

Padmanabhan, Rajeswari 150
Parsi theatre 140, 143
Parsi theatrical companies 141
Pischel 7
Pisharoti, K.P. 75
Puran 149
Prasāda etc. 142
Public theatre 41
'puppet show' 7
'puppet play' 8, 140
Prithvi Theatre 142
Prithviraj 142, 150

Ram Gopal 148
Rectangular theatre 23, 25
Ravi Shankar 150
Ridgeway 7
Roth 48

Sangeet Natak Akademi 144, 150
shadow play 7, 16
Shakespeare 110
Sītābeṅgā cave 6, 46
Square theatre 23
Subbulakshmi, M.S. 150

Tagore 142
Tagore, S.M. 46, 53
Tamil theatre 138, 140, 150
Telugu theatre 140
Telugu stage 141
Temple theatre 19
Thakur, Omkar Nath 150
Triangular theatre 23

Uday Shankar 148, 150
University of Hawaii 139

'vegetation spirit' 7, 8
Vyjayantimala 150

Wilson, H.H. 6, 17, 47
Windisch 5, 49
Winternitz 127

Yajnik, R.K. 140